a little history of canada

h.v. nelles

OXFORD
UNIVERSITY PRESS

1904 ❦ 2004

100 YEARS OF
CANADIAN PUBLISHING

OXFORD
UNIVERSITY PRESS

70 Wynford Drive, Don Mills, Ontario M3C 1J9
www.oup.com/ca

Oxford University Press is a department of the University of Oxford.
It furthers the University's objective of excellence in research, scholarship,
and education by publishing worldwide in

Oxford   New York

Auckland   Bangkok   Buenos Aires   Cape Town   Chennai
Dar es Salaam   Delhi   Hong Kong   Istanbul   Karachi   Kolkata
Kuala Lumpur   Madrid   Melbourne   Mexico City   Mumbai   Nairobi
São Paulo   Shanghai   Taipei   Tokyo   Toronto

Oxford is a trade mark of Oxford University Press
in the UK and in certain other countries

Published in Canada
by Oxford University Press

National Library of Canada Cataloguing in Publication

Nelles, H.V. (Henry Vivian), 1942-
A little history of Canada / H.V. Nelles.

Includes index.

ISBN 0-19-541837-9

1. Canada—History. I. Title.

FC165.N44 2004   971   C2004-902268-7

2 3 4 -   07 06 05 04
This book is printed on permanent (acid-free) paper.
Printed in Canada

contents

becoming Canada   v

home and native land   1

british americans   55

dominion limited   113

distinct society   183

another opening   255

index   258

For Jen and Geoff

becoming canada

⌒

History lives and is a constant guiding, confining, and sometimes intractable presence in the life of Canadians. When travellers land in Canada, and if they are observant, they will be brought face to face with it. Arriving passengers in Vancouver will take note of the extraordinary Haida sculpture *The Jade Canoe* in the airport, the signage in both official languages, English and French, the portraits of the Queen in the arrivals and immigration halls. If Toronto is the destination the plane will actually land in Mississauga, a suburb named after a Native tribe, at Pearson International Airport, named after a mid-twentieth-century Canadian diplomat/prime minister, and the taxi will crawl through traffic with the weary visitors to, perhaps, the Royal York Hotel. In Montreal, La Reine Elizabeth will be a figure on the money, a portrait on the airport wall by the Maple Leaf flag, and a hotel destination. The signs will be bilingual, at least in the airport, but the language on the street will be French.

Contemporary Canada is a bewildering mix. Toronto, the largest city, is said to be the most cosmopolitan on the planet and its streets, schools, and subways are home to more than 200 ethnicities. This extraordinary multicultural diversity may be somewhat startling to visitors expecting to meet the Canadians they imagined, perhaps patterned on the image of the stalwart Mounties. There is, to be sure, a massive social experiment underway in Canada, but I would argue that the change is not unprecedented. That is the story of Canada. The enduring theme of Canadian history is transformation.

The indigenous peoples of the Pacific Coast possess the ideal symbol for Canadian history, one that I want to appropriate as a metaphor. For their elaborate rituals the coastal tribes carved evocative, brightly painted wooden masks. One particular type has been called a Transformation Mask. The wearer appears first as a raven or an eagle. With a tug on a hidden set of strings, the mask opens up to reveal a sun, a moon, a killer whale, or a human face. Some particularly elaborate masks open up to three layers, revealing a different motif each time.

That mask serves as a symbol for my interpretation of Canadian history in this little book. Canadian history is not the story of a single people realizing their nationhood along the European model. Nor is it the story of a revolutionary society forging an integral new nationality out of the old through struggle, along the lines of the United States. Canadian history is a story of transformations that continue. Canada has fundamentally changed several times in its past. And it is doing so yet again. But in each transformation the past is not obliterated. As in the Transformation Mask, something of the eagle can be seen in the sun. Something of the past persists and has to be incorporated into the present. Contemporary Canada is thus a composite, the latest in a series of metamorphoses, but it carries forward living attributes of its previous incarnations.

For that reason I have organized this interpretive essay around a series of from–to transitions. 'Home and Native Land' shows how the arrival of French and British traders and colonists not only added new social elements to indigenous societies of northern North America, but also led to fundamental transformation of those societies. 'British Americans' reveals how this huge territory was reconfigured in different ways under contested British imperial authority. In the standard version a colony becomes a nation.

That does not happen in the Canadian case. 'Dominion Limited' shows how diverse colonies were only loosely integrated into a national federation, how the country opted for something in between colonial status and independence, and how in economic affairs and international relations Canada remained dependent on the United States and Great Britain. 'Distinct Society' shows how within the last 60 years a new volatile social and political order has emerged out of the chrysalis of the old, a unique country and at the same time one that has seemed to be constantly on the verge of falling apart.

Such a narrative structure calls for substantial revision to the usual chronology of Canadian history. My starting and ending points are not major political events—the Conquest, Confederation, prime ministers—but rather moments of relative equilibrium when a new order has been consolidated. 'Home and Native Land' covers the period from the Ice Age to approximately 1740, the height of the French Regime. 'British Americans' carries the story forward from 1740 to the 1840s, by which time a distinctive British North America had emerged as a durable alternative political configuration on the northern borders of the United States. 'Dominion Limited', covering the period from the 1840s to 1939, takes us from a collection of British colonial societies to transcontinental, quasi-autonomous Dominion. 'Distinct Society', seeing Canada from the 1940s to the present, charts the transformation of an essentially white-settler Dominion, heavily influenced by its British heritage, to a distinctive bilingual, statist and open society.

> *Canada emerges and changes; it becomes.*

Canada emerges and changes; it becomes. Canada has always been open to the world, to the flow of peoples, goods, technology, and ideas. It has flourished, grown, and changed under influences emanating from the outside. At the same time, Canada has been able to exercise a collective will, choosing, asserting, setting policy, and in its own way acting upon the world stage. Though Canadians may not be able to articulate precisely what it means to be Canadian, for many different reasons they take pride in being Canadian (yes, even the majority of Quebecers) and project a sense of themselves collectively to the world. At the same time, the notional Japanese and European visitors, though they might see things that remind them very much of Los Angeles, Chicago, London, or Paris, know instantly that they are not in the United States, Britain, or France. Canada is an entity unto itself; it is not a shadow of something else. It is a product of a history that is unique but not isolated.

Canada might be thought of as a triumph of politics. Major confrontations have been avoided, irreconcilable differences muted, absolutes suspected, and final solutions deferred. Indeed, students often complain that Canadian history is not interesting enough; that is, it does not contain enough bloody civil wars, great ideas locked in mortal combat, bandits, flamboyant characters, or charismatic leaders. I would insist Canada does possess some of these dubious attributes, but I would agree with the general proposition that Canada presents an alternative story of adjustment, accommodation, and continuous negotiation. But it should not be thought of as a Peaceable Kingdom on that account. Canadian history has its share of violent conflict, bigotry, repression, injustice, and deprivation. Because it has avoided overt civil war for the most part, it should not be thought to be without deep-rooted, long-lasting, and unresolved conflicts. Nor should its tragic potential be downplayed.

Though the traveller from abroad on landing in a major

Canadian city—where almost 80 per cent of the population now lives—will encounter a Canada that is new, it is nonetheless a country in continuous contact with its past. Canadians too bump into their history in all seasons and in the most unexpected places. History is not so much the story that is over, but rather a gift and a burden to be carried forward into the future. As Canadians refashion themselves, so too the past is reshaped. What follows is my attempt to capture the essential elements of that story so that visitors and citizens, as they walk the streets, read the papers, watch television, and listen to the voices of Canadians, can savour the ongoing dialogue between past and present through which Canadians remake themselves.

As Canadians refashion themselves, so too the past is reshaped.

This is a personal interpretation, not a textbook. I have not tried to be comprehensive. My goal throughout is to provide the reader with an essential understanding of the main themes of Canadian history. I address *A Little History of Canada* to several audiences. The first are Canadians in search of a brief introduction to the history of their country. The second are the many hundreds of thousands of travellers visiting Canada either on business or on vacation each year who want a concise overview of the history of the people they are about to encounter, and have only a six- to eight-hour flight in which to learn what they need to know. The third are those who come to this country from elsewhere and decide to stay. Each year more than 200,000 people choose to become citizens of Canada. They may wonder, Who am I becoming? I have crafted *A Little History of Canada* with these readers in mind.

⌒

The word 'Canada' is used in several different ways depending upon the time and the context. In the beginning, Canada did not exist. The word was first spoken by Native peoples to describe their village. Early French traders applied it generally to the region of the St Lawrence. The word acquired a legal meaning when the French gave the name Canada to their North American possession, which grew eventually to cover about half the continent. Afterwards the name denoted one and then two colonies along the St Lawrence River and the Great Lakes, and later and informally the whole collection of British North American dependencies. At Confederation in 1867, Canada consisted of the four former colonies: Canada East, Canada West, Nova Scotia, and New Brunswick. Eventually the jurisdiction of the government of Canada would extend from the Atlantic to the Pacific to the Arctic Oceans, absorbing the other British realms and encompassing British territorial claims in the North. Canada is a chameleon word; it can be a space on the map, a country, and a people, all of which change over time. I have not been as arbitrary as Humpty Dumpty was with Alice over the meaning of words—'When *I* use a word it means just what I choose it to mean—neither more nor less'. I hope the precise meaning will be apparent from the context.

I recall once on a train in Thailand, my local dining companion, when he learned I was from Canada, wanted the answer to a question that had been burning in his mind: Why do the policemen in Canada wear such funny hats? Sadly, I did not have an answer. I do now, though it's 25 years late. His question and other encounters with students and scholars outside of Canada remind me that visitors have a different angle of vision; they do not connect with the sometimes private language insiders unconsciously use. I have tried, as much as possible, to use language that translates meanings into universals rather than to employ the particular usage common in Canadian historical discourse.

Many years ago when I was teaching Canadian history in

Japan, my students complained to me that Canadian history had too many names. They might have added that most of them were confusingly the same—how do we keep the Macdonalds, Mackenzies, and Cartiers sorted out? Thus I have tried to reduce the number of names to a minimum.

⁓

I am acutely conscious that I have left things out; many important matters remain uncovered in these pages. I am aware, too, that my sometimes sweeping generalizations and deceptively simple assertions do violence to generations of subtle historiography. It is my hope, however, that inquiring readers will want to fill these gaps, or capture the nuances and matters of detail that I have necessarily tucked under the metaphorical carpet. An introduction should lead on, rather than exhaust the subject. Here then is a taste of Canadian history that I hope stimulates an appetite.

home and native land

⌒

Even in anthropological terms Canada is a new country. Human beings evolved on the African continent about 160,000 years ago. By contrast, the earliest archaeological evidence of human habitation in North America dates back only 14,000 years. This late arrival can be attributed in part to the time it took for human culture to spread from Africa, across Eurasia to Siberia. But for most of the early epochs of human history, Canada lay buried under a huge icecap. That icecap advanced southward and retreated northward at least four times before a final gradual withdrawal that began about the time the first humans appeared on the scene. Canadian history begins with the melting of the ice.

Glaciers blocked human occupation of the Americas beyond Alaska until a north–south corridor along the Rocky Mountains opened up between retreating lobes of ice. With so much water locked in ice, ocean levels were much lower and Alaska was connected by land to Siberia across what is now Bering Strait. Immigrants from Asia crossed this land bridge, slipped south through the narrow gap in the ice, multiplied in the generally benign environment, and rapidly spread out to populate the vast expanses of North America, Central America, and South America. It is possible, too, that the Americas may have been partially peopled somewhat earlier by migrants travelling by water, but the decisive migratory wave, which inundated any isolated earlier residents, occurred about 12,500 years ago.

As the climate warmed and the glaciers retreated northward,

the area we know as Canada experienced significant environmental change. Tundra, shrubs, and glacial lakes gave way initially to poplar, birch, and spruce forests. Then grasses, pine, and oak insinuated themselves northward. By approximately 5,000 years ago, when the icecap had finally melted, the climate, water levels, and ecology of Canada had evolved into something recognizably similar to today's features.

The earliest human inhabitants thus had to adjust to a dynamic environment; their presence, in turn, contributed to some significant change. As the ice margins retreated, hunting and gathering populations moved northward. Climate and vegetation changed constantly. Hunting by humans with fluted-stone pointed spears, along with shifting ecologies, led to the fairly sudden extinction of the indigenous mega-fauna, the 10-ton mammoths, mastodons, and giant bison.

The first peoples of Canada negotiated in some ways the most dramatic transformation.

Humans adapted, building their lives around the search for other prey—tapirs, jaguars, spectacled bears, llamas, peccaries (all of which sought refuge further south), and caribou, elk, moose, and the bison, which also migrated to North America from Asia about the same time as humans. Thus the first peoples of Canada negotiated in some ways the most dramatic transformation in the history of Canada, from an ice-covered barren to a temperate mountain, plain, and woodland environment.

Across the vast distances of the Americas, amid many different geographical, ecological, and climate regimes, a profusion of indigenous cultures developed, closely adapted to their regional environments. Indigenous cultures did not arise in total isolation, however. Population growth, migration, warfare, and trade brought peoples into contact with one another. Through these contacts, tools and practices spread across space and cultural boundaries. For example, the bow and arrow appeared first among people in the North about 1,800 years ago. This weapon's superiority for hunting medium-sized and smaller game led to its widespread, but not universal, adaptation by Native peoples across the continent. Similarly, the knowledge of pottery making gradually spread northward from its South and Central American points of origin. Rope making, basketry, and net weaving were taken up by neighbouring tribes and passed on through cultural exchanges as conditions allowed.

Around 1,500 years ago, settled agriculture based upon corn, a practice learned from peoples further to the south and west, had become established in the Great Lakes region, and 500 years later, beans, tobacco, sunflowers, and squash had been added to the inventory of cultivars. Items unique to specific places—silver for ornaments, flaked stone for spear points, obsidian and copper for blades, amber and marine shells for jewellery—moved surprisingly long distances through trading networks. In short, Native societies were constantly adapting, moving about, and acquiring new tools and cultural practices. Before European contact, Canada's Natives were not timeless and unchanging peoples living before history. Transformation and accommodation to new challenges were as much part of their lives as they are of ours.

About 1,000 years ago, when Europeans established contact with North America, Canada was home to six main regional cultural groupings of Native peoples, 12 linguistic families, and more than 50 identifiable languages. Canada and Western Europe, regions of comparable size, shared this characteristic of cultural and linguistic diversity. The two regions differed, however, in the complexity of their social organization, technological capabilities, and population size. By comparison with Europe, there were no towns in Canada, no institutions extending beyond a particular region, no iron, and relatively few people. At a time when Western Europe contained approximately 50 million people, the Canadian population probably numbered under 1 million, perhaps as few as 500,000 but possibly as many as 2 million. Though Canada looked empty to its first intercontinental visitors, given existing modes of subsistence, it was in fact populated at close to its carrying capacity; hunting to sustain a population required enormous space.

<2—

On the narrow margin between the sea and the mountains and along misty fjord-like inlets of the Pacific West Coast, indigenous peoples built a rich, hierarchical, and populous civilization on the basis of harvesting abundant salmon and marine life, and foraging in the verdant rain forest. About one-third of all Canada's Native peoples lived in this region, in the most densely settled communities north of Mexico. Divided into 13 tribes speaking 6 main languages, most coastal cultural groups were male dominated, but matrilineal with respect to clan memberships. The northern tribes were the most sharply differentiated into hereditary classes—chiefs, nobles, and commoners with status, slaves with none—while southern communities tended to be more egalitarian. Living in semi-permanent villages marked by clan totems, the coastal tribes were nonetheless united in harvesting the forests, rivers, and seas, in sharing their sustenance and worldly goods, and in performing spiritual rituals. Straight-grained cedar, readily carved and split, provided posts and planks for building materials, fibres for clothing, war canoes for hunting and transportation, as well as the signature totem poles, masks, and boxes of these cultural communities. The salmon, extraordinarily numerous during the spring and fall runs up the coastal rivers to spawn, could be easily netted, dried or smoked, and stored for later consumption. Pacific Coast peoples traded with one another, organized sea-going whale hunts, and fought each other for slaves, territory, honour, and prizes. Abundant food made possible an elaborate social structure, a rich material life, and also a wondrously beautiful symbolic universe that still lives in the indigenous arts of the region.

On the vast Prairie interior, an ocean of waving grasses in the summer and a howling, exposed steppe in mid-winter, a quite different and less populous cultural community evolved. The nomadic Plains Indian tribes for the most part built their lives around the buffalo, which was their source of food, clothing, and hides for their portable teepee dwellings. Shields could be fashioned from the tough neck skin, drinking cups from the horns, thread from the sinews, and the dried dung could be burned for cooking. In spring and summer small tribal groups would follow individual herds of buffalo as they migrated about the Prairie. Using Medicine Wheels sculpted of loose stones on hilltops these people communicated with the gods to ensure the return of large herds. To harvest a winter store of food several tribes would gather at specific sites in the late summer and fall, and, hunting on foot in coordinated parties, they would stampede herds of buffalo off cliffs, called buffalo jumps, and then slaughter the wounded beasts writhing on the rocks below. The most famous of these sites, Head-Smashed-In Buffalo Jump in southern Alberta, drew large numbers of Natives annually for over 5,000 years, according to archaeological evidence. In a few places buffalo could be driven into pounds or corrals where they could be butchered. The tongues of the buffalo and the fetuses of pregnant cows were especially favoured delicacies. Alternatively the hunters would set the Prairie ablaze to encourage the regrowth of succulent green shoots, which would in turn attract grazing buffalo to the hunting grounds. This type of hunting could sustain only a relatively small population scattered over an enormous space, perhaps as few as one person per 26 square kilometres.

In the forested regions, which stretched from the mountain cordillera in the West in a sweeping arc north of the Prairies for thousands of kilometres and then continued across the Great Lakes region to the Atlantic Coast, distinctive hunting-fishing-gathering cultures emerged. In the dense woodlands, around the many lakes and along the rivers, Native peoples hunted deer, moose, and elk; snared smaller game; speared or netted whitefish, sturgeon, and trout; and foraged for nuts, seeds, berries, and edible plants. Tribes would typically gather into larger groupings in the spring, summer, and fall for social occasions, to fish, to harvest resources, and to trade, and then to disperse into smaller family groups for winter survival. Natives fashioned the lightweight canoes used to navigate the often turbulent waterways and countless lakes of this region using the bark of the white birch, a framework of saplings, and the pitch of pine to make things watertight. These resources and the available technology could only support a small population, perhaps only 200,000 or 300,000 people spread thinly across a continent-sized territorial range.

By contrast, on the sandy, easily tilled soils found on both sides of Lake Ontario, more settled, more densely populated agricultural societies arose. About 1,500 years ago, earlier hunter-gatherer peoples took up the cultivation of corn in woodland clearings or burned-over patches. Beans, squash, sunflowers, and tobacco followed. Over time these Iroquoian people became increasingly dependent upon agriculture and supplemented their diet with hunting, gathering, and trade with other woodland tribes. About 1,000 years ago palisaded villages of up to 250 people appeared across the lower Great Lakes region. Inside the stockades, Natives lived in communal longhouses made of stacked elm bark lashed on a framework of poles. Every so often, as the soil became depleted, crop yields fell off and firewood became scarce, and so these villages had to be relocated. Warfare to gain territory, to seize food, for sport, and to obtain captives for ritual torture was endemic to the region. The cultivation of new crops permitted an increase in village size to upwards of a dozen longhouses containing perhaps 600 people; later the villages would grow even larger. At its height, before European contact, this Iroquoian enclave in the central Canadian woodlands numbered approximately 60,000 people and constituted the second most densely populated portion of the country.

The woodlands peoples who inhabited the Gulf of St Lawrence, and the bays and rivers of the Atlantic shore, depended mainly upon the sea for their sustenance. In addition to game and wild plants from the land, these northeastern peoples harvested shellfish, migrating salmon, seals, seabirds and bird eggs, walrus, and small whales. The eastern shore was not as bountiful as the western, and the harsher climate and more exposed rocky coast discouraged settlement. As a result, tribal groups were smaller. In southeastern New Brunswick small villages of excavated dugouts and rock mounds provided shelter in extreme conditions. The indigenous peoples of Nova Scotia and Prince Edward Island, although they possessed a similar language and tools, were nevertheless migratory. They located their temporary shelters of bark and skins in protected bays and riverside settings, and developed light watercraft for navigation on rivers and coastal bays.

Canada before European contact was in a state of constant change as indigenous peoples migrated in search of food, followed game, took advantage of their neighbours' weaknesses, occupied enemy territory and assimilated their populations, or fell back from enemy attacks. For example, Athapaskan people moved south onto the central plateau of British Columbia about 1,300 years ago, and about 700 years later the Iroquoian peoples expanded down the St Lawrence Valley. Native peoples moved constantly, sometimes incrementally and sometimes in long-distance migrations. In this process of ceaseless mingling, and as technologies and cultural practices penetrated new territories, some cultural groups disappeared and new ones emerged. Native peoples continuously adapted and changed while confronting the challenges of survival in a harsh climate and competition for control of territory.

Nowhere was this pattern of constant change more evident than in the Arctic. Eskimo people arriving near the end of the first migrations from Siberia infiltrated the Arctic regions as the glaciers retreated. Climate warmed and cooled in cycles, and with each change food became more or less abundant. Several dominant cultures, identified by different spear points and tool modifications, succeeded one another: Shield Archaic, Paleo-Eskimo, and Dorset. In some parts of the Arctic these peoples lived off caribou and muskox; in other parts fish and sea mammals formed the basis of the diet. These early Arctic peoples lived in tents and hunted at sea in kayaks made from sealskin. Some hunted only on foot with spears and arrows. The Newfoundland Beothuk were more closely related in culture to these peoples of the Arctic, Labrador, and northern Quebec than they were to the tribes of the Atlantic Coast.

Around the year 1000, the Thule people, who would later be known as the Inuit, began expanding eastward from their base in Alaska. As they spread across the Arctic, they adapted local techniques, becoming adept whalers skilled in using harpoons and kayaks. They travelled across the ice using dogsleds and built permanent semi-subterranean wooden villages. The Thule were, apparently, more efficient hunters than the Dorset people whom they drove off or assimilated in their relentless progression eastward during the auspicious period of climate warming after AD 1000. Within a period of 600 years, Thule people completely displaced Dorset people across the Arctic.

A major event in world history occurred at approximately the same time as the Thule people began their eastward expansion, somewhere along the east coast of Labrador, the north shore of Newfoundland, or perhaps along the Gulf of St Lawrence. After thousands of years of evolution and wandering, the eastern and western branches of humanity encountered one another, and the circle of global human migration closed from east to west.

After thousands of years the circle of human migration closed from east to west

For such a momentous event it is perhaps surprising that scoundrels played starring roles. Eric 'the Red' Eriksson, a twice-exiled murderer, had led the colonization of a sheet of ice he had the temerity to call Greenland. Later, following in his father's wake, his son, Leif 'the Lucky' Eriksson, ventured further westward, lured by the tales of sailors, driven off course, who had seen land. These were hard men even by Norse standards. Escorted by squadrons of puffins and a flotilla of flightless great auks—now extinct—Leif found new lands: a barren land of stone slabs to the north (Helluland); a flat wooded territory he considered adequate but unexceptional for his purposes due west of the Greenland settlements (Markland); and a third region further south that he called Vineland, a verdant, heavily forested realm that abounded in salmon, game, desirable timber, and that most luxurious of foods for a Norseman, wild grapes. On one of his subsequent reconnoitring voyages along the coast of Vineland between 993 and

1000, Leif Eriksson spotted smoke rising in the woods by a river. He and some of his crew landed to investigate, and there, on a nameless shore, representatives of the European and American branches of the human family finally met face to face.

We do not know exactly where this encounter took place, or indeed what people the Norse met. *The Norse Sagas,* our only source, are vague and contradictory on such details. We do know that the meeting took place only after the Greenlanders explored extensively along these shores without finding any indigenous peoples. Occasionally, they came across evidence of human activity, but they had not seen the people themselves. The Amerindians whom Leif Eriksson approached could have been woodlands Algonkian Indians such as Montagnais or Mi'kmaq.

Staring at each other in wonder, puzzlement, and fright, the two branches of humanity would have noticed some similarities and differences. From this distance we can see more. In the first place they both recognized each other as human—not Gods or animals. The indigenous peoples were dark haired and the Norse travellers blonde, red-haired, and bearded. They were all, however, similar in height, health, and longevity—though later the Norse would emphasize how small the Natives were with their dismissive name *skraelings.* They inhabited comparable dwellings: the Norse lived a semi-subterranean lice-plagued existence in sod longhouses cut from turf; Native peoples similarly lived close to the earth in dwellings fashioned out of rock and timber. Upon meeting they instinctively set about exchanging objects as they sized each other up.

But important differences immediately became apparent to the Native peoples. The Norse possessed iron for axes, swords, knives, and elegant ocean-going boats of split planks held together with iron rivets. They were clothed not in furs and skins but rather in woven fibres from sheep and goats. They possessed knowledge of navigation: knowing how to get to North America and, if the weather co-operated, how to return to Greenland. While the Natives were hunters and gatherers, the Norse were farmers who brought with them animals, agricultural techniques, and, unknowingly, portions of a transatlantic biological regime such as weed seeds, microbes and vermin. These voyageurs came ultimately from a Kingdom, Norway, and from organized communities numbering in the hundreds in Greenland and thousands in Iceland. The Native peoples, living in small tribal groups, were well adapted to their environment, which they exploited with stone tools; they were linked to neighbouring peoples through trade and combat. The Norse ranged thousands of kilometres across the ocean; they had conquered and occupied many lands, including much of England, coastal France, Ireland, Iceland, Greenland, and now they stood poised to extend their reach to continental North America.

Despite their fierce mien and seafaring prowess the Norse were essentially pastoralists. They set out on their epic voyages to find grassland to pasture their cattle, sheep, and goats, and fodder to keep them over the winter. Prospecting for pastures, a scarce commodity in northern latitudes, the Norse established a base at L'Anse aux Meadows on the northern tip of Newfoundland and perhaps others as yet undiscovered along the Labrador coast. The L'Anse aux Meadows site consisted of three groups of stone buildings covered with turf laid on a wooden framework. There, for a decade or more, parties from Greenland and Iceland wintered in this then-wooded site in preparation for, or following, summer voyages to the south. They were also on the hunt for wood to build and repair their ships, and for roof frames for their houses and outbuildings in sparsely timbered Greenland and Iceland. In time they operated a forge to smelt and shape the native bog iron into metal. From these bases Leif's brothers and brothers-in-law made extensive exploratory voyages into the Gulf of St Lawrence where, along the New Brunswick coast, salubrious summer climes, abundant salmon, grassy riverbanks, butternut trees, and tangles of coveted wild grapes drew them ashore. In a few places, they built small encampments and enclosures for their cattle. And, in one of these verdant enclaves, the first European child in North America was born and given the less than heroic name Snorri.

Over time these cultural differences between the indigenous North Americans and their occasional European visitors would grow wider. But in the year 1000, on a strand in the Gulf of St Lawrence, the two branches of humanity met on roughly equal terms. And if by chance the encounter had taken place on the West Coast, the European advantage would have been even less apparent. But this first European contact by the Norse around 1000 did not lead to successful colonization. The Greenland settlements, numbering at most 600 inhabitants, could not long sustain inconclusive explorations involving hundreds of men and women. And those settlements themselves soon came under strain. In the Gulf of St Lawrence, relations with the indigenous peoples quickly deteriorated in a series of tragic and violent misunderstandings. The Natives did not appreciate Norse attempts to kidnap them to take home as exhibits. The Norse resented the Natives' casual appropriation of Norse weapons. What was interpreted as theft was avenged. Misunderstandings led to violence and death. Murder led to retaliation and punitive raids on both sides. In this conflict, the outnumbered Norse were at a disadvantage. Iron swords were no match for well-aimed stone-pointed arrows. The Norse eventually retreated from their most advanced encampments. In time, they also abandoned L'Anse aux Meadows.

Moreover, the Greenland colonies, which had given rise to these probes, had begun a long, slow process of disintegration. Pastoralism in this delicate ecosystem degraded the environment as deforestation and overgrazing led to irreparable soil erosion. Long-term climate change brought cooler summers, longer winters, and increasingly extensive offshore ice floes that blocked navigation. Gradually, during the onset of this Little Ice Age, the Greenlanders lost regular contact with Iceland and through it their Scandinavian homeland. For the next 400 years, these communities experienced an agonizingly slow decline. They nevertheless appear to have maintained occasional contact with the Labrador coast, for timber, and with Baffin Island and northern Greenland, where hunting caribou and sea mammals supplemented their dwindling diet. In these latitudes the Greenlanders continued to encounter Dorset peoples with whom they probably engaged in some trade. The Norse objects in Dorset archaeological sites could have been obtained through direct trade with the Norse, from salvaging shipwrecks, or from conquest. In any event, encounters between these anonymous Norse and Native North Americans continued sporadically in the northern regions for about 400 years after contact had been broken off in the Gulf of St Lawrence. Then, at the beginning of the fifteenth century, the Greenland settlements disappeared. Possibly the isolated eastern and western settlements, much reduced in numbers and morale, came under attack from Thule–Inuit peoples descending from the north. Sometime around 1450 a last desperate goat curled up in an abandoned farmhouse and died, to be buried by the drifting sands of this now-desolate wasteland. The Viking era had ended.

⌒

The Norse had reached Canada around 1000, explored the coastline extensively, but then retreated. Like modern air travellers from

Europe they approached Canada from the north Atlantic, crossing Greenland, making landfall in Newfoundland and Labrador. However, they possessed neither the population to sustain these explorations, nor the diplomatic skills to establish peaceful relations with indigenous peoples. Where conditions were most favourable to pastoral agriculture, Natives were also most numerous. The Norse lacked the numbers and military hardware to displace the Natives or sustain their occupation in the teeth of hostility. Indeed the reverse occurred; the Natives drove them off. The Norse sought to practise a temperate pastoralism in an environment that could not sustain it. Their cattle and sheep made a desert of the northern environment. A cooling climate and thickening ice weakened the long supply line from Norway to Iceland to Greenland to Canada, and led to its final collapse. But the oral traditions of these adventures, captured in writing in the *Sagas*, became part of European lore, adding substance to the dream of agreeable lands beyond the sea.

As the Norse communities in Greenland silently expired in the fifteenth century the quest for protein for the table and light for the home brought new European visitors to the eastern shores of Canada from a southeasterly direction. French, Portuguese, Basque, and later English fishermen discovered the teeming Bank and inshore cod fishery around Newfoundland. In the later 1400s and early 1500s, they came in ever-increasing numbers to catch the fish so important to the Southern European diet. Basque whalers pursuing their prey across the Atlantic were drawn to the Labrador coast, where they rendered the fat into oil to be carried home to fuel smokeless lamps. Portuguese seamen in a satirical mood chose the name Labrador (*Tierra del Lavrador,* land of the farmer), and Basque words mingled with Native phrases as the language of contact. For a brief time, a Portuguese colony fought for survival on the Cape Breton shore. In the mid-1500s, more than 400 ships carrying thousands of men regularly plied these waters, more ships and men than in contemporary Spanish convoys to Mexico and the Caribbean. Among these venturesome commercial people, vernacular knowledge of winds, currents, shores, shoals, and navigational secrets gradually accumulated, to be passed on by word of mouth among the fraternity, jealously guarded against competitors, and shared with professional navigators for a price.

These whalers and fishermen were only incidentally interested in the land; they had come great distances at considerable danger to themselves to harvest the wealth of the sea. The cold, dank, rocky, heavily forested, coniferous shores of Newfoundland, Labrador, and Nova Scotia were not particularly attractive to people from Iberian latitudes. They migrated to their fishing grounds and whaling stations each year, coming ashore for water, fuel wood, repairs, and to escape storms. The fishermen usually salted their catch on board, but occasionally they built wooden stages on the beach to dry fish for shipment back to Europe. And the whalers found abundant fuel to boil down whale blubber into oil. But neither needed elaborate or even permanent onshore structures to accomplish their seasonal tasks. These land-based activities brought them into accidental contact with indigenous peoples, who in turn came to anticipate the seasonal arrival of Europeans. Such encounters led to an informal but growing trade on the Labrador coast, on the shores of Cape Breton, and along the Gulf of St Lawrence, the Europeans valuing furs and the Natives seeking metal weapons, utensils, textiles, and alcohol. The European newcomers also competed with the indigenous population for fishing grounds. Relations were not always peaceful. Europeans casually kidnapped Natives to take home as trophies. Natives harassed and destroyed European proto-settlements. As the sixteenth century progressed the indigenous peoples of Atlantic Canada were brought into regular contact with a mainly South European fishing and whaling system. However, since the fishers and whalers stayed mainly offshore, contact was episodic and their lives continued without much disruption by European influences.

The growing wealth and power of Europe in the sixteenth century led to a new kind of overseas expansion: state-sponsored voyages of exploration to locate more direct routes to the Orient, to claim new lands for Renaissance European princes and Christendom, and to expand knowledge of and control over the wider world. The belief that through the capture of treasure and trade in exotic commodities these voyages could become financial bonanzas—a conviction justified by the experience of some of the earliest ventures—quickened interest in the major European courts and commercial centres in voyages of exploration. Following in the wake of Christopher Columbus, Spanish and Portuguese navigators mapped, claimed, and conquered large portions of the Caribbean and Central and South America, carrying shiploads of gold and silver back to enrich their princes and sponsors. A Papal Decree in 1494 divided the known New World into Spanish and Portuguese spheres of influence.

But the competition for gold and the lure of the Orient drew others into the quest. To break the Spanish–Portuguese monopoly, capture territory, and enrich themselves, the English and French kings also sponsored transatlantic voyages further to the north. In 1497 an Italian mariner, Giovanni Caboto (John Cabot), sailing for King Henry VII of England, formally 'rediscovered' Newfoundland. Another Italian, Verrazano, in the service of Francis I of France, cruised the eastern seaboard of North America in the 1520s and established that a continent-sized landmass blocked passage to the Far East. These and other famous voyages of discovery drew upon the marine technology and tacit knowledge of the anonymous fishermen who had gone before and who were at the same time expanding European understanding of the New World with their commercial activities.

Jacques Cartier's voyages of exploration for the French Crown in 1534, 1535–6, and 1541 permanently altered the destiny of what was to become Canada. On his first voyage, he reconnoitred the Labrador and Newfoundland coasts through the Straits of Belle Isle, and then explored the lower reaches of the Gulf of St Lawrence before returning with two Native captives. On his second trip, during which he and his crew wintered-over in the region of Quebec, Cartier, against the wishes of his Native hosts, travelled up the St Lawrence as far as the site of Montreal, a route he followed again upon his return in 1541. On the last trip Cartier's fortune-hunting associates established a fortified village manned by convicts from French prisons and furiously set about digging for gold and diamonds. The settlement did not last. In the winter scurvy decimated their ranks. The quarrelsome colonists fell upon each other. Murders and hangings destroyed the venture from within. Native attacks killed many more before spring, when the survivors fled back to France.

At one level Cartier's voyages brought back disappointing news: the St Lawrence was not a passage to Asia but a river draining a continent blocking the way to the Orient. Cartier found no gold, and the diamonds his expedition had gathered proved on analysis, once he got home, to be pyrite and mica, giving rise to the dismissive crack 'phoney as diamonds from Canada'.[1] The land he 'discovered' could by no stretch of the imagination be turned

---

1   This fine example of ancient regime French ridicule now rings a little hollow as Canada produces an abundance of gem-quality diamonds.

into a kingdom of fabled riches like Mexico, Peru, or Brazil. Instead, it was a place of more prosaic commodities and simpler peoples, and a curiosity containing its own distinctive but esoteric wonders. Still, it too was a vast and mysterious land upon which Europeans projected their hopes and readily imagined that what they were looking for lay beyond the hills on the horizon. Canada would not dazzle the European imagination or fire great ambitions, but it would capture the attention of some well-placed French courtiers and merchants who saw opportunities there.

Jacques Cartier's explorations marked the formal beginning of a process that would permanently transform Canada. Fishing fleets and merchants had already led the way. Cartier had apprenticed as a sailor on voyages to Brazil and possibly Newfoundland. On his first voyage Cartier's vessel was overtaken by a large French commercial fishing boat out of La Rochelle. The indigenous peoples he encountered a few weeks later in the Baie de Chaleurs clearly demonstrated that they were quite familiar with European visitors and wanted to trade. Indeed, they were so clamorous to trade, holding furs aloft on sticks as their canoes encircled the ship, that Cartier felt compelled to drive them off with his canon. Routine contact and exchange between Europeans and Amerindians obviously had preceded the arrival of the great explorers. (Native women, perhaps put on their guard by prior unpleasant experience with European sailors, apparently lurked in the background.) Cartier was not alone, nor was he the first European to sail these waters, but he was the first to do so with the authority of a King and something more than fish on his mind.

If in some respects the forbidding, lower St Lawrence landscape appeared to him to bear the mark of Cain, it would soon also bear the mark of Cartier and his countrymen. First, Cartier was responsible for naming Canada, or rather he adopted the word his two kidnapped interpreters uttered to describe their homeland. Used first in the limited sense of describing tribal territories lying between Grosse Isle in the east and Trois-Rivières in the west, the name (meaning town or village) came to be applied to this region of North American territory in general.

Second, Cartier assumed possession of the place. He not only made a ceremony of raising a cross bearing the name of the King of France, but he also emphasized the importance of that religious and political symbol to his somewhat alarmed Native hosts. At a more profound level he assumed Canada to be a place where he could do what he wanted without seeking anyone's permission. He and his friends sought no one's leave to establish their fledgling if doomed colony. The savages, as he called them, were there to be commanded, if possible improved, and if necessary removed. The land, he believed, was France's for the taking.

Third, Cartier penetrated deep into the interior of the country following the pathway of the magnificent St Lawrence, until rapids—later called Lachine in reference to the dashed hopes of finding China upstream—impeded his passage. European influence, previously confined to Atlantic shoreline, now extended hundreds of kilometres into the interior, much to the initial delight of indigenous peoples inland who sought direct and unmediated contact with the foreigners. The gatekeeper rule of the coastal tribes had been broken. Cartier prevailed in the face of Native remonstrance and even open hostility. His ship's canons, hand weapons, and body armour established a new power relationship between the European visitors and their more numerous Native hosts.

Finally, Cartier conducted an inventory of the plants, animals, birds, landforms, and peoples of the new world that, with the publication of his travel narratives in Italian, English, and French, greatly broadened European knowledge of the characteristics of the new world and publicized its possibilities. He possessed the place and its occupants by naming and describing them, and in doing so he attached Canada firmly to Europe. For Canada, Jacques Cartier was the future, and it was French.

From a Native point of view, Cartier's voyage foretold a world turned upside down. The French gave every appearance of claiming land that Natives thought of as theirs. They displayed open contempt for indigenous cultural and spiritual practices, insisting upon the importance of the Cross and Christian religion. Cartier seized sons, daughters, even a chief, Lord Donacona himself, and carried them off to France, most never to return. However much the Iroquois people of the village of Stadacona—now Quebec—might plead, bargain, declaim in their most powerful oratory, invoke their most fearsome sorcery, and offer bribes, gifts, and substitutes, the French would not be deterred.

For Canada, Jacques Cartier was the future, and it was French.

Nor, since they possessed a frightening canon, could they be forcibly prevented from taking whomever they wished without tragic loss of life. The French brazenly advanced upriver to consort with rival tribes in the interior, against all custom, civility, and honour. Above all, deadly diseases accompanied the French. The Natives helped the French when scurvy visited their mid-winter fortification, but the French could offer nothing but prayer when a devastating European epidemic raged through Stadacona that same winter, carrying off more than 50 Iroquois inhabitants. The invisible companions of the early French visitors—their viruses, vermin, and bacteria—would wreak even greater havoc in the years to come as, through Native trade and community activities, they were transmitted widely to devastate the continental population. The power of the cross, the gun, and the microbe, and that unshakable European assumption of superiority and possession felt first by the Iroquois of Stadacona in the 1530s, would over the next two centuries change the indigenous way of life throughout the continent.

⌒

But change would happen gradually. For the rest of the sixteenth century the French, racked by their own internal wars of religion, directed their official energies towards the likely more profitable task of competing directly with the Spanish and Portuguese in southern explorations. They would not return in significant numbers to Canada for more than 60 years. The English too were pre-occupied elsewhere. Elizabethan pirates preyed upon the Spanish galleons in the Caribbean. English colonizing energies were spent subjugating Ireland.

During this period a few seafarers, most notably Martin Frobisher, Humphrey Gilbert, and Henry Hudson (after he was wooed away from the Dutch), continued to probe the Arctic on behalf of the English Crown and mercantile interests searching for the elusive passage to China and, of course, gold. Breton, French Basque, and English fishermen consolidated their hold over the growing Newfoundland fishery. Dried and salted fish found a ready market in Southern Europe as an inexpensive food for the numerous Saints days. The English, lacking salt, focussed their activities in the bays of the Avalon Peninsula and the northern shore of Newfoundland where they dried their catch on wooden flakes. This dried fish, which recovered its texture in cooking, stored well, shipped with minimal losses, and commanded premium prices in European markets. The French fishing fleet, operating mainly offshore, frequented the harbours along the southern and western shores of Newfoundland and in the course of the fishery a growing trade with indigenous peoples developed. Natives wanted knives, kettles, glass beads, mirrors, and items of clothing. At first the Europeans did not much value Native articles, but they took the furs the Natives freely offered and seemed to have in great abundance. In time these furs, especially the finely woven felt of the beaver pelt, found a ready market among French hatters.

In the Gulf of St Lawrence by the 1580s the village of Tadoussac, at the mouth of the Saguenay River, had become the main trading point where furs from the interior were bartered with the 20 or so French boats that gathered there each summer. Quietly and informally the commercial possibilities of Canada became known in the ports of western France and England as cargoes of fish and bales of furs landed with increasing regularity on the quays. By the end of the sixteenth century, enterprising merchants in Basque and French seaports outfitted several hundred vessels and recruited several thousand sailors and fishers each year, specifically to engage in this trade along the Maritime and Gulf coasts.

Natives of the Arctic, the Beothuk of Newfoundland, and the woodland peoples of the Maritimes felt the impact of the European presence most acutely. In the Arctic, for example, the newly arrived Inuit peoples forcefully resisted the incursions of Frobisher and Hudson. The Basque, Breton, English, and Irish fishermen displaced the Beothuk people of Newfoundland from their shores. Driven inland with its scarce food resources, sometimes murdered on sight as thieves, the Beothuk slowly starved to death. After prolonged contact in the Maritimes, the Mi'kmaq and Malaceet tribes, who formerly spent the bulk of their lives as fishers on the coast, reoriented themselves inland to obtain the furs they now needed to maintain commerce with the newcomers upon whom they now depended. A trade language developed as the *lingua franca* of the region, combining elements of Basque and Algonquian dialects.

The word *Iroquois,* for example, is a modification of a word from this language, *Hirokoa,* meaning 'the killer people'. Thus, Natives acquired names not their own and often from their enemies.

⌒

Around 1600 the French Crown decided for strategic reasons to exercise more authority over its Canadian possessions, whose commercial prominence had been noticeably growing. The King of France used the instrument of the royal monopoly grant to carry out his policy. The holder of the monopoly—at first a series of individuals, later a succession of incorporated companies—gained the exclusive right to trade in the region in return for promises to settle a certain number of colonists, provide civil government as in France, and convert the indigenous peoples to Christianity. After reconnoitring the St Lawrence, the first expedition of the Canada monopoly established a beachhead in the Bay of Fundy, initially on an island along the western shore, and then on the eastern mainland. Port-Royal, built on the shore of the Annapolis Basin in 1605, marked the beginning of what would become a permanent French colony in Canada. For three summers, the employees of the monopoly engaged in a futile search for gold, silver, and gem stones. They barely survived the winters, though on their third they amused themselves with ample wine, amateur theatricals, and a competitive culinary contest they called the Order of Good Cheer. The colony survived, but it could not exercise its strategic function of defending the royal monopoly. Trading vessels from other countries as well as France simply ignored the royal warrant with impunity.

In response, Samuel de Champlain, a mapmaker, sailor, and the most energetic lieutenant of the monopoly, relocated the little settlement to the St Lawrence River above Tadoussac, to a commanding site where fur trade traffic could be controlled from the heights by canon. In 1608 at Quebec (an Algonquian word meaning 'narrowing of the river') on the flats below the cliff, Champlain built what he called a habitation, a fortified trading post, where he and 27 comrades settled in for the winter. More than half of them died of scurvy before ships arrived in the spring to restock the post with food, trade goods, and more men. Despite this rough beginning, the enterprise survived. The next year Champlain planted wheat and rye and surrounded the walls of his habitation with roses. From this tiny beginning, the frail colony of New France would haltingly flower throughout the seventeenth century.

Champlain did not have to contend with the awkward and possibly hostile presence at Quebec of Donacona's Iroquois successors. Indeed, he built his habitation virtually on the site of the abandoned village of Stadacona. Sometime between the visits of Cartier in the 1530s and Champlain in the first decade of the seventeenth century, the Iroquois had disappeared from the lower St Lawrence Valley. No one knows for certain what happened to them. Better-armed rivals supplied with European weapons may have driven them out. They may have retreated from the region, decimated by European diseases. Tribes further inland, determined to break their hold over intercourse with the Europeans, could have dispersed them. For whatever reason, the powerful Iroquois people had vanished from the banks of the St Lawrence, leaving something of a vacuum into which Algonquian peoples from the north had infiltrated.

These were the people who now greeted Champlain, upon whom he depended to gather furs from the interior tribes, and with whom he formed a tacit military alliance. These woodland peoples, Montagnais and Ottawas, traded with the French and guided Champlain as he explored the region. In return Champlain agreed to join his Native allies and lend his arms to an attack on the Iroquois, their mortal enemies, who had now consolidated their power in villages stretching from the northern Adirondacks into the lake district south of Lake Ontario. With the aid of his loud but not particularly accurate harquebus (a primitive shotgun that sprayed metal fragments rather indiscriminately) they defeated the Iroquois in a pitched battle in 1609. Champlain's action made sense from a strategic point of view; it pleased his friends and secured their aid in his endeavours. But it won him the undying wrath of a powerful enemy, the Iroquois Confederacy.

After a few years of struggling for mere survival, Champlain began to dream of much bigger things for his fledgling colony. In a memorandum to the King and the merchants of France in 1618, he spun a vision of a rich economy exporting fish, fish products, minerals, dyestuffs, timber, fur, gems, and livestock to France. He predicted the customs revenues on goods flowing down the St Lawrence River from the short route to Asia would exceed those of all of France by ten times. On the banks of the St Lawrence at Quebec, Champlain could imagine a magnificent city, Ludovica, about the same size and grandeur as central Paris. More than 300 of the King's soldiers would secure the settlement from three great forts. A similar number of families would till the soil while missionaries from the Recollet religious order would settle the indigenous peoples in peaceful Christian villages. It was a vision of France in America, designed to appeal to the ambitions of both court and counting house, built in equal parts upon firm knowledge, pious hope, and speculative pipe dreams.

Quite apart from the faulty premise that China lay somewhere in the vicinity of present-day Toronto, there were several reasons why Champlain's vision of an idealized French 'city upon a hill' did not come to fruition in his lifetime—or ever. For most of the seventeenth century, the fledgling colony could not depend upon substantial or consistent support from France. The erratic fur trade was a frail reed upon which to build a stable economy. The colony came under constant attack, both from other European imperial powers and from indigenous peoples. As a result of its tribulations, New France acquired a fearsome reputation that tended to deter both potential colonists and investors.

Royal charters so grandly granted could just as arbitrarily be rescinded. Fickle royal favour, heavy indebtedness, and intrigue on the part of merchants who had an interest in breaking the monopoly meant frequent changes of management that bedeviled the colony. Individual merchants could rarely command the capital on their own to sustain the enterprise; companies of merchants once they received the royal charter also collapsed under the strain. In truth, neither individuals nor companies willingly wished to undertake the expense of recruiting, transporting, supplying, and defending settlers, or supporting priests in the field, especially when profits from the fur trade often failed to meet expectations. The French backers of the various New France ventures, whether out of necessity or choice, rarely fulfilled the settlement obligations demanded by their royal charters. The French Crown further weakened the colonization effort by banning Protestants from New France. The intention was to create a society loyal to the King, held together by religion rather than divided by it, but this edict effectively eliminated the very Protestant commercial classes that had been most energetic in promoting the colony.

The fortunes of the colony depended largely upon the returns from the fur trade, which were inherently unstable. The flow of furs to Quebec could be highly variable depending upon Native alliances, warfare, trade with enemies, and disruptions in the transportation system. Ships from France could be intercepted by enemies, lost in storms, or arrive in greater numbers than expected. Free traders floated on the margins of the colony, defying the system by skimming off some of the best pelts. Fur was also a luxury good, whose price in France fluctuated with available supplies and changing fashion. New France was not built upon a foundation of sugar, tobacco, agriculture, or silver or gold mining—each of which required labour in the form of immigrants, indentured servants, or slaves. The fur trade, drawing heavily upon Native labour, could manage with a relatively small European complement of more or less itinerant merchant traders and shippers.

The survival of this emerging colony required adaptation by the French to a North American environment and by the indigenous peoples to the presence of the French. Through contact, the two cultures developed mutual respect—and, it must be said, reciprocal animosity. The French borrowed indigenous technologies—canoes, snowshoes, and toboggans—to travel in the new landscape, adopted some aspects of Native clothing, and had recourse to herbal remedies for sickness and injuries. Native peoples coveted European knives, textiles, utensils, and weapons. They also developed a fondness for French uniforms, rituals, and brandy. The French admired the bravery and physical endurance of indigenous peoples, especially their immunity to pain, but deplored what they considered the savage customs of the Natives, their wanton cruelty, and their pagan religion. Reading between the lines of the missionaries' and explorers' accounts it would seem that indigenous peoples regarded the bearded French as physically inferior, deformed, hairy, morally depraved creatures who spread disease as they went and drove off the wildlife. The symbolism of the Christian religion terrified them. The heavy timber and stone houses of the French struck the Natives as excessive and ridiculously immobile. Natives apparently thought well of the French attentiveness to the sick and dying but were puzzled by their apparent indifference to the needs of the poor. Each society reacted to the other according to its needs, biases, and fears, a process of cultural hybridization that would be ongoing.

Constant warfare was the most serious impediment to the growth of Canada. New France struggled into existence in a hostile world, a pawn in the dynastic quarrels of European monarchs. In 1629, for example, English pirates seized Quebec when the French King refused to pay his sister's dowry to the English King. It was returned after three years when the French King finally made good. Rival colonies and trading competitors tried to put Quebec out of business. In 1635 Virginia colonists burned the French community of Port-Royal on the Bay of Fundy and carried off some of its inhabitants. And all the while English privateers constantly harassed French ships in the Gulf of St Lawrence.

Each society reacted to the other according to its needs, biases, and fears.

However, the most deadly threat to the colony lay close by. In 1649, to gain control of the flow of furs and the benefits of trade, the Iroquois Confederacy of Five Nations set out to destroy the colony of New France and disperse its Native allies. Armed with guns by the Dutch traders in New Amsterdam and English merchants from New England, the Iroquois maintained a constant guerrilla campaign against the settlements along the St Lawrence and launched a full-scale frontal attack on the Ottawa and Huron fur-trading allies of the French. The Iroquois invaded Huronia—already weakened by European epidemic diseases—and killed, captured, or scattered its inhabitants. In a ruthless attempt to control the fur trade, the Iroquois annihilated their Huron brethren. Outside of the fortification of Quebec no one was safe in New France. The mission village of Montreal came under constant siege. In lightning raids on isolated farmsteads, the

Iroquois brutally murdered men, women, and children and carried off captives for ritual torture. In the year 1661 Iroquois raids killed 61 inhabitants of the small community. In the face of this sustained, well-armed, and organized Iroquois campaign of terror New France had to fight for its survival.

The ferocity of the Native attacks considerably damaged the already tarnished overseas reputation of Canada as a colonizing frontier. The few people in France who knew anything of Canada thought of it as a barren place, beset by a howling climate, peopled by criminals and prostitutes, and tormented by nightmarish Native raids. The Jesuit Order, when it took over the responsibility for bringing the indigenous peoples to Christianity in 1632, provided a regular flow of information back to its supporters and sponsors in France. These most disciplined forces of the Catholic counter-reformation willingly sought martyrdom as they established their missions among the indigenous peoples. The horrific tales of Jesuit suffering and death along with stories of barbaric torture and Native cannibalism conveyed back to France in their letters did little to relieve anxiety at home. Canada seemed an unpleasant, dangerous place with few attractions to compensate for its considerable risks.

For all of these reasons, very few inhabitants of the most populous country in Europe willingly sought to emigrate to New France in the early seventeenth century. It is true that few French subjects left the country for any overseas colonies in that century, but Canada was a particularly unpopular destination. In fact, when one group of settlers bound for Canada passed through a Normandy village, the inhabitants rioted to set them free, thinking they would not willingly seek exile from France in Canada.

At first, the French government did not subsidize the transatlantic migration; nor did it offer much encouragement. The most likely migrants, Protestant Huguenot facing persecution in France, were barred from the colony. With varying degrees of conviction, the owners of the trading monopoly tried to bring out settlers, usually as indentured servants bound for a certain number of years to work under contract, after which their return passage would be provided. Many immigrants to Canada during this period were in effect conscripts who grudgingly performed their duties and then left at the first opportunity. The religious orders imported their own lay servants to sustain their missions. Merchants, traders, sailors, and craftsmen came and went with each shipping season.

By the mid-seventeenth century, the people of Canada consisted of a floating population of young males, most of whom planned to reside only temporarily in Canada. Because the French kept such good records, we know that between 1608 and 1659 about 5,000 migrants crossed the Atlantic from France to Canada. Of that number 40 per cent were indentured male servants and only 9 per cent women. The rest were soldiers, members of the colonial administration, merchants, artisans, agriculturalists, and clergy. Only a handful of families made the voyage. About 1,200 of the 5,000 migrants, less than one-third, remained in the colony. At mid-century, when the English colonies on the eastern seaboard probably claimed more than 40,000 European immigrant inhabitants, New France had fewer than 5,000 permanent and transient residents. Indeed, by the end of the seventeenth century there were more French-speaking Huguenot in New England and New York than in all of New France. After 50 years of fitful administration under a succession of private contractors, the colony of New France still scarcely existed.

⌒

All of that changed dramatically in 1663, in what is usually thought of as one of the great 'moments' in Canadian history.

French authorities had not been satisfied with the development of Canada under private auspices. In their view the fur trade, with its inherent expansionist characteristics and long supply lines, exposed the colony to too many risks. Mercantilist administrators preferred a tightly knit community based upon agriculture with a supporting artisanal sector. Such a settlement could be more easily defended when it came under attack; indeed it could more readily defend itself. It was also more stable, less subject to external cataclysms and cyclical economic swings.

In 1663, the French Crown, recognizing the strategic importance of Canada on a continent increasingly controlled by the English, took over direct responsibility for the feeble colony. The young King Louis XIV and his energetic minister of the marine, Jean-Baptiste Colbert, in effect made Canada a province of France under royal control. A strong, interventionist government, with a coherent economic and social plan, well supplied with taxpayers' money, and served by an able and imaginative public service, restored the colony to health, made it a vital player in North American geopolitics, and set its course for the next century. This is the sort of effort—systematic public policy, properly pursued—that Canadians instinctively respect. In this regard they are very French. This latent admiration for *dirigiste* government is perhaps an enduring cultural legacy from the *ancien régime*.

This is the sort of effort—systematic public policy, properly pursued—that Canadians instinctively respect.

France sent out a governor with full authority to lead the colony, maintain order, and defend the inhabitants. The military force to back up his mandate came initially from a troop of marines that accompanied him and then a French regiment dispatched to Canada a short time later. Along with a governor, an intendant, or chief operating officer—the first being Jean Talon—took charge of the civil administration, and social and economic development of the colony. A bishop already in the colony, with responsibility for the missions to the Indians and the loyalty as well as the spiritual and social welfare of the inhabitants, completed the administrative triumvirate.

The French plan for the colony came straight from the mercantilist pattern-book. Canada was to become an easily defended compact agricultural community of villages, fields, and churches—a little France. Ideally it would feed and sustain itself in most respects, exporting raw materials—timber, fish, and furs—to the home country. Its agricultural surplus would also help sustain France's Caribbean colonies, which exported vast quantities of sugar, but otherwise could not feed themselves. Canada would not only become self-sustaining, but it would also enrich the home country's manufacturers through the purchase of textiles, hardware, household utensils, weapons, and farm implements. Once the Native peoples had been pacified, the Church would organize them in Christian settlements where they would be gradually assimilated. A dynamic, growing colony such as this, situated astride the main river leading into the heart of the continent, served strategic purposes as well. It divided the English realm in Hudson's Bay from the Atlantic colonies in the south, and effectively pre-empted English possession of the interior. That, at least, was the plan. It could only be realized with substantial resources, state involvement, and consistent political will. It is somewhat remarkable in retrospect to observe how many of the French royal objectives actually were achieved.

⌒

To make the plan work Canada desperately needed settlers and manpower. To that end France subsidized overseas passages. New estates, or seigneuries, were granted to landlords who in turn had an obligation to settle them with colonists. France shipped agricultural supplies and breeding stock, particularly cattle and horses, for Canadian farms. Over a decade the Crown hired about 4,000 *engagés*—tradesmen, labourers, and agriculturalists—and transported them to Canada. Members of the army were offered incentives to settle in Canada when they were discharged. Still, a heavily male and young population could not reproduce itself. In one of the most imaginative population policy measures of all time, the French government gathered up about 800 young women from hospices and orphanages, provided them with suitable dowries, and shipped them out to Canada. In a colony starved of women, these 'Daughters of the King' were wed within a surprisingly short time of their arrival, usually in less than two weeks. But just to make certain that the marriage market would be cleared, the government fined reluctant bachelors or prevented them from engaging in the fur trade while brides remained to be taken. This balancing of the sex ratio in the latter half of the seventeenth century provided the fecundity upon which the remarkable demographic growth of the colony would subsequently be based. Public policy also helped in that respect as well. Families of more than 10 children received government subsidies.

During this period the French government poured hundreds of thousands of livres into Canada, investing in a number of local activities to diversify the economy, most notably construction, public works, shipbuilding, and brewing. An aggressive population policy supported these objectives. Between 1660 and 1700 the French government oversaw the immigration of about 10,000 people, 50 per cent of them soldiers, 7 per cent indentured servants, and 13 per cent women. By 1700 a reasonably prosperous agricultural settlement had developed on the banks of the

St Lawrence River between Quebec and Trois-Rivières, and around the island of Montreal.

Of course, not all went according to plan. The settlers could not be confined to compact villages as in France, preferring to spread themselves out in a thin line of farmhouses along the river-front. Agriculture became increasingly important, emerging as the main economic activity by 1700, but the fur trade still provided the most lucrative opportunities for ambitious young colonists. Governors even extended a series of military posts into the interior of the country, protecting and expanding the range of the trade. French-Canadian *engagés,* called *coureurs de bois* ('runners of the woods'), employed by merchants in Montreal and Quebec, took over the transportation, gathering, and supply aspects of the trade from indigenous peoples in the interior. Debate still rages in historical circles as to whether the fur trade siphoned off the energies of the agriculturalists at key times in the season and diverted the profits of trade from the colony to the metropole. The proposed gradual assimilation of Native peoples through settlement faltered. Indeed, the Jesuits and other religious orders preferred to keep Natives apart from the corrupting influences of European society. Diversification of the economy proved difficult. The high cost of labour and perennial shortages of skilled labour made many colonial businesses uneconomic. The colony, importing more than it exported, was perennially short of hard currency. Specie—coin money—could not be retained in the country. Nor could fresh supplies from government coffers be assured. For a hard-pressed royal treasury with many obligations closer to home, Canada remained a fairly low priority. Even when resources were committed they could be lost at sea or intercepted. On one memorable occasion in 1685, when the ship bearing the summer payroll failed to appear, the governor inscribed playing cards that passed as the currency of the colony.

Defence remained the biggest challenge facing the reinvigorated colonial administration. Under this new management, New France went on the offensive, declaring war on the Iroquois. French troops and Native allies descended into the heart of Iroquois country, slaughtering inhabitants, destroying villages, laying waste fields—until the Iroquois sued for a truce. In 1701, weakened by disease, overwhelmed by the need to incorporate many captives, internally divided between Christian converts and non-Christians, and humiliated by the vicious repression of the French, the Iroquois negotiated The Great Peace of Montreal, which proved lasting, and which permanently removed the threat of Native massacres from the St Lawrence Valley. Following this treaty the French were able to install missionaries in the decimated communities, whose converts created an effective fifth column within Native councils. Over time, some of the Iroquois were induced by missionaries to establish villages within the territory of New France, in the vicinity of Montreal. These Mohawks—one of the five nations making up the Iroquois Confederacy—and mission Indians became staunch allies of the French when war broke out once again.

New France had other enemies too. Whenever France and England went to war—which happened quite often—their surrogates in North America seized the opportunity to fall upon one another with murderous enthusiasm. The War of the League of Augsburg (1688–97) and the War of the Spanish Succession (1702–13) provided occasions for a renewal of hostilities in North America locally known respectively as King William's War and Queen Anne's War. Accompanied by their new-found Iroquois allies, French guerrillas descended upon outlying New England settlements, especially in the Connecticut Valley, burning farmsteads, slaying inhabitants, and scalping and carrying off terrified captives. An estimated 1,000 men, women, and children were taken captive from these English settlements and removed to New France. Frantic relatives ransomed many of these captives, but the majority remained unredeemed, settling into their new lives among their Native or French 'hosts'. One of these female English captives, Esther Wheelwright, rose to become Mother Superior of the Ursuline Order at Quebec in the mid-eighteenth century.

New Englanders, of course, retaliated with a seaborne assault. The orphaned and undefended French settlements on the Bay of Fundy, descendants of the very first French colonizing efforts, were particularly vulnerable. Even the heart of New France came under attack. Twice invasion fleets from New England appeared in the river below Quebec, but failed to mount an effective assault. An overland invasion force from New England got swallowed up in the mountains, forests, and swamps of the Adirondacks. Canada's formidable geography, climate, and faulty English tactics preserved and protected the outnumbered French colonists.

New France remained a relatively minor element of a much broader set of French strategic concerns. The fortunes of war in Europe and in the colonies overseas did not always run in parallel. The French, along with their Native allies, proved particularly adept at war in North America, extending their influence deep into the interior, into the Hudson's Bay regions in the far north, and into the area south of the Great Lakes. Nevertheless, French losses in Europe could be compensated for by territorial concessions in the colonies. Such proved to be the case in 1713 when the Treaty of Utrecht ended the War of the Spanish Succession, a period of protracted conflict in Europe. In the peace the French paid for their losses in Europe by giving up possessions in North America. They surrendered Hudson's Bay and Acadia to the English and gave up settlements in Newfoundland, though they retained important fishing rights to the northern coast of Newfoundland. Though France lost Nova Scotia, it retained Cape Breton Island. These wars showed that the Atlantic approaches to Canada had to be secured against the British. Beginning in 1719, the French Crown undertook construction of the largest fortification in the Americas on Cape Breton Island at English Harbour, appropriately renamed Louisbourg. France positioned this massive geometrical marvel of Vauban military engineering, along with its resident garrison and naval squadron, to guard French interests in the fishery and protect the St Lawrence River gateway to Canada.

New France flourished during the 30 years of peace following the Treaty of Utrecht. Certainly it grew up as an extension of France, greatly dependent upon the mother country, but it would not become a miniature replica of France. It was a colony of French origin, but that was its point of departure. As this population responded to available economic opportunities in a particular North American environment within a loose framework of political authority, a distinct culture would evolve, something with a character of its own, properly called New France.

Immigration continued into the eighteenth century, though at a somewhat reduced rate. Most of the immigrants came from the port cities of western France, their hinterlands, and from the Paris region. Towns accounted for five times as many immigrants as did the French countryside. However, population growth in the colony depended less upon immigration than upon natural increase because, as previously, fully two-thirds of the immigrants to New France either returned to France or left the colony. Of the estimated 27,000 immigrants to Canada before 1760 only about 9,000 remained. Those who stayed behind, however, formed a population that experienced one of the highest birth rates ever recorded. New France could count upon approximately 55 births for every 1,000 inhabitants compared with something in the order of 40 per 1,000 in seventeenth-century France—and fewer than 10 in Canada today. Not surprisingly the large number of unruly and badly behaved children caught the eye of visitors. The higher proportion of married couples in New France largely explains its extraordinary birth rate. Once the sex ratio had been balanced, fertility drove population growth in New France. Fertility rates within marriage were somewhat higher than in France itself, largely because of better diet, earlier marriage, shorter intervals between births, and longer life in Canada. Each year New France escaped the crises of subsistence and the visitations of epidemics that periodically devastated the French population at home. However, high infant mortality rates comparable to those in France restrained population growth somewhat. Still, by 1740 the European origin population of the St Lawrence Valley exceeded 50,000, of whom some 5,000 lived in Quebec and 3,500 in Montreal. For the most part they were born in Canada. Canada was their home; they were no longer immigrants.

Population growth produced a much more densely settled core settlement about 400 kilometres long between Quebec and Montreal. Habitants and their numerous children pushed the forest back from the riverbanks at a rate of about one hectare per farm per year. Settlers usually set fire to the forest to begin the clearing process. Stands of maple, pine, and oak gradually gave way to lush meadows and grain fields. By the 1730s in the older seigneuries, about 30 per cent of the land had been cleared. Usually no trees were left standing in the swath of European landscape under construction a kilometre or two deep on either side of the river. Ironically, wood quickly became scarce in the bald landscape in the immediate vicinity of settlements. But the forest was never too far away, as the long narrow landholdings were only one or two ranks, or rows, deep. At the beginning of settlement the forest provided timber, firewood, and wild game for the table, but the importance of game diminished as it became more difficult to obtain, and domestic livestock increased in numbers. By the 1730s in older settlements habitants kept an average five or six cattle, slightly fewer sheep. Wheat, oats, and peas—in that order of importance—were the primary crops. Small quantities of native corn (maize) were also grown. Government subsidies at the time temporarily encouraged the growth of hemp for rope making and flax for fibres. The habitants grew their own tobacco. Potatoes and other indigenous American crops at this stage did not perform a significant role in the habitant diet. Visitors complained the men smelled of onions.

What seemed backward and lazy to outsiders made perfect sense in the Canadian environment.

In many respects, the habitants created a European agricultural landscape, but they rejected the French village model of settlement. Instead, they preferred to locate their farmhouses, made of whitewashed cut stone or squared logs laid one atop the other and pierced by small paper windows, in a row at the front of their long, narrow seigneurial allotments. The St Lawrence became in effect an extended village of continuous settlement along its north and south shores, and up the Richelieu Valley. The rivers provided ready communication in summer, of course, but also when they were iced over in winter. European travellers commented upon the backward agricultural practices of the habitants—the stump-ridden fields, ramshackle fences, and the manure heaped up on the ice to be carried away in the spring. But given the abundance of fertile, newly cleared land and the shortage of labour, what seemed backward and lazy to outsiders made perfect sense in the Canadian environment. Habitant families fed themselves by their own labour from their own land. Most habitants did not produce a surplus to sell into local markets (though a few did), but their rents in the form of agricultural produce to the seigneurs and their tithes to the Church in kind did help create a local market in agricultural commodities.

By the mid-1730s Canada as a whole had gone beyond self-sufficiency in agriculture and had begun to export surpluses to feed communities along the lower St Lawrence and Louisbourg, and to supply France's Caribbean possessions. Still, more than 80 per cent of the exports from New France consisted of beaver pelts, furs, and hides bound for France. Iron forges, for example, briefly flourished in the vicinity of Trois-Rivières, but the low quality of the ores and the high costs of labour eventually sank the enterprise. Thus in the eighteenth century, despite the growth of the agricultural sector and attempts to develop local industries, New France remained a fur trading enterprise, especially since labour costs hindered the development of local industries.

A well-understood hierarchy structured society in New France as in old France, but there were some significant differences. Both societies recognized subordination as the underlying principle of civil society—though it should be noted that the relative absence of authority structures in the original Acadia settlements around the Bay of Fundy made for a much more egalitarian social formation than in New France or old France. People of different standing possessed different rights and responsibilities. A clear hierarchy of such mutual obligations ordered civil society, extending up and down from the peasant to the seigneur to the King and ultimately to God. Security flowed from having a recognized place in this hierarchy. Below the King a nobility of the sword, descendants of old landowning and military families, and a nobility of the robe, high officials serving the Crown, stood at the apex of society. Social standing came more from birth and ascribed status than it did from wealth, though in time wealth could usually acquire status.

In New France a small caste of mainly transient government officials and military officers from France occupied the commanding social heights. A military-aristocratic ethos at the top thus set the tone for Canadian social formation. The peculiar conditions of Canada softened the edges of this system. Not many of noble status chose to make their careers in Canada. Thus the nobility necessary to a proper order of things had to be partly invented. Access to these ranks thus remained somewhat more open in Canada than at home. Merchants, for example, could acquire minor noble status in Canada but not in France. An abundance of land made it relatively easier to obtain the landed estates required for titles. Military officers could acquire seigneuries upon their discharge. The rents from seigneurial lands, however, usually did not provide sufficient income to seigneurs by themselves to finance a style of life much more elevated than that of the habitants around them. Outside the main towns and the military messes, the nobility remained a largely invisible social presence but one whose influence could be felt nonetheless.

Historians examining dowries, wills, estate inventories, and census data have discerned a tacit social order arrayed within the somewhat narrow band of society in Canada. Wealthy wholesale merchants and highly skilled craftsmen such as silversmiths mingled with the nobility at the top. Most of these people, like the nobility above them, were essentially birds of passage who would return to France after a time serving their trading house in Canada. A secondary group of ship captains, contractors, skilled tradesmen, and tanners maintained polite social relations with the group above. A third class of military men, notaries, tailors, joiners, and metalworkers formed a recognizable and respectable group slightly lower on the scale. The vast majority of the population found itself ranked further down the social ladder among a class of modest occupations such as habitant farmers, shoemakers, masons, carpenters, and private soldiers. Most marriages took place within each group or just across its margins. Still further down, one encountered journeymen, carters, and day labourers.

Usually not mentioned in this list, because they were not considered part of civil society, were the 900 or so slaves counted in New France. Two-thirds of these slaves were young, indigenous peoples, casualties of Native wars in the interior, who were kept as servants. Invariably they died young from European diseases. About 300 Black slaves, imported from the Caribbean, provided domestic service in the houses of government officials, ostentatious merchants, and the religious orders. Slaves toiled in houses rather than fields or workshops, and they certainly chafed in their servitude. But in Canada they were more of a social adornment than an essential source of labour. New France was a society with slaves, but not a slave society with an economy dependent upon non-free labour. Native peoples in the mission villages outside of Montreal and Quebec occupied a social limbo. They were in the society but not of it. They were wards of the state, like children, to be kept apart and protected especially from European vices such as alcohol. Upcountry a quite different order of things prevailed.

There remains some disagreement among historians as to who provided social leadership in the countryside and the extent of social gradations within the habitant class. In law, the seigneur possessed superior social status. In return for rents and dues the seigneur in theory had to maintain a manor house, build a mill, hold court, and summon collective labour for public works on roads and bridges. A special pew was reserved for him in the parish church, and he was owed privileged standing at local fetes. But in practice the seigneurs were frequently absentees. Seigneurial courts rarely functioned. Modest seigneurial manors were scarcely distinguishable from habitant dwellings. Thus in reality habitant communities do not seem to have been organized along axes of seigneurial influence.

The parish priest might also claim the role of social leadership. He baptized, married, and buried habitants, and administered the sacraments to the community. His counsel could be sought or freely given. The parish priest would organize the community to build and maintain the church, which, once constructed, usually formed the central gathering place for the community strung out on either side. On its steps major announcements were made; its bells sounded warnings and punctuated joyful celebrations. In the towns, nuns and priests provided education, hospitals, orphanages, and a seminary, and distributed charity to the needy. The bishop, of course, occupied a position of high spiritual and also civil authority in the counsels of the colony. But out in the countryside the clerics were not numerous at first; not all parishes had resident priests. When they were present, the clerics were often resented as much as they were respected. In difficult times the priests bore the unenviable burden of pronouncing moral opprobrium on habitant conduct and demanding the parishioners pay the tithes they owed. Their strictures and their exactions frequently stung.

In fact, the local captain of the militia, a respected habitant chosen by the habitants themselves, seems to have played the role of leader at the local level. He was usually a well-established habitant with some military experience. He commanded the respect necessary to muster his neighbours in self-defence and, in the absence of the seigneur, for local works. He could also represent them in relations with higher authority and when called upon resolve petty disputes, and it was through him that the colonial government communicated with its subjects. In a society plagued by an almost constant state of war, the captaincy of the militia was not an honorific position.

Military officers serving abroad and visitors from other countries frequently commented upon the development of what might be called a Canadian character markedly different from that of the home country. Canada had begun to develop an identifiable language of its own containing many Native terms and expressions from the polyglot North Atlantic trading system. Because of the importance of trade, the military, and transatlantic communication, more people lived in towns in New France than one might expect. Canadians were considered independent, even haughty. They were especially sensitive to slights and insults, and they bristled at the notion that they were peasants. The elaborate headgear, beauty, and flirtatiousness of the young women occasioned frequent comment, as did their saucy habit of exposing ample expanses of flesh, even upon occasion in church. Puritanical clergy regularly upbraided their female parishioners for their unseemly or extravagant dress. The men were considered strong, healthy, proud to a fault—but, in the eyes of outsiders, somewhat indolent. Habitant men displayed an inordinate fondness for spirited horses. A smart, good-looking horse commanded considerable esteem, something reflected in the unusual number of horses recorded in surviving documents. Some critical observers, who

Canadians were considered independent, even haughty. They bristled at the notion that they were peasants.

lacked a similar appreciation of horses or believed such equine indulgences appropriate only to persons of higher quality, thought habitant energies could have been directed more profitably to their cattle and fields. The indifferent housekeeping of the women observed by strangers seemed to extend to the men's lax management of the fields as well. The high birth rate in New France speaks to an active habitant sex life, but illegitimacy rates were low. Brides were often pregnant at marriage, sexual relations having been sanctioned with the pronouncement of the bans. Indeed some habitants' determination to be married—because sexual relations could only be conducted within that institution—scandalized the clergy and their communities. Eager couples simply stood up together and pronounced themselves married in a public place, a practice called *marriage à la gamine*.

Superstition, magic, and folk beliefs exerted a powerful influence over popular thinking in a society haunted by night demons and living in the dark shadow of sudden, often violent death. Religious piety and folk traditions carried by immigrants from many parts of France combined in the society of the St Lawrence to create a colourful and somewhat fervid imaginative life. New France also possessed its own rich sources of popular legends. For almost a century Native raids, descending suddenly with murderous fury from the bush, created constant and quite justifiable terror. The Great Peace lifted this menace after 1701, but the memory and nightmares remained. Children did disappear by day and night. Habitant families made their lives in lonely places, beset by long nights, fierce storms, and wild animals. Many people never returned from canoe trips on rivers strewn with rapids, fishing expeditions in rough weather, and long voyages to the interior. Drowning was a surprisingly common form of early death. The forest lay close at hand too, ready to swallow up the unwary.

In a dangerous and extreme environment, the natural readily became the supernatural. Fiery portents and apparitions in the sky accompanied earthquakes. Howling wolves and creaking branches in the dark of night became werewolves, half men, half wolves. Fireflies and will-o'-the-wisp haunted the troubled. The devil, a crafty, evil presence in the habitants' midst, tempting, tormenting, and possessing, provided an all-purpose explanation of misfortune, accidents, lost souls, and missing belongings. Not surprisingly on stormy nights amid the dancing shadows of the glowing hearth, Canadians thought themselves tormented by witches and spectres. They fought back with curses, folk remedies, and religious incantations. When conventional exorcism or folk remedies failed, colonists occasionally sought protection in the courts from the evil of witches. Paper folded in just the right way helped make wishes come true. These popular beliefs, it would seem, were much more firmly held by the habitant classes than the more educated colonial elite, who dismissed these popular delusions.

_⌒_

Many people in New France lived or had lived a double life. The European settlements along the St Lawrence maintained continuous contact with another world upcountry. Young men frequently spent a portion of their lives as *coureurs de bois,* carrying trade goods into the interior and fur bundles out, manning the fur trading posts in the interior, and maintaining Native alliances. Each year approximately 400 men were involved, one-third of whom wintered-over upcountry. In the interior, far from the authority structures of home, these intrepid youth acquired the outlook and manners of unbridled, habitual adventurers. Living among indigenous peoples, they adopted Native ways. Many formed semi-permanent liaisons with Native women and had second families in the interior. The fur trade thus gave birth to a new people between

Native and European cultures. Some mixed-blood, or Métis, children of the fur trade remained with their mothers in their tribal groups, others formed resident members of the fur trade labour force with either Native or other Métis life partners, and still others returned with their fathers to the St Lawrence settlements. When fathers and children settled down in their parishes on their seigneuries they necessarily brought back with them a somewhat looser, devil-may-care, freedom-loving attitude. Perhaps too they displayed disdain for the drudgery and constraint of life on the family farm.

Seen in a comparative colonial perspective what was truly remarkable about New France was its extraordinary expansion and territorial scope, especially given its relatively small population. Although the core of the colony remained situated on the St Lawrence, Canada expanded rapidly to include most of the central interior of North America. Champlain himself had explored the Ottawa River, Georgian Bay, and what is now central Ontario. By the 1660s other adventurers had penetrated north as far as Hudson's Bay and west as far as Lake Michigan and the north shore of Lake Superior. In the mid-1670s Jolliet and Marquette explored the upper half of the Mississippi marvelling at the huge herds of buffalo they spotted on the banks. A few years later La Salle, searching now for buffalo skins, expanded the trading network south to the mouth of the Mississippi. In the late-seventeenth century fur traders had established themselves in Illinois Country, throughout the Ohio and northern Mississippi river systems. The first half of the eighteenth century found French and Canadian exploration parties venturing westward on the Great Plains of what is now the United States and as far as the Spanish missions in Texas. At about the same time, the La Vérendrye family and their Native guides ventured out from the woodlands onto the Prairie of present-day Manitoba, continuing southwest to explore the upper reaches of the Missouri River.

What can explain this relentless expansionary zeal that led the tiniest colony to control the majority of North America? Geographically the French were fortunate. The St Lawrence system provided a virtual highway into the heart of the continent. Its endless lakes, rivers, and short portages to other watersheds drew the French ever deeper inland. In contrast, English settlers on the East Coast found their way west blocked by mountains. The fur trade was by its nature expansionist. Not only were furs quickly depleted, but also traders had strong incentives to get to the source of their supplies, to strike a better bargain with primary producers rather than middlemen, and to obtain finer quality furs which in turn commanded higher prices. These forays necessarily made enemies of the indigenous peoples who had previously managed transactions as middlemen. Geographical expansion of the fur trade was thus rarely peaceful. Once the interior was legally opened to trade after 1700, hundreds of licensed *coureurs de bois* established posts throughout the Great Lakes region and southwest along the Mississippi. The summer of 1740, for example, saw between 500 and 600 men departing Montreal for the interior posts.

The state, too, adopted an expansionist strategy. Initially the French government was torn between its domestic goals of maintaining a compact, agricultural, easily defended settlement on the St Lawrence and its competitive strategic goals of hemming in its British and Spanish rivals. Competition won out. As early as 1671, at a ceremony at Sault Ste Marie, agents of the French Crown raised a cross and claimed the entire western interior of the country for France. In pursuit of its own diplomatic goals, the Crown established military posts at Kingston, Detroit, and Michilimackinac to command the Great Lakes. A short time later, the French built strategic outposts in the Illinois Country to secure the trade, manage hostilities with Native peoples, and pre-empt western expansion by the English. Thus a string of military posts—which also doubled as fur trading posts as officers capitalized on their opportunities—asserted French claims to the interior.

Other desires also played their part in this expansion. The quest for glory and immortality on the part of all participants should not be discounted. Adventurers wanted to know more about the unknown continent. As late as 1700 they still sought that elusive route to Asia. As that possibility faded, explorers directed their energies to finding the mysterious western and southern seas. Some quest always pulled the French deeper, usually their own desires reflected back to them by their Native interlocutors. Militant evangelical religion also carried the French far into the interior, especially during the late-seventeenth century. Jesuits, Recollets, and Sulpicians, supported both by the state and by pious sponsors in France, went to extraordinary lengths bringing the reformed Catholic religion to Native villages to save heathen souls. Priests frequently accompanied soldiers, explorers, and fur traders on these advanced missions. Church, state, and commerce were mutually reinforcing institutions in the exploration enterprise. Undoubtedly geography favoured Canada. But all of its sinews—religious, scientific, military, and economic—stretched to support its ambition to command the continent.

During the first half of the eighteenth century New France extended from Louisbourg at the tip of Cape Breton, up the St Lawrence, into the Great Lakes Region, and out onto the Great Plains. French Canada controlled the entire Mississippi basin southward to France's Gulf Coast colony, Louisiana, and west as far as the possession of New Spain. Each summer, the port of Louisbourg bustled with the arrival and departure of more than a hundred naval ships and cargo vessels, most headed for France's Caribbean colonies or back to France. The sailors and garrison behind Louisbourg's massive masonry ramparts guarded the Atlantic approaches to Canada and asserted France's military might in North America. Louisbourg, the central point of the French North Atlantic fishery, delivered huge quantities of dried and salted cod to metropolitan French markets and the Caribbean, but it could not feed itself. Food for the rock-bound fortress came from the nearby Acadian settlements, now under nominal British control, and from the St Lawrence settlements of New France. Some of the fishermen from Louisbourg and Cape Breton exploited fishing grounds on the northern peninsula of Newfoundland, territorial rights retained after the Treaty of Utrecht in 1713 ceded Newfoundland to England.

By the 1740s the St Lawrence River served as the effective main street of the colony of New France. A dozen or so sea-going vessels landed each summer at Quebec, maintaining direct communications with metropolitan France. Quebec itself was a town of about 5,000 divided into upper and lower regions. Quebec was above all the political, military, and spiritual capital of the colony. Royal officials, the armed forces, and ecclesiastical establishments commanded the heights of the upper town of Quebec. The walls and spires perched on the cliff gave Quebec the look of a fortified hilltop village in France. On the narrow riverfront below the cliffs, ships loaded with manufactured imports emptied their cargoes onto the quays. Labourers hoisted these goods into the merchants' storerooms and manhandled bales of beaver, deer, moose, and weasel fur into the holds for the return journey. Upstream from Quebec, smaller coasting vessels and bateaux rowed by oarsmen forwarded goods to the main trading entrepôt of Montreal and returned with the season's take of furs. Along the shore, habitant families tended their crops in long narrow fields stretching back from their rows of neat cottages surrounded by huge vegetable gardens and current bushes. Though the winters were harsh, given the miserable state of the roads, they preferred the winter months when they could glide up and down the smooth ice-bound river, bundled up in furs, snug in their sleighs, behind their prancing horses. Montreal, the headquarters of the interior fur trade, had begun to rival Quebec in economic importance. Settlements on the fertile plains in the region supplied the town with food and the fur trade with labour.

The heart of New France beat along the cultivated banks of the St Lawrence, but the colony thrived on its extensive trading links with the Native peoples of the West and Northwest. Above the rapids of the St Lawrence, European settlement clustered around the combined military forts and fur trading posts in the interior. In the Northwest a mixed society of regular soldiers—formal members of the French army—merchants, missionaries, indigenous families, and fur traders with their Native wives and Métis children mingled within the palisades. Agricultural colonies spread out around the Mississippi posts, growing food to feed the trade. In this region slaves from Louisiana supplied much of the agricultural labour. Canada, then, was a string of quite different kinds of communities from the seaports, towns, and seigneurial settlements of the East, to the military-commercial enclaves along the lakes and rivers of the continental centre.

The requirements of Empire and the imperatives of the fur trade drew the French ever deeper into the interior of the continent. By the 1740s the French maintained posts and conducted fur trading operations throughout the Great Lakes region and southwest beyond the height of land into the Mississippi territories. A second major line of operations extended the French commercial and military reach northwest across the Upper Lakes to Lake Winnipeg and beyond. Each year more than 100 men wintered-over at these upcountry posts; in the summer more than 500 canoe men carried trade goods inbound as far as the western Prairies and returned over the vast distances of the continental interior with bound packs of furs.

◦◦

This extraordinary French colonizing thrust disrupted Native communities but did not destroy or completely overwhelm them. In many places Natives were completely displaced from their traditional territories, but over much of the interior, indigenous communities maintained their presence, resisted, adapted, and selectively incorporated aspects of European culture. Through diplomacy Native leaders negotiated a fragile degree of relative autonomy between the contending European colonizers. The arrival of European trade goods—knives, axes, pots, kettles, guns, fabric, blankets, mirrors, and beads—made Native lives easier, but the importance of acquiring furs to exchange for these items largely reoriented Native life. Over vast regions of the continent the fur trade became the major axis of indigenous culture. Tobacco and brandy brought the spirit world closer, but excessive use led to a disintegration of social structures. Possession of European weapons also strengthened Native power, making them much more formidable foes.

War necessarily accompanied trade, and though war was nothing new to indigenous cultures, these battles rent asunder old alliances and, with European weapons, were much more deadly than what had gone before. However, the most destructive agent of European colonization, epidemic diseases, raced ahead of the settlers, carried by Native middlemen, French missionaries, fur traders, and explorers. European diseases effectively emptied the continent in advance of the colonists. Indigenous populations had disintegrated under the combined influence of European contact, and their cultures had been profoundly ruptured long before the first wave of settlement.

Even in the Arctic and on the Great Plains, indigenous peoples could feel the impact of European expansion long before the Europeans themselves appeared on the scene. The fur traders of the Hudson's Bay Company, for example, resolutely confined themselves to their factories along the shores of Hudson's Bay. Native peoples carried their trade goods deep into the northern rivers, lakes, and forests and returned each spring laden with thick, prime pelts to trade. The influence of traders on Hudson's Bay extended as far as the woodlands of the northern Prairie hundreds of kilometres distant. On the Arctic Islands, recently arrived Inuit people spreading into the region retreated north to avoid the inevitably fatal contact with the newcomers. On the Prairie, wild horses, descended from escapees from New Spain far to the south, ranged north in huge herds. In the early eighteenth century Native peoples domesticated these mustangs and in the process acquired an effective new weapon to deploy in the buffalo hunt. Previously confined to hunting on foot, they now mounted horses, an unintended gift of European colonization. Soon they would acquire knives and guns—long before the first eastern explorers and traders ventured into their territory. The wild horses of New Spain fundamentally altered the human–animal balance on the Great Plains of Canada. In the last quarter of the eighteenth century the coastal tribes of the west began to experience the impact of Europe contact as Russian ventures began probing their territory from the north and Spanish seafarers pushed up the coast from Mexico. Directly and indirectly these European influences from the north, south, west, and especially the east had changed the human face of Canada. Continuous contact, invasive colonization, and mutual cultural adaptation slowly but surely tugged at the strings of the Transformation Mask, pulling open the panels, to reveal a new Canada.

⌒

Like a string of pearls, French possessions in North America hung in a great crescent from the Gulf of St Lawrence down the Mississippi Valley to the Gulf of Mexico. European power, both military and cultural, had penetrated deep into Native territory and fundamentally affected indigenous ways of life. Indigenous peoples had to come to terms with the powerful transforming European presence in their midst—trading, adapting, resisting, negotiating, and relocating as circumstances required. The bastion of French imperialism in North America was the agricultural and commercial colony of New France, which, as its population grew from natural increase in the eighteenth century, increasingly acquired a distinct native-born Canadian character. Within the framework of a French political and social regime, and under the protection of the French army, a robust, well-fed, reasonably prosperous community of farmers, artisans, townsfolk, and fur trade workers flourished on the banks of the St Lawrence. Upcountry contact gave birth to wholly new Métis societies, peoples 'in between'. Many Canadians may have been of French origin, but they had been changed by contact with North Americans and they too were now at home and native in their land.

Contact, colonization, and mutual cultural adaptation tugged at the strings of the Transformation Mask.

british americans

Within a relatively short period the Transformation Mask that was Canada would unfold yet again to reveal a new creation. If Canada was thoroughly French in 1740, how did it become demonstrably British over the next century? The short answer, of course, is by conquest. But that does not explain why Canada stayed British through an era of revolutions, invasions, and insurrections, or why at the end of the period not only British inhabitants, but also French Canadians and indigenous peoples too, professed allegiance to the British Crown and British ideals. How did Canadians become British in their minds if not their hearts when there were other possibilities? That will require a somewhat longer explanation.

Canadians were not alone on the continent in the mid-eighteenth century, of course; nor was their presence uncontested. The territorial aggressiveness of the Canadians, their Catholic religion, not to mention their terrifying guerrilla raids, had earned them the undying enmity of their mainly Protestant and English neighbours. Moreover, French possessions in the Americas were chess pieces in a much broader global game being played by the major European powers: France, Spain, Holland, and England (after the Union of 1707, Great Britain). The Dutch, though they remained an important global imperial power, had long since retreated from North America with the surrender of New York in 1664. The empires conducted their main combat in Europe; for the most part colonial wars were sideshows. However, the North American colonies of

European powers had their own reasons for fighting each other. Occasionally, when the stakes were high enough, the main battles in the bigger imperial struggle were played out in this theatre—as would be the case in the 1750s.

Skirmishes, raids, battles, and military preparations for battles were normal features of life all along the disputed borders of New France. In the far south, the French claims in Louisiana rubbed up against the Spanish possessions on both flanks, on the east in Florida and on the west in Texas. Along the Atlantic seaboard, the thirteen British colonies had begun to push land-hunting expeditions across the Alleghenies into the Ohio country, where they inevitably came into conflict with the French and their Native allies. Beginning in 1754, two years before formal hostilities between France and Britain broke out in Europe, an undeclared war, known locally as the French and Indian War, raged along this inland frontier. A young George Washington cut his military teeth in these campaigns, though his record was far from distinguished (one victorious raid and an ignominious surrender). New England resumed its more or less perennial war with New France in the 1740s. Stung by overland raids from the north, the New Englanders lay siege to Louisbourg with British backing, forcing its surrender. Louisbourg had to be returned in 1748, much to the annoyance of the New Englanders, but they had proven the vulnerability of the French even at their supposedly strongest point.

To counter the threat of Louisbourg and provide a North American base for its fleet, the British established a naval base in a harbour they named Halifax and laid plans to colonize lands they retained from the French they called Nova Scotia. Further north in the Atlantic the British had forced the French from their fishing 'rooms' along the south shore of Newfoundland. French fishing rights to the north shore of Newfoundland continued to be protected by an international treaty. By mid-century, as more and more of the English and Irish fishermen began to winter-over to secure the best fishing grounds, the resident population that inhabited Newfoundland year round was about 5,000, a number that swelled to over 15,000 when the migratory fishermen arrived for the summer. The strategic Newfoundland fishery had largely fallen to the British, though the French clung to their landing rights on the northern shores. In the far north, the mainly Scottish factors and servants of the Hudson's Bay Company asserted British claims to the entire northern interior of the continent from their fortified trading posts on the Bay.

The French in America were not as strong as they seemed. In fact, they were surrounded and outnumbered. The French did possess two great advantages that allowed them to survive much longer than might otherwise have been expected: firm alliances with indigenous peoples which

French troops had to spread themselves thinly to defend the long string of forts in the interior.

strengthened their numbers, and a mastery of the tactics of frontier fighting with few scruples about terrorist attacks on civilians. But they also displayed glaring weaknesses. A small number of French troops had to spread themselves thinly to defend the long string of forts in the interior. The French supply and communications lines stretched out over thousands of kilometres. This chain of command was most vulnerable at a key point: the Atlantic link between France and New France where the growing British navy had begun to assert its dominance. Should British sea power sever this vital cord, the French grip on the continent would quickly release.

Overall the British were much stronger in America than were the French. Numerically the British population overwhelmed that of the French; it grew more rapidly on account of steady immigration and by most measures it commanded greater wealth. In 1760, when New France counted approximately 60,000 European-origin inhabitants along the St Lawrence and a few thousand more upcountry, the 13 British colonies contained more than a 1.5 million people. Though tiny and poor by comparison, New France had been spared defeat by the resourcefulness of its military, by divisions and irresolution among the 13 colonies, and by the sheer complexity of mounting a coordinated land-sea attack on Quebec. The French Empire in America survived as long as it did, in large part because the British Americans could not find the united determination to muster a concerted campaign against their audacious foe. That would change.

⌒

The first years of the French and Indian War went badly for the British, and they did not respond well to the reverses. French defenders humiliated the combined British and American expeditionary forces sent to attack forts in the Ohio country and New York frontiers. Only on the borderland of Nova Scotia and New France did the British and New England troops achieve success, capturing two French outposts. This resumption of open hostilities once again placed the French-Acadian residents of Nova Scotia in a delicate position. Since 1713 the Acadians of the Bay of Fundy had been nominally British subjects. The British and New England forces in Nova Scotia had long suspected the Acadians of supporting the French war effort. The British believed with some justification that the French priests in Acadia acted more as French agents than pastoral advisors. When the British overran the two French forts in 1755 only to discover several hundred Acadians ensconced inside, their darkest fears were confirmed.

Up to this point, the British had responded to the anomalous presence within their empire of a Roman Catholic, French-speaking population largely by overlooking the problem. They settled their conscience and squared their policies with legalism, by demanding the Acadians swear an oath of allegiance to the British King. After some negotiation, the Acadians complied, with the agreed-upon proviso that they would not be required to bear arms on behalf of their new monarch against their former compatriots. Within the latitudinarian logic of empire in the mid-eighteenth century, the declared loyalty and neutrality of the Acadians compensated for their language and religion. Neutrality, then, was the essential condition of their being left in quiet possession of their lands under British rule. When that neutrality was called into question the Acadians found themselves in deeper trouble than they could have imagined.

British officials adopted a policy that today would be called ethnic cleansing.

At first the British responded in the traditional way by calling for a new oath of allegiance, this time without qualifications. When the Acadians insisted upon taking an oath that preserved their customary neutrality, the British interpreted this as a hostile act. Fearing war in which French forces from Louisbourg, and Native warriors supplied by Acadian sympathizers, might overwhelm Nova Scotia, the British officials on the spot adopted a policy that today would be called ethnic cleansing. In 1755 as news of British defeats on the western frontier came in, the governor and his council took it upon themselves to deport the entire Acadian population. The decision to evacuate the Acadians was taken at the local level, by British army and navy officers concerned about the strategic situation and by councilors, mainly from New England who hoped perhaps to inherit the vacated lands. In the first summer, soldiers rounded up about 8,000 men, women, and children, bundled them onto troop transports, burned their crops and villages behind them, and shipped them off to the major port cities of the 13 colonies. In doing so, the British and New England forces removed settlers of doubtful loyalty from a geographical position where they might tip the strategic balance, and put them in places far away where they would be swallowed up by the majority. The deportation also opened up new land for settlement on New England's northern frontier. It was a shameful policy, brutally but not lethally administered.

Deportation, which continued for almost a decade, scattered the Acadian people to the four winds. Most disappeared in the polyglot mix of peoples swarming into the British colonial seaports to which they were consigned. Disease spreading rapidly on the crowded ships in midsummer claimed many lives. A few colonial administrators, taken by surprise by the sudden arrival of unannounced, sickly, and decidedly unwelcome refugees, shipped them on to Great Britain. Some deportees ended up in France.

The Acadians, of course, resisted their forcible removal in whatever ways they could. Hundreds of families fled to the woods. Some tunneled out of the stockades holding them for deportation. A mutiny turned one poorly guarded ship around and forced it back. The deportation initiated an epic and ultimately poetic wandering on the part of Acadians to reunite families, to rebuild their communities, and, if possible, to return to their homeland. Acadian deportees in the southern colonies eventually made their way to Louisiana via Haiti to start life anew in a French, tidewater milieu. The Acadian exiles even in France grew restless and with Spanish assistance they too made their way to Louisiana. After 1764 Acadians could legally return to Nova Scotia. Several hundred families did make their way back but not to their former homes; in the interval, New England settlers had occupied their lands. By the end of the eighteenth century the returned Acadian population which settled on the shores of the Gulf of St Lawrence exceeded in size the population of the original Acadian colony on the shores of the Bay of Fundy. A century later the Boston poet William Henry Longfellow would craft a lachrymose lyric poem based upon legends of the expulsion. *Evangeline,* a tale of feminine courage, fidelity, and the cruelty of fate, followed a young bride on her epic journey throughout the United States to find her love. This poem attained enormous popularity in England, despite its British villains. Through an imperial cultural network, this poem returned to Canada, was translated into French in Quebec, and subsequently became a symbol of the New Brunswick Acadian national revival in the late-nineteenth century.

⌒

Meanwhile the fortunes of the French and Indian War—after 1756 the Seven Years' War—had begun to turn. No longer troubled by Scottish insurrection at home and determined to put an end to the French nuisance, the British government poured military assets into the American theatre in 1757. The next summer 13,000 soldiers of the British army, about 500 American troops, and 1,842 guns besieged Louisbourg, the French strongpoint. Once again the seemingly invincible fortification fell after a month of relentless pounding by the British batteries. Gunners set fire to the French fleet moored in the harbour. The poorly built masonry on the seaward side, from which the French had not expected an attack to be mounted, crumbled under the assault. Louisbourg surrendered without much of a struggle. A few months later in the far West a massed advance of more than 10,000 British and American troops in the Ohio country overran the 300 French defenders of Fort Duquesne, renamed in triumph after the British prime minister who had reinvigorated the war effort, Fort Pitt. The Native tribes of the region, previously allies of the French, concluded a separate peace with the British. In one calamitous year of British campaigns, the French had thus lost both their hold on the Ohio country and the bastion on their Atlantic approaches. The stage was thus set for a moment of high drama, an attack on the heart of French America—Quebec itself.

Early in the summer of 1759 a huge flotilla of British ships landed about 8,500 British regular soldiers under the command of Major General James Wolfe on the south shore of the St Lawrence River opposite Quebec. Wolfe, who had commanded troops in the siege of Louisbourg the previous year, had been eager to attack New France via the St Lawrence. The Marquis de Montcalm, the French general, dug his army of 13,000 into defensive positions commanding the river flats and the sloping north shore downstream from Quebec, the most likely assault points, and waited patiently for Wolfe's attack. At first Wolfe appeared daunted by the geography and frustrated by his enemy's unwillingness to be drawn into the open. At the end of July the French repelled an attempted invasion, ordered by Wolfe over the objection of his officers at the most heavily defended part of their line, resulting in heavy losses to the British.

In the aftermath of this defeat, Wolfe seemed to lose control of the situation. Racked by pain from kidney stones and dysentery, but even more badly torn apart by indecision, Wolfe behaved badly. While he dithered about where to launch his attack he directed his aggressiveness towards the defenceless civilian population rather than his entrenched foe. He ordered the settlements on the south shore of the river put to the torch. He commanded his gunners to launch a bombardment of the City of Quebec across the river to reduce it to ruins. These were punitive acts of no strategic importance beyond revenge. Meanwhile, as time ran out on the summer expedition, he more or less turned planning of a final assault over to his three brigadiers. A half-mad James Wolfe, locked in his sickroom brooding over Gray's 'Elegy in a Country Churchyard' ('The paths of glory lead but to the grave . . .') became the butt of jokes among the junior officers.

Under this less than resolute command, the British forces belatedly decided upon a landing further upstream which would cut the supply lines from Montreal to Quebec, divide the French defenders in two, and position the St Lawrence army to act in concert with General Amherst's overland invasion force, which was poised to strike up the Lake Champlain–Richelieu River corridor. Wolfe concurred, though the pessimistic tone of his dispatch to the prime minister informing him of the plan revealed both his state of mind and the likelihood of success. Arrival of word that Fort Niagara had been taken by the British momentarily buoyed hopes that the pincers were tightening on Canada. Early in September, navy troopships took up positions in the river above Quebec, drifting up river and down river with the tide. The British apparently intended to land on lightly defended, hilly terrain well upriver from Quebec. A visible effort on the part of other British troops to prepare for another invasion below Quebec held the majority of the French army in their positions downstream. After heavy rains delayed the invasion, Wolfe decided without consultation to reroute the landing from the roundabout, more easily taken ground upstream to a risky assault up the formidable cliffs directly in front of the fleet just above Quebec.

In a daring amphibious operation against a fast-running tide, the navy put the troops ashore at the foot of the cliffs in the dead of night on 13 September 1759. French sentries mistook the landing for a convoy of their own much-needed provisions slipping past the British from Montreal. The British soldiers then clambered up a narrow defile in the cliff face and took up defensive positions on the heights while the navy hauled a number of field artillery pieces up the path onto the field. By eight o'clock in the morning Wolfe had formed six regiments into a line of battle facing Quebec in Abraham Martin's fields, known locally as the Plains of Abraham. It was an audacious combined operation, as risky as it was unexpected, and brilliantly executed. When Montcalm recognized that the main assault had occurred upstream and that Wolfe had surprisingly gained the heights, he quickly moved his best troops back to Quebec and, as the morning mist cleared, marched them out to meet the enemy.

On the field that morning the two armies of about 4,500 men faced each other; perhaps the French held a slight numerical advantage. The British had several pieces of field artillery in position; the French had none. The British had moved up closer to the town in the open fields, but the French occupied slightly higher ground overlooking their enemy. The main difference in the two armies lay in their training and support. The French troops were for the most part untried, many of them militiamen inserted among the regular troops to fill out the ranks. The British troops were all well-trained, highly disciplined, battle-hardened regular soldiers. The French lacked provisions to sustain an extended siege. Montcalm doubted the fighting ability of his men. He also worried about the British digging themselves in across his supply lines. As the two generals manoeuvred their troops into position for the first European set-piece battle between regular armies in North America, the British held the upper hand by a slight margin.

Montcalm's sense that this advantage would grow with time led him to make a fatal mistake. Instead of waiting for reinforcements, bringing up artillery of his own from the city, or holding off for the anticipated arrival of a relief force coming from Montreal to overwhelm the British from their rear, Montcalm chose to attack before the British could entrench themselves. At about ten o'clock silken banners unfurled and drums sounded. The predominantly grey and white masses of French troops charged down the slope towards the British, a central column flanked on either side by two extended lines. The British received the attack arrayed in a thin red line, two or three deep across the field. The French commenced fire immediately. The advance became ragged as untrained troops stumbled over one another when those in the front fell to the ground to reload. Despite taking heavy casualties, particularly from the sniping of irregulars and Natives on the flanks, the British line held firm and held its fire. When the French advanced to within 30 metres, a fusillade erupted in rolling volleys along the British line. The British field guns did their deadly work, spraying grapeshot into the French charge. Disciplined fire at close range tore the French attack apart. The British line moved forward through the smoke a few metres and fired again. The centre of the French advance faltered, drifted to its right, and then reeled backward. A wholesale rout followed as the right side of the French army collapsed. The British pursued in more or less good order, raking the retreating French with lethal fire. It was all over in less than half an hour.

Leading the charge on the right side of his line, Wolfe fell just as the momentum shifted, killed by a sniper's bullet. Montcalm too received a mortal wound during the French retreat. Each side suffered approximately 650 casualties, the British slightly more than the French. About 60 British soldiers were killed in the fighting, many of them senior officers. The loss of Wolfe and his immediate subordinates momentarily left the British without command, during which time the French army escaped. Had Montcalm waited until afternoon he would likely have prevailed. French reinforcements marched in from the north too late to be of assistance. The Montreal soldiers, arriving on the scene some time after the battle had ended, sensibly withdrew back to Montreal, where they were joined later by the remnants of Montcalm's army.

⌒

Rarely does the fate of a continent turn on the outcome of single engagement. The French had lost a battle, but not necessarily the war. They still maintained a large army in the field; controlled the upper St Lawrence, the Richelieu, and the fortified town of Montreal; and had the advantage of fighting in territory they knew well, supported by a sympathetic population. Nonetheless the Battle of the Plains of Abraham was decisive in one important respect: the British had accomplished their objective of the capture of Quebec. This had enormous symbolic significance in North America, but also in Great Britain, where bonfires on hilltops greeted the news, and in France, which had done all it could to defend its interests in this remote corner of the world. It remained to be seen whether the French could recover or whether the British could follow up their victory.

By spring the tables had been turned. In late April the reinvigorated French army manoeuvred into position on a slushy field not far from the Plains of Abraham. It was the turn of the British, perhaps overconfident from their victory the previous fall, to march out to engage the French head-on. On this occasion the French prevailed with a ferocious bayonet charge, inflicting heavy losses (259 killed and 829 wounded) on the retreating British. The French now surrounded a bloodied, demoralized, and hungry British army huddled within the walls of Quebec.

British sea power finally decided the issue. On 9 May a British warship sailed up the St Lawrence to Quebec. A week later two more arrived. The British navy relieved and resupplied its expeditionary force; the French navy could not. Their fleet had been cut to pieces by the British in Quiberon in November. The French army before Quebec thus retreated to Montreal to meet British land forces advancing methodically from the south through the Richelieu Valley. In September 1760 the army of the St Lawrence and the land forces driving north met at Montreal. For this final act in the 'Fall of Canada' the British mustered some 17,000 troops outside the walls of Montreal against a mere 3,500 French defenders within. To a French emissary, the British commander, General Jeffrey Amherst, demanded imperiously, 'I have come to take Canada and I will take nothing less'. To avoid a bloodbath and the devastation of the region the defenders had little choice. On 8 September 1760, Vaudreuil, the Canadian-born governor of Canada, and his French military commander, Lévis, capitulated without a fight. The British piled humiliation upon defeat. The French army had to surrender without receiving the honours of war.

'I have come to take Canada and I will take nothing less'.

What could be won in war could be lost in the peace. That had happened many times before. The final outcome of the Seven Years' War would not be settled until the Treaty of Paris in 1763 ended hostilities between England and France. This treaty represented a global settling of accounts, not just an end to the war in North America. On the whole the French had lost ground in India, the Caribbean, and Canada. Louisiana was confirmed as a Spanish possession. After some internal debate the British decided to keep Canada, if they could, to prevent further wars with its American colonies. It does nothing for Canadian self-confidence to be reminded that the French surrendered Canada with equanimity in order to recover their two island colonies in the Caribbean.

Beyond that, the French could happily bid Canada *adieu,* but not Newfoundland. For France a presence in the all-important fishery was of greater strategic importance than the possession of Canada. To that end the French kept two islands in the Gulf of St Lawrence (St-Pierre and Miquelon) and retained landing rights for French fishermen on the north coast of Newfoundland. After the expenditure of 80 million pounds and heavy human losses, the British controlled the entire eastern half of North America from the Arctic to the Caribbean. As to why the French would give up Canada so willingly, historians have concluded that the French believed Britain would be weakened by the acquisition rather than strengthened, that Canada within the British Empire would hasten the day when the other 13 colonies would want to be rid of it.

The French may not have been as Machiavellian or as prescient as this interpretation would suggest. But undoubtedly the French realized that it would be easier to unite the continent militarily than it would be to harmonize the conflicting interests of the colonies politically. After all, Britain's first attempt at incorporating a different people within the ambit of empire had ended in tragedy and infamy with the deportation of the Acadians. After 1763 the really hard part of governing on a continental scale would commence. And who at that time, other than the French, would be bold enough to predict that within 20 years the only part of America remaining British would be Canada?

ᡗ᠆

Canada now had to be incorporated within the British Empire. To accomplish that difficult task, British imperial policy towards Canada veered back and forth over the first few years. At first Britain proposed to make Canada into a colony just like the others, namely by endowing it with British colonial institutions, and Anglicizing and Protestantizing it. When that failed, in order to secure loyalty in tempestuous times, British policy reversed direction completely and recognized Canada as a special exception within the Empire. Britain shifted from a policy of conformity as spelled out by the Royal Proclamation of 1763 that provided for civil government in Canada, to exceptionalism in 1774 with the passage of the Quebec Act. More changes would come with time. In drafting these policies, Britain had to trade off several conflicting objectives: the security of British interests, and the satisfaction of the new British subjects in Canada; peaceful relations with the Native peoples of the West; and recognition of American colonial aspirations towards greater autonomy and western expansion. No policy could accomplish all of those objectives at once.

The Royal Proclamation confined Quebec to a small parallelogram along the shores of the St Lawrence stretching from the Ottawa River to Gaspé. This arbitrary bit of map-making severed the core of Canada from the fur trading territories upcountry and the fishery downriver. The governor of Newfoundland received jurisdiction over the seal-hunting and fishing villages of the Gulf. The former French possessions around Cape Breton were incorporated into Nova Scotia. The Great Lakes Basin and the Mississippi Valley, all of the territories west of the Allegheny Mountains, were to be set aside as Indian Territory. And the British faced their first test in this region even before this policy could be announced.

During the summer of 1763 a charismatic Native leader named Pontiac led a pan-Indian confederacy in a quasi-religious crusade to rid the region of British influence. In a violent campaign marked by treachery, torture, and the massacre of civilians on the Native side, reprisals, and callous germ warfare on the part of the British, many but not all of the posts in the western interior fell to Native forces. Pontiac and his people wanted a space of their own beyond British and American control. They also wanted to treat with the contending European and American factions as political equals, negotiating agreements when it served their own interests. The revolt gradually died out when French help failed to materialize, as indigenous peoples turned to the business of provisioning themselves for the winter, and as the British forces of repression began to regain control.

But something of great significance did emerge from Pontiac's rising on the one hand and the Royal Proclamation on the other, that did much to nurture Native belief in the role of the British Crown as protector of indigenous peoples. The British realized that to maintain peaceful relations with the militarily important and numerically superior societies in the interior, Natives must be assured of the security of their territory from encroachment without their consent. The Indian Reserve set aside within the terms of the Royal Proclamation represented the first formal recognition in British law of Native rights. Indian lands could not be surveyed, occupied, or settled until they had been purchased by the Crown with Native consent. Land would no longer simply be claimed by the Crown as had been the case under French rule, or occupied without consent as had been the case in most of the American colonies. In effect, the British determined to deal with Native peoples on a government-to-government basis. However much this policy soothed Native anxieties, it enraged land-hungry American colonists who had already begun to push through the gaps into the tramontane interior. The Royal Proclamation in law at least denied them their destiny.

The new policy also signalled a major regime change within Quebec. A military governor would rule with an appointed advisory council, but a representative Assembly, like those in the other colonies, was promised in due course. The imposition of English criminal and civil law, it was hoped, would attract English-speaking migrants from the other colonies that would eventually overwhelm the French-speaking population. As in the rest of the Empire, the Proclamation barred Catholics from holding public office; the proposed Assembly would be accessible to only the English newcomers. The new governor received instructions to encourage the inhabitants 'to embrace the Protestant religion'. Migration, intermarriage, and assimilation, it was thought, would be the main instruments of social and thus eventual political transformation. Thus at first British policy aimed to wipe out everything that was distinctively French and Catholic about the Canadians and turn them into model, fully acculturated British colonial subjects. The Royal Proclamation sought the same outcome as the Acadian deportation but without the messy business of actual removal. The project failed and in the fullness of time the policy had to be reversed.

Governments may dream up policies in a higher register, but life often continues at its own accustomed lower octaves. Bluntly put, the New Englanders did not come in the numbers expected. About 7,000 New England farmers seized the farmlands and harbours of western Nova Scotia that had been involuntarily vacated by the Acadians. A smaller number of English and Scottish immigrants followed. But Quebec was another story. Large-scale agricultural migration did not accompany the change in government. Instead, a disputatious gang of merchants and fortune hunters swarmed about in Quebec supplying the army and the fur trade. Under the military governor a small number of administrators and judicial officers reconstructed the machinery of civil government. Even after a decade, the English-speaking immigrants numbered only in the hundreds. Meanwhile in the countryside, the habitant population continued to reproduce itself at the same merry rate as before. Hundreds could not assimilate thousands; indeed, there was a distinct possibility that the reverse might happen as English immigrants married into French-Canadian families. As the second governor sent out to administer the policy ruefully confessed, barring a catastrophe Canada would be French 'to the end of time'.

At higher levels, the military conquest and the change in regime profoundly altered Canadian society, but at the more basic level in the parishes and towns, life went on much as before. Most of the army, civil administrators and many of the merchants, who were itinerant in any event, returned to France after 1760. War thus removed most of the French military, mercantile, and governing elite. Historians have long debated whether this loss of former leaders represented a 'decapitation' of the society. On balance the answer seems to be no. British counterparts slipped into their places; business resumed under new management; and Canadian fur traders formed equally effective partnerships with British merchants. In short, Canadians accommodated themselves to the new order, actively participated in it, and quietly recast the new regime in their own image. The French face of Canada persisted under British proprietors.

The French face of Canada persisted under British proprietors.

This process of mutual accommodation can perhaps be illustrated in the realm of religion. The last bishop of New France died in 1760. In theory this would not be a matter of concern to a British colonial government for whom the Roman Catholic Church had no standing and whose policy was to eliminate it. But governors in the eighteenth century could not imagine civil government working effectively without the social cohesion of religion. The established Anglican Church could scarcely play this role for the Catholic majority of the population. Besides, the new administrators saw in the Roman Catholic Church an institutional ally in securing the continued loyalty of its flock to the new regime. So in effect the British governor hand-picked the candidate he thought best suited to this role, lobbied his home government to look the other way, and Rome happily obliged by appointing the new bishop. Under British auspices and with official sanction the Roman Catholic Church continued its spiritual, pastoral, welfare, medical, and educational roles.

Once in place the British governor and his advisors found they had to equivocate on the promised representative Assembly for roughly similar reasons. If instituted under prevailing British law barring Roman Catholics from office, such an institution would necessarily exclude the vast majority of the population from participation in civil government. Its membership would be confined to that small, fractious and, it must be admitted, somewhat unsavoury clutch of newly arrived merchants. Aristocratic military officers and judges, with their customary class disdain for people in trade, tended to look down their noses at the merchant community who, in their opinion, were merely 'hard-faced men who had done well in the war', to employ an epithet coined much later but with similar malice. To give government over to such rascals would be a travesty of British justice. On the whole the British authorities preferred the counsel of the more refined seigneurs and some of the old French families who remained. To the outrage of the merchants, who fumed about tyranny and the denial of British institutions, the promised representative assembly never materialized. After a decade of practical experience in the government of Canada, Great Britain had to choose between a stricter adherence to established policy or practical recognition of the exceptional administrative arrangements that had evolved. They did not enjoy the luxury of deliberation in relaxed circumstances.

In 1774 the British did what might be expected under the circumstances: they recognized the reality on the ground by providing a unique administrative structure for Canada. The Quebec Act of that year brought the commerce of the western interior back under the control of the governor of Quebec by effectively annexing the Ohio country once again to Canada for administrative purposes. As for Quebec itself, this act formally re-established the Roman Catholic Church, instituted a joint regime of English criminal and French civil law with respect to property, and provided for government by a governor and an appointed Legislative Council, for which Roman Catholics would be qualified. British policymakers decided against both an elected assembly restricted to Protestants and one fully open to the French-speaking majority. Neither seemed to offer stability or loyalty, especially in time of crisis. Britain thus chose to provide a manageable government, agreeable to the majority, rather than try to impose a system that would satisfy only a volatile minority and antagonize the country. For most Quebecers of French origin the Quebec Act represented an important recognition of their distinctive culture within the British Empire. By the same token the Quebec Act denied the English-speaking residents rights they expected as British subjects.

∽

Settlement of the question of government for Canada took on added importance given the political context of growing hostility towards Great Britain in the 13 colonies. There is no need here to rehearse in any detail the prelude to the American Revolution. Put simply, restraints imposed by Britain upon the independence of colonial legislatures, limitations on territorial expansion, interference with the freedom of trade, and the imposition of taxes without consultation—all led to mounting tension between the government of Great Britain and the colonial assemblies through the 1760s and early 1770s. Then in 1774, in response to the Sons of

Liberty destruction of the East India Company's tea shipment in Boston, Britain passed a series of Coercive Acts giving the colonial governors greater autonomy from the popular assemblies, measures so inflammatory in their intent that they came to be called the 'Intolerable Acts' by indignant colonists who now began organizing resistance. One of these Acts was the Quebec Act.

What seemed perfectly sensible to the majority of Canadians about the Quebec Act appeared totally intolerable to the majority of American colonists. In the first place, it recognized the Roman Catholic religion, and even brought the authority of the state behind its collection of tithes. Americans wanted the viper of popery in America stamped out. Second, by denying the citizens of Quebec proper representative institutions the British held a timorous people under their military thumb. Quite rightly Americans interpreted the Quebec Act as a tool to secure a northern power base from which the British might more effectively control America. In Quebec, the tyranny the 13 colonies resisted could be seen most clearly. Finally, the Quebec Act delivered the presumed territorial inheritance of the American colonies, the Ohio country, into the hands of their erstwhile enemies, the Canadians.

The American Revolution had a major impact on Canada, both directly because it came to Canada in the form of an invasion, and indirectly because its consequences did much to shape subsequent Canadian history. When colonial resistance to British authority turned to open rebellion in 1775, the American colonists urged their brethren in Quebec to join the Continental Congress. Energetic agents and provocative pamphlets failed, however, to arouse much interest. Canadians rejected their first invitation to join the nascent Republic, more from indifference and preoccupation with their own affairs than open hostility. The Continental Congress then decided upon a pre-emptive strike against British power in Quebec to liberate the Canadian people. (The dangerous delusion of the United States that the world is waiting to be liberated by them goes back a long way.)

In the late summer of 1775 two armies marched on Canada. One under the command of General Montgomery advanced easily over the well-travelled route up the Lake Champlain corridor towards Montreal, and another under Benedict Arnold struggled overland through the trackless woods of what is now Maine to Quebec. Despite urgent appeals from both the Roman Catholic Church and the governor, the Canadian population showed no desire to defend themselves against the advancing Americans. While the French-Canadian social elites rallied to the British cause and the Church literally preached resistance, the militia, however, remained inert. The Americans easily captured Montreal and marched on to Quebec where the governor had concentrated British forces. In Montreal and in the countryside the invaders were warmly received as long as they paid hard currency for their supplies and behaved respectfully. But even emissaries as talented and bilingual as Benjamin Franklin could kindle little enthusiasm on the part of Canadians to join actively in the Revolution.

In a blinding snow-storm British regular troops easily defeated the misguided attack.

At the beginning of winter the combined Continental Congress forces lay siege to Quebec. The American invasion collapsed however when it collided with the geography and climate of Quebec. Unable to strike at the fortified Upper Town, the Americans chose instead, on the night of 31 December, to plunder the storehouses of Lower Town. In a blinding snowstorm British regular troops easily defeated the misguided attack, killing Montgomery, wounding Arnold, and taking 300 prisoners. More as a comedy than a tragedy, the siege persisted throughout the winter, losing strength daily through disease and desertion. At one point several hundred Americans offered to volunteer in the British army when their term of recruitment ended. Arrival of the British fleet with reinforcements in the spring dispersed the invaders, who had already begun to wear out their welcome among the local population. The more ideological revolutionaries who succeeded Montgomery and Arnold appear to have offended the very people they hoped to liberate, as a result of open hostility towards their language and religion and their purchases with paper currency of dubious value. The crusading desire to free a people from British tyranny and stamp out popery was not well understood among the largely contented and staunchly Roman Catholic population.

To the despair of both sides the Canadian population appears to have decided to adopt a strict non-partisan stance in the conflict. They refused equally to defend the British or to join the Revolution. The Nova Scotians adopted the same calculated neutrality as the Quebecers. Nova Scotians had only recently arrived themselves from New England. Their invitation to join the rebellion came from cousins and uncles, not former enemies. Yet they too chose the Acadian option; namely, to stay scrupulously neutral on the sidelines, let other people do the fighting, and come to terms with the victor when the dust settled. It was not a heroic position. Certainly it does nothing to help the historian understand where popular sympathies lay. A poorly supported and unenthusiastic invasion of Nova Scotia petered out before it began; thus the question of their loyalty was never practically put to the Nova Scotians. But their conduct does allow us to say that when invited by their relatives to join the Revolution they chose to sit it out. After the summer of 1776 a British military build-up and consequent stimulus to the local economy won over public opinion in

Canada. Halifax bustled and the countryside thrived with the relocation of the British fleet. Quebec similarly prospered as the British army gathered its forces for a major invasion of the rebel colonies.

⁓

The greatest impact of the American Revolution on Canada occurred after the end of hostilities. Politically, the Revolution represented a path not taken for Canadians. Henceforth Canadians would have to define themselves in opposition to the revolutionary tradition or at the very least in contradistinction to it. The British, in their eagerness to end the war and placate the newly independent United States in the peacemaking process, gave the Americans all they requested—except Canada, which the American delegates insouciantly listed as one of their demands. However, Britain did cede all of the Ohio country to the new republic, much to the distress of the Canadians. In the Treaty of Paris of 1783 that formally ended the American Revolution, Canada lost its natural hinterland, even though it had retained most of it in the fighting. The French held on to fishing rights in Newfoundland, though the 'French Shore' was moved from the northern to the western coast, a privilege the French retained until 1904. Finally, in the geopolitical sense, Canada acquired new value within the imperial scheme of things as Great Britain's strategic North Atlantic and North American bastion. This represented a benefit in one sense, as Britain had to pay attention to Canada's welfare, but it also meant that Canada remained an imperial hostage to fortune on the North American continent.

The American success in the Revolution directed streams of refugees towards Canada that fundamentally changed its social composition. At the end of hostilities about 60,000 refugees fled by ship from East Coast ports to Nova Scotia. Another 10,000 or so found their way to Quebec, where officials relocated them on lands along the St Lawrence above the Ottawa River and around Kingston. Women accounted for about 40 per cent of this first modern refugee movement, men slightly less, and children just over 20 per cent. Many of the Loyalists were not political refugees, in the sense that they moved on the basis of ideological conviction. Rather, most of them simply found themselves on the losing side. Their pre-war interests and associations connected them to the British. Some were members of the former colonial administration or served it in some capacity. Others fell under suspicion of collaboration, whether justifiably or not. As the Revolution concluded those most compromised either abandoned their property and left, or had it seized and fled. Far more, however, stayed behind to accommodate themselves as best they could to the new regime.

The Revolution was in many respects a civil war. Interests and convictions divided brothers and sisters, fathers and their kin. The fault line of revolution ran through families as well as between them. Loyalists thus left behind relatives and friends as well as their homes. Long afterward, the separate branches of families kept in touch through regular correspondence and occasional travels. The Revolution divided Native peoples in the same way. In New York, for example, most of the Iroquois remained neutral in the conflict, though some eventually sided with the revolutionaries. A number of Mohawks, under Chief Joseph Brant, remained actively allied to the British. During the hostilities, British forces, Native warriors under Brant's leadership, and counter-revolutionary irregulars conducted a vicious guerrilla war in upper New York directed in part against their own people. They murdered relatives, and torched farms and churches they had built themselves. They could hardly return to the homes they had destroyed. After the war the British opened up land to receive these refugee combatants at the western end of Lake Ontario close to their wartime base on the Niagara Peninsula. The Mohawk, too, sought relief. The British purchased a huge tract of land from Mississauga Indians along the Grand River to provide a new homeland for their displaced Native allies.

The migration of the Mohawks and elements of the other Iroquois tribes to the Grand River reminds us of the ethnic pluralism of the Loyalist experience. About 2,000 Loyalists were indigenous peoples. About 3,000 were Black, either free Blacks or slaves who became involuntary Loyalists with their masters; most of them were from the east coast colonies and resettled in Nova Scotia. More than half of the Loyalist refugees had been born in the 13 colonies and could thus be considered 'American'. Slightly fewer originated in Great Britain, but a significant minority came from other countries. Religious minorities were overrepresented in the Loyalist population. In Quebec the British acquired title to land in the name of the Crown through treaties of purchase with Native peoples before settling the émigrés. British officials began negotiations with resident indigenous peoples as early as 1781. Within a few years most of what is now southern Ontario had been acquired as Crown Land. Native peoples received reserves of land set aside for them and payment in goods in return for the surrender of their land. Interestingly, the indigenous peoples involved were themselves immigrants to the region, having moved into the territory from the north onto lands vacated by the destruction of the Huron sometime after the mid-seventeenth century.

The Loyalists may not have been as political as later commentators would make out, but their migration precipitated significant political adjustment. So numerous were the newcomers to Nova Scotia and so pressing their needs, that another colony, New Brunswick, had to be carved out in 1784 to accommodate them. Prince Edward Island had already been separated, its lands parcelled out to 67 great landlords who proposed to rent to settlers. This cozy piece of court patronage saddled the colony with a problem of how the tenants might obtain clear title to their land from their absentee landlords, an issue that tormented island politics for more than a century. The refugees may not have been ideologically driven, but most of them were British Americans in their bones. Instinctively they believed that the legitimacy of government derived from its willingness to serve the interests of the people. They also expected certain things as British subjects, such as British law, property rights, and political institutions. They also expected to be compensated for their losses with land, provisions, tools, seeds, and preferment in public employment. Thus many found the institutions of Quebec inimical, in particular seigneurial land tenure and French civil law for property and marriage. They added their voices to those of the English-speaking mercantile minority in demanding change. Within a decade the British government was forced to make the third major adjustment to the government of Canada.

The British too believed they had learned something from the American Revolution; that is, that the colonies should be endowed with a constitution and social make-up resembling that of Britain itself. Having lost the first empire, the British were determined not to lose the second. The Constitution Act of 1791 created two colonies, Upper and Lower Canada, each with its own administration and Legislative Assembly. In Upper Canada, British law and institutions would prevail. In Lower Canada, a mixed system of English criminal law, common law, and French civil law would continue; seigneurial tenure would apply in most of the province and an English freehold system would govern in the newly settled townships. Popular representation within a limited franchise was deemed necessary if only to vote for taxes and thereby relieve the burden of empire from the British treasury. Catholics, and therefore French Canadians, could sit in this Assembly. But the incipient democratic tendencies of legislative assemblies needed to be held in check.

To that end an upper house, a Legislative Council, like the House of Lords and representing propertied interests, was added to counterbalance the Assembly in the colonies. The governor, with ample means, and a council of his own choosing to advise him, exercised a fairly wide sway of independent authority. To preserve political stability and authority within the Empire, layers of appointed administrative authority overwhelmed, it was hoped, the modicum of legislative liberty needed to express the popular will and raise taxes. Crown and Clergy Reserves were set aside to finance civil government and a state religion. Outside Quebec, provision was made for the establishment of 'the Protestant religion'. In practice this meant that the Church of England and in time the Church of Scotland received lands, privileges, and the right to marry. In this way religious sects, thought to be hotbeds of sedition, would be kept in their place and the levelling spirit curbed. The spiritual and the emotional realm—never far from politics—would remain in the hands of 'sound men'.

The first governor of Upper Canada arrived in 1792 with the intention of reproducing in this rough pioneer society 'the image and transcript of the British constitution', including a colonial aristocracy. Such were the ambitious plans, but they would have to be built with the crooked timber of humanity, much of it migrating into the region in the 1790s from the American frontier.

⁂

Beyond the staterooms and battlefields, ordinary people, through their toil and the nurture of their families, also created new realities that shaped the destiny of Canada. Social and economic change did not just happen; human effort drove change. Men and women going about their daily lives, wrenching their living as best they could from a hard land, made history too.

The gradual growth of a resident fishing population in Newfoundland forced Britain to rethink its policies towards the island. For many years Britain forbid settlement on the grounds that the migrant fishery served as a nursery for seaman for the royal navy. Regulations compelled fishing expeditions organized in the ports of Devon and Dorset to take a certain number of 'green men' for training each year. As the outgoing fishing vessels regularly victualled and recruited in southern Ireland, a sizeable minority of the Newfoundland population became Irish and Roman Catholic. After three centuries of migratory fishing, the end of the eighteenth century saw the rise of a land-based fishery exploiting the inshore grounds of northern Newfoundland, the Avalon Peninsula, and the formerly French-controlled south shore. By the 1790 these 'planters' accounted for as much as half the annual catch.

Permanent settlers dramatically altered the environment. The residents denuded the shores of trees around their coves as they gathered fuel, lumber for their houses, and construction timbers for their wharves, boats, drying stages, and flakes. They also eliminated the indigenous population. As the displaced and desperate Beothuk people raided these isolated settlements on a regular basis, the residents pushed them further into the barren interior and hunted them to the point of extinction. By 1800 almost 20,000 permanent residents called the Newfoundland home, three-quarters of them men and almost half of Irish Roman Catholic origin. Belatedly Britain had to recognize that Newfoundland was no longer a great vessel, moored in the north Atlantic as training ground for its sailors. A colonial administration had to be organized to provide civil government. Meanwhile, out at sea a substantial migratory fishery flourished. The French operating out of St-Malo and the English from southwestern ports sent as many as 300 and 500 boats respectively to fish the Grand Banks and the offshore grounds each year. Newfoundland continued to provide fish for European markets, and with the Americans excluded, a significant dried cod trade with the British sugar islands in the Caribbean opened up. It is thus that Newfoundlanders acquired their taste for rum.

After the American Revolution the fur trade in the Northwest entered its Heroic Age with two great trading systems vying with one another—that of the Hudson's Bay Company in the north, and that of the Northwest Company, a virtual transcontinental business, operating out of Montreal. They competed over vast distances to control the lucrative fur trade of the western interior. Each spring, flotillas of the Northwest Company's great canoes set off from Montreal for the north shore of Lake Superior laden with trade goods. At a fort near present-day Thunder Bay, the brigades from Montreal would meet the wintering partners coming in from the network of fur trading posts further west carrying the season's haul of furs with them. The rafters of the great hall rang with boozy song and laughter as old friends reminisced, mourned the departed, and heard only slightly embellished tales of the exploits of their colleagues. Wreathed in pipe smoke and smelling of whiskey, the Montreal merchants and their upcountry partners would compare market intelligence, plan the next season's campaign, invest in new posts or explorations, exchange goods for furs, and divide the profits and losses from previous years.

The rafters of the great hall rang with boozy song and laughter as old friends reminisced.

The Hudson's Bay Company, seeing the Montrealers preempting the flow of furs at the source, moved inland themselves to build rival fur trading posts along the rivers of the interior. By the early nineteenth century the entire woodland interior from Lake Superior to the Rocky Mountains, and north as far as Great Slave Lake was dotted with hundreds of competing fur trading posts, most of which lasted less than 15 years. The competition to obtain the best sites often turned violent as traders literally fought for furs and, as inducements to trade usually involved alcohol, the rivalry proved socially destructive as well to Native peoples. In 1811 the Hudson's Bay Company established the Selkirk Colony of Highland Scots, Irish, Germans, and Swiss on the Red River, strategically placed to thwart the Montrealers' east–west supply lines. A massacre inevitably ensued in 1816 as the two groups fought for control of the region.

The Hudson's Bay men and the Montrealers competed as well to discover new fur trading areas. By the 1770s most rivers of the Prairie West had been charted. Samuel Hearne, an employee of the Hudson's Bay Company, crossed the northern barrens, reaching the Arctic Ocean by the Coppermine River in 1772. Alexander Mackenzie, working for the Northwest Company, ventured north as far as the Arctic Ocean in 1789 and overland west to the Pacific Coast in 1793. His colleague Simon Fraser explored the mountainous interior of British Columbia, reaching the Pacific on the river that bears his name in 1808. At about the same time, David Thompson extended the Northwest Company's reach down the Columbia River system to the Pacific through a region called New Caledonia. Fur trading companies financed these expeditions to extend their hinterlands and to find new transportation routes for goods. In doing so these commercial interests greatly expanded knowledge of the geography of the continent built upon a trading network that tied these new regions economically to Canada.

The rapid geographical expansion of the fur trade in the West disrupted the lives of Native peoples in the northwestern woodlands. Along the transportation corridors of the fur trade they congregated around the posts for food, protection, and work. In some heavily exploited areas disease and displacement both reduced the numbers of Native peoples and increased their dependence upon the trade. Historians have estimated that the total indigenous population of Canada fell to about 175,000 in the early 1800s, a decline of more than 30 per cent in a century. By the beginning of the nineteenth century the Northwest Company maintained about 1,000 employees wintering in the interior, the Hudson's Bay Company about half that number. Apart from the small number of Scots merchants at the top who managed the Montreal fur trade business, the traders and voyageurs who made up the large majority of the personnel consisted almost exclusively of French Canadians from the St Lawrence parishes. The Hudson's Bay men came mainly from Scotland.

As they had since the beginning of the fur trade, Native women developed long-lasting relationships with the European traders. For the French Canadians, Native women secured lasting alliances between traders and tribes, acted as interpreters for their partners, and worked in the post to prepare the furs for shipment. Far more than 'comfort women', Native women acted as guides, diplomats, and workers. Over time, these liaisons took on the character of common-law marriage. The Métis children of the fur trade grew up with a dual heritage: the French language and economic associations of their fathers, and the intimate knowledge of the people and the land of their mothers.

The Orkneymen of the Hudson's Bay Company formed similar domestic unions. From these English alliances with Native women, an English-speaking mixed-blood people emerged, called the Country Born. These two groups of children of the fur trade married, creating their own second- and third-generation communities around the posts. In time Métis and Country Born people specialized in supplying the fur trade with a portable, high-energy food based upon buffalo grease and berries called pemmican, and providing the labour force necessary to maintain the extensive transportation system of the trade. Thus working people, men and women, explored, mapped, exploited the resources, and together populated the continental interior.

Russian traders pressing south from Alaska drew Spanish counter-expeditions north from Mexico into the waters of the Northwest Pacific Coast in the mid-eighteenth century. Belatedly, the British dispatched Captain James Cook to assert their interests in 1776 on his fatal third voyage of exploration. Subsequently, Captain George Vancouver mapped the coastline for the British during a three-year voyage beginning in 1792. Eventually, the Spanish withdrew from their forward base on Vancouver Island. British sailors and Russian traders independently discovered that the Chinese highly prized the pelt of the sea otter, so luxurious and numerous in the region. Thus out of official exploration, a new trans-oceanic fur trade developed on the Pacific and with it the Native peoples of the West Coast were drawn into the web of global commerce. They provided the pelts and other furs in return not only for the usual trade goods, but also for dyes, metal axes and tools for carving, and copper for ritual shields. They were more successful than most indigenous peoples in being able to channel the proceeds of the trade into enriching their cultural life, though they too succumbed in large numbers to European diseases. The West Coast was also attached to the British colonial system from the East, across the continent. Venturing overland and along the great rivers of the West, Montreal fur traders had advanced to the Pacific by 1793. The West Coast thus became tied to Britain and British interests in Canada both by land and by sea.

◦——

The disruption to world trade that accompanied the French Revolution and especially the Napoleonic Wars created new opportunities for Canadian products in the British market. However, the political fallout from this continental conflict, as the United States found itself compelled to declare war on Great Britain, indirectly made Canada a major theatre of war. British power and colonial loyalty would be tested once again in combat.

Napoleon closed most of Europe to British commerce. Britain retaliated by blockading French seaports, preventing all vessels, including American ships, from reaching the French market. Britain further infuriated the Americans by boarding US vessels on the high seas to seize suspected deserters and impress often innocent sailors into the British navy. Coming at the end of a long series of commercial insults at the hands of the British, the Americans considered these blatant provocations a cause of war. In addition, in the Northwest, a renewal of raids to prevent US expansion onto Native lands led by a Shawnee Chief Tecumseh, with British covert support, gave the citizens of frontier states their own local reasons for seeking revenge. Aggravated commercial interests in the East and War Hawks in the West combined to tip the Congressional balance towards war. Striking out against Canada was the most convenient means of dealing a blow to Great Britain, even though there was no strong desire in the United States to own Canada.

Napoleon kept British forces fully occupied on the continent and in other theatres of war. No reinforcements could be spared for the time being; Canada would be on its own. The American regular army outnumbered the relatively small contingent of

British troops (5,600 in the Canadas and 4,200 in Nova Scotia). The local militia were numerous, but poorly trained, badly equipped, and of dubious loyalty in parts of Upper Canada. A military campaign focussed on taking the relatively defenceless strategic city of Montreal might have brought the Americans victory. Instead they dissipated their forces across a broad front. The war unfolded in a series of land battles along the Great Lakes–St Lawrence border, naval engagements on the Great Lakes and Lake Champlain, and a naval blockade of the East Coast of the United States maintained by the British fleet operating out of Halifax.

In 1812 the Americans launched a three-pronged assault from the west at Detroit, across the Niagara River in the centre, and in the east up the Lake Champlain corridor. Aggressive tactics by the Upper Canadian commander, Isaac Brock, pre-empted the western attack and hurled back the Niagara invasion, though this action cost him his life. In the east, Canadian militiamen under the command of a French Canadian, Michel de Salaberry, repelled the invaders advancing on Montreal from Plattsburgh. The French- and English-Canadian militia jointly beat back another invasion near Cornwall along the St Lawrence. Thereafter most of the action occurred in Upper Canada. In the summer of 1813 American forces captured the Upper Canadian capital of York (Toronto) and met little resistance invading the Niagara Peninsula. In the fall British regular forces and Native warriors drove the invaders back. In the west, the United States defeated the British and their Native allies (Tecumseh was killed in the fighting), and continued to occupy the western part of Upper Canada until the end of the war. On the Great Lakes, the Americans under Admiral Perry gained naval mastery in a series of battles. The following summer British forces and Upper Canadian militiamen defeated the Americans in a pitched battle at Lundy's Lane near Niagara Falls. About the same time the British briefly invaded the city of Washington in retaliation for the capture of York, setting fire to the Capitol and to the presidential residence. This building became known thereafter as the White House as a result of the whitewash used to cover the smoke damage.

The war ended in 1815 with Napoleon's final defeat, with no significant changes in the status quo in North America. Canada's boundaries remained unchanged. Once more, Canadians had declined the opportunity to become Americans. In Upper Canada, among a population largely American in origin, there had been visible support in some quarters for the US cause. Several members of the Upper Canadian Assembly defected; the militia responded to the call to duty with the utmost reluctance and at times defiance. The Upper Canadian militia did eventually rouse itself late in the war, serving with distinction particularly at the bloody Battle of Lundy's Lane. The defence of Upper Canada rested primarily upon the shoulders of the regular British army. Important credit must also be given to the Native fighters whose participation in several engagements turned the tide, the Battle of Queenston Heights being but one example. In Lower Canada, the French-Canadian militia did rally to the British cause with considerable enthusiasm. The Roman Catholic Church and the old seigneurial families regarded the Americans and their anti-clerical, republican French friends as a threat to the French-Canadian way of life. In the war of 1812 French-Canadian militia showed more zeal in defending their homeland and British interests than did the Loyalist Upper Canadians. In the upper province, the Americans were tolerated as occupiers—they were after all cousins—but not welcomed as liberators. And when they were

> *Once more, Canadians had declined the opportunity to become Americans.*

driven out, their departure did not occasion much regret. In Upper Canada the war was regarded more as a falling-out between friends, but its outcome did serve to draw the boundary line more emphatically between kindred peoples.

⌒

Seen from a lofty academic perspective the War of 1812 turned out to be a tremendous benefit to Canada. Increased British military spending and the construction of defensive fortifications in Halifax, Quebec, Kingston, and other places provided a direct stimulus to the Canadian economy. Britain's exclusion of foreign shipping from the Empire encouraged the growth of shipbuilding and a shipping industry in Maritime Canada. The Atlantic forests provided a convenient source of masts and ships timbers for the British navy at a critical time. A commercial timber business also grew up alongside this military trade. Interference with the flow of timber from Britain's traditional source of supply, the Baltic, created an opening for wood from Canada to enter the British market. When wheat prices soared in Britain because of disruptions in supplies from the continent and tariff wars, occasionally it paid merchants to freight Canadian wheat across the Atlantic. The commercial warfare that accompanied the Napoleonic Wars inadvertently opened up lucrative trading opportunities for the Canadian colonies.

The post-war years witnessed a significant boom in Canadian forest products exports to Great Britain and, for the first time, a major flow of British emigration to Canada. Enterprising shipbuilders and lumbermen quickly stripped the Nova Scotia shoreline of its merchantable timber. The lack of rivers in the region meant that the interior forest remained relatively untouched on the peninsula for the time being. However, New Brunswick with its thick pine forests and long, swift-flowing rivers possessed almost ideal geography for the nascent timber trade. The St John River in the south and the Mirimachi in the north became the two main axes of the Maritime timber trade. Even by 1810, revenue from timber exports from Quebec to Great Britain exceeded the value of furs by a substantial margin.

After the war the St Lawrence Valley, the tributaries running into it, and the Ottawa River became the home of a thriving and varied forest products industry. At first the British resisted the importation of what was considered inferior quality colonial wood. But given the high duties blocking foreign timber from the market, British shipbuilders, contractors, and carpenters eventually overcame their prejudice against the Canadian product. Early in the nineteenth century Canada exported a variety of forest products to Britain—in decreasing order of importance, square timber (red pine and oak logs hewn square with a broadaxe and adze), deals (large rectangular slabs of wood), planks, boards, barrel staves, and ashes. In Britain the square timber would be sawn according to British specifications for the lumber trade. Some of these huge colonial timbers became the posts and beams of the great Victorian factories then under construction. The deals, planks, and boards would be roughly sawn in Canadian mills for shipment and finishing abroad. Ashes from the burned-over forest were used for soap making, fertilizer, and gunpowder production. In total Canadian timber exports rose from about 140,000 cubic metres in 1810 to more than 550,000 by the late 1820s, approximately two-thirds of these totals originating in New Brunswick. After a slight decline in the early 1830s, exports continued to increase, reaching more than one million cubic metres by the end of the 1840s. Over time the proportion of sawn lumber to squared timber tended to increase and the Quebec business expanded relative to its Maritime counterpart.

Each winter a small army of axemen invaded the Maritime and St Lawrence forests. Housed in rude shanties and fed a calorie-rich diet of pork, beans, bread, and potatoes, the loggers chopped their way with alarming speed through the virgin forest. The logs would either be squared by hand where they fell, or at a riverside dump after they had been drawn by oxen or horses over tote roads of snow and ice. Come spring breakup these huge sticks of timber would be driven down streams into the main rivers where they would be formed into rafts. A gang of skilled raftsmen steered these enormous trains of timber downstream, breaking them up occasionally to run treacherous rapids. The St Lawrence River below Quebec became a vast sea of wood each summer as a waiting armada of freighters loaded the timbers and lumber bound for Liverpool, Bristol, London, Glasgow, and Ireland. Between 1823 and 1834, for example, the number of ships clearing the port of Quebec doubled from 600 to over 1,200 annually on account of this trade. It took crews of about 13,000 men to load the cargo.

Abundant water power in the colonies encouraged the development of a sawmilling industry along virtually every stream and river to provide lumber for export and for the growing domestic market. By the 1830s, for example, about 500 sawmills of various sizes operated in Upper Canada, a number that would rise to over 1,500 by 1850. The St Lawrence River carried the hardwoods, sawn lumber, and ashes of the Great Lakes region to Quebec in volumes that exceeded those of the Ottawa River system up into the 1840s. The forest industry became the largest employer of wage labour in the colonies, providing seasonal employment to young men, farmers in the off-season, and a small number of full-time skilled workers. The Ottawa trade employed an estimated 1,500 hands in the 1830s, rising to 8,000 in the 1840s. In Lower Canada, forestry, river driving, sawmilling, and shipbuilding provided important supplementary employment for a rapidly growing population whose agricultural sector had begun to slip into relative decline. The forest industries also became a significant market for provisions, fodder, horses, harness, equipment, axes, and clothing. The timber trade for both domestic and export markets became one of the main motors of economic growth.

The economic importance of the rising forest industry has often been heralded in historical accounts. The environmental cost of this kind of relentless forest exploitation has not, however, received the attention it deserves. After logging, forest fires inevitably raged through the discarded limbs and smaller timber left behind. Natural regeneration took generations; quite different tree species rose in succession on the abandoned timber limits. Stripped of its trees the hydrological character of the land changed; rain and snow ran off more quickly; nearby rivers filled with silt. Bark dislodged from logs during the river-drive sank, lining their bottoms with a poisonous, anaerobic layer of muck. The damming of rivers for sawmills changed stream flow, altered the local ecology, and barred the way for migrating fish species. New fish such as carp flourished in the slacker, warmer water. To be rid of great piles of nuisance sawdust, the millers habitually dumped it into the rivers to be carried away, adding further to the indigestible biological load of the streams. In a variety of ways, the early forest industry transformed the environment.

⌒

During this period after the Napoleonic Wars, agriculture served as the main motor of economic growth, the principal occupation of the population, a leading export industry, and of course it too reshaped the environment in countless ways. The lands of Upper Canada when they were cleared of trees provided ideal conditions for the growing of wheat. Fields in this region regularly yielded on average 12 to 15 bushels of wheat per acre. Wheat could be readily milled into flour in the region at the hundreds of gristmills that shared the streams with sawmills. Packed in locally made barrels it would then be shipped down the St Lawrence system to market. Wheat could also be shipped as grain in bulk. Over these years a growing proportion of the Upper Canadian surplus went into feeding Lower Canadians. Between one-half to two-thirds of Upper Canadian wheat was exported to Great Britain, encouraged, after 1827, by much lower British Corn Law duties against imported grains. Of course a great deal of flour was consumed in Upper Canada, on the farms, in villages and towns, and in the lumber camps. With the population doubling every generation, agricultural productivity had to keep up with an ever-larger number of mouths and still produce an exportable surplus. Exports were important, but the main agricultural activity remained feeding and supplying the rapidly growing local market. Oats and hay flourished in the temperate climate, providing food for draft animals, cattle, sheep, and pigs. In the early nineteenth century, as settlers swarmed in, slashed and burned the forest, planted and harvested their first crops, and steadily improved their cultivated acreage, Upper Canada grew into the leading agricultural colony of British North America.

Lower Canada experienced a different trajectory. The most populous colony and an early producer and exporter of wheat underwent an agricultural and demographic crisis of sorts between the War of 1812 and the 1840s. There traditional agriculture and economic growth could not keep pace with the rapid growth of the population. Moreover, crop diseases in the older fields of the region and the loss of nutrients led to declining wheat yields. Farmers responded by shifting out of wheat to the production of oats and hay to feed cattle, sheep, and swine destined for urban markets. The question whether there was a widespread crisis of subsistence in the rural areas of Lower Canada remains a matter of scholarly debate. Certainly the adjustment occasioned much distress. By the 1830s, Lower Canada, which had once exported a surplus, could no longer do so. It tended increasingly to purchase its wheat and flour from Upper Canadian sources, practise subsistence agriculture to meet immediate family needs, and raise livestock to provision the towns, cities, and the lumber camps.

For the thirty years after the wars, economic opportunities in the British North American colonies combined with post-war economic distress in Britain led to large-scale migration from Britain to Canada. The conditions in the British Isles that converged to provide a powerful 'push' to emigration included overpopulation, post-war political unrest, social dislocation as a result of changing agricultural practices, and restructuring of the manufacturing trades. In the neutral language of the economic historian, the enclosure of larger fields from smaller plots and the raising of sheep released underused labour for other occupations. These changing farm practices produced growing unemployment among agricultural labourers and widespread distress as people were displaced from their homes. The agricultural revolution and the early stages of the industrial revolution set the rapidly growing British population in motion. The sudden emergence of industrial cities was accompanied by squalor and urban poverty. In such circumstances, many enterprising single men and families of the middling sort sought ways of escaping to new opportunities. Various public and private schemes too were launched to alleviate distress and forestall social revolution by relocating surplus population to the colonies, where it would be a benefit rather than a liability to the Empire. The British government also tried to address British North America's chronic security problem by settling demobilized soldiers and others in group settlements. But assisted immigration provided only a small proportion of the total; most immigrants made their way to British North American on their own.

From the end of the Napoleonic Wars to 1830, an annual average of about 25,000 British émigrés left their homeland, usually about half of them were bound for the British North American colonies and half for the United States. During the 1830s and 1840s the exodus increased to approximately 100,000 annually, with slightly more favouring US destination over Canadian. During the 1830s about one-third of British immigrants to Canada originated in England and Scotland; fully two-thirds arrived from Irish ports. The immigrants headed overwhelmingly towards the abundant free land available in Upper Canada. Only 17 per cent were drawn to Nova Scotia and New Brunswick; another 17 per cent found employment largely in the urban areas of Lower Canada. The remaining 66 per cent continued on to Upper Canadian destinations, though some pressed on to the United States. About 50 per cent of these immigrants classified themselves as common labourers, slightly under 40 per cent as farmers or farm labourers, and only about 6 per cent considered themselves semi-skilled or skilled workers.

The settlers brought with them their own crops, grasses, and breeds of livestock. In the process of introducing European species from carp to starlings, settlers also wiped out indigenous species, from the rattlesnake to the passenger pigeon. In a couple of generations they turned a North American Carolinian forest into a denuded rolling prairie. They created their own distinctive landscape out of imported and domestic materials. This massive migration of people from Great Britain to Canada between 1815 and the 1840s served to make the British North American colonies more

British than French in cultural terms. But, it should be noted, much of that 'Britishness' was actually 'Irishness'.

Immigration on this scale expanded local markets, brought new knowledge and skills, and provided additional labour to expand production of timber and agricultural products. But in the port cities, the arrival of the overcrowded immigrant vessels also inevitably delivered unwelcome waves of epidemic diseases (mainly smallpox and cholera) and cargoes of abject poverty. Halifax, Quebec, Montreal, and to a lesser extent Toronto bore the brunt of this human flood as local urban labour markets had to absorb the newcomers in wage-earning employment and provide rudimentary social services to alleviate distress and contain contagion.

Much of that 'Britishness' was actually 'Irishness'.

But it must be emphasized that in all of the British colonies the major source of population growth remained natural increase. Birth rates both in the Catholic rural parishes of Lower Canada and the Protestant back townships of Upper Canada remained astonishingly high throughout the early nineteenth century—more than 50 births per 1,000, for example, in Quebec. The steady arrival of new immigrants, but more importantly the regular arrival of new babies drove up the population of Upper Canada from about 40,000 in 1800 to almost 500,000 in 1842, a twelve-fold increase. The Lower Canadian population rose in the same period from approximately 200,000 to about 800,000, or roughly four times. Estimates suggest the Maritime population experienced a five-fold increase during the same period from about 80,000 in 1800 to just over 400,000 in the 1840s. The growing population in Upper Canada found ready employment clearing land, ploughing, planting and harvesting, occasionally logging, but also constructing the houses, commercial buildings, roads, bridges, wharves, and mills of a new society. But in Lower Canada, even by the late 1820s, there appeared to be too many hands for the available opportunities. Quebec began at this early date to export its surplus population not west to Ontario but rather south to the industrial towns of New Hampshire and Massachusetts. Canada thus became both the destination for immigrants and a source of emigrants.

෨

Following the War of 1812 the British North American colonies were blessed with several generations of relative peace. In the Northwest, the Hudson's Bay Company's acquisition of the Northwest Company in 1821 restored order and consolidated the monopoly in the region. Fur traders, agriculturalists, lumbermen, merchants, and fishermen could respond to expanding markets as best they could, without fear of invasion, monetary instability, or confiscation of cargoes on the high seas.

In the 1830s British North America witnessed a classic struggle for self-government. Going about their daily business, the colonists found many obstacles close to home that they believed stood in their way. Their vociferously expressed complaints led to locally grown political instability that shook the colonies in the 1830s. In a very general way, political unrest in the British North American colonies shared much in common with earlier discontents in the American colonies. Essentially, a rising democratic reform movement, chafing under colonial authority and local oligarchic control, struggled to reform political institutions to better reflect popular will. Authority could be tolerated as long as it served broader public interests at not too high a cost. Rights and liberties in the abstract may not have had much of a following in British North America, but when governments demanded too much, behaved in a high-handed fashion, or fastened a burdensome agenda upon their subjects, popular forces had at hand a well-stocked rhetorical arsenal with which to fight back. Colonial reformers also drew strength from the progress of similar populist, democratic movements in Britain and the United States. But in each colony this struggle took on its own unique character, involving varying combinations of social and economic distress, demagoguery, authoritarianism, blunders, popular support, concessions, and even violence. And in contrast to the familiar story, British authority emerged from the conflict more thoroughly entrenched.

In Upper Canada popular discontent festered over control of government institutions by an interrelated elite called by its detractors the Family Compact or Tories. In the eyes of its critics, the unelected Family Compact, which populated the Legislative Assembly and the governor's Executive Council, or cabinet, effectively controlled the elected Legislative Council and thereby managed the affairs of the colony in its own interests. Specific grievances focussed on land policies that reserved large tracts of prime land from settlement for the benefit of the Anglican Church, the government, and the social elites. Critics complained too of nepotism and patronage, the disenfranchisement of citizens of American origin, and heavy expenditures on canals and public works, which were thought to have little direct benefit to the general population. The harsh treatment meted out to popular leaders, Robert Gourlay in the early 1820s and William Lyon Mackenzie later, became themselves examples of the abuse of power by the oligarchies. Gourlay was forced into exiled, and the newspaperman Mackenzie had his types thrown into Toronto Harbour by a gang of Tory hooligans. The electoral fortunes of the reformers and the Tories ebbed and flowed during this period with neither side being able to gain firm control of the Legislative Assembly. Reform support came mainly from the expanding rural areas north and west of Toronto and from immigrants of American origin. The Tory elites found support among the urban commercial classes, the recently arrived British immigrants, and the Loyalist Orange Order among the Protestant Irish.

In Lower Canada the reform movement set out to gain more popular control. The British governors of Lower Canada traditionally appointed their Executive Councils and Legislative Councils from the ranks of the English-speaking commercial classes and the seigneurial elites who themselves were more and more British as time passed. Thus the executive came largely from the English-speaking minority of the province. From a fairly early date, however, the French-speaking majority controlled the elected Legislative Assembly. Here a group known colloquially as the Parti Canadien resisted executive domination by refusing to vote funds for the government. The political reformers in Lower Canada fought for popular control of government institutions to advance a fiscally and socially conservative legislative agenda. Lower Canadian reformers objected to expensive canals and public works, promoted by the commercial classes, to improve transportation along the St Lawrence corridor. That program not only cost money, but also undermined local producers by making imported products from Upper Canada cheaper. The Parti Canadien sought to maintain traditional institutions such as seigneurial tenure and rural life against the inroads of commercialism, agriculture, and urbanization.

Louis-Joseph Papineau, a scion of an old seigneurial family, led the fight for an elected upper house to check the policies of the military-business elite running the province. Papineau and his growing number of followers drawn from the ranks of the liberal professions—mainly notaries and lawyers—effectively created a political deadlock by refusing to vote funds required for civil government. Like Mackenzie in Upper Canada, Papineau was well acquainted with popular movements in Britain and the United States. Both men had mastered the well-honed grievance, the orotund formal petition, theatrical appeals to the British government, and the grandstanding parliamentary manoeuvre. Papineau's political resistance drew strength from the growing social distress of the rural population as a result of crop failures, overpopulation, and the need to reorient agriculture towards new markets and produce. Thus in Lower Canada the discontent took on the flavour of a conflict between English and French, and between commercial versus rural interests, in a context of mounting rural economic distress. After 1826, as the political struggle took on more overt nationalist dimensions, the Parti Canadien renamed itself the Parti Patriote. As the conflict evolved, Irish nationalists and some disaffected Irish Roman Catholics played a disproportionately important role in the leadership of the organization in opposition to Britain.

The contest between the elected legislative and the appointed executive branches of government in British North American had actually developed first in the Maritime colonies. Nova Scotian settlers had insisted upon an elected Assembly in the 1760s. From the mid-1830s Joseph Howe, a renowned orator and talented newspaper publisher, led the movement against the ruling clique and in favour of popular government in Nova Scotia. In New Brunswick a reform movement demanding greater control over the revenues from Crown Lands appeared about the same time, even though a homogeneous population largely descended from Loyalist settlers generally supported the colonial administration. Early in the nineteenth century, the tenant farmers of Prince Edward Island used their Assembly to launch a campaign to acquire clear title to their lands from the absentee landlords. As the proprietors were well protected in the appointed branches of government, but more importantly in the British Parliament, these long-running remonstrances always came to naught. In Newfoundland, which gained a resident governor in 1817 and an elected Assembly in 1832, a similar reform movement had to negotiate the finely balanced traditional antagonisms of Protestants and Catholics, English and Irish, merchants and fishers, the city of St John's and the outports. In 1842 conflict became so intense that Britain suspended the Legislative Assembly, creating in its place a combined elective and appointed house. Thus the Canadas were not unique; throughout British North America in the 1830s, popular campaigns to obtain greater self-government, and to curb the authority of governors and their councils, gained strength. Only in Upper and Lower Canada did the struggle turn to armed rebellion.

Seen from a British perspective the reform agenda required the governor to serve two masters: the British government and the colonial legislatures. British authorities did not habitually care much about Canadian affairs, but when they were forced to turn their minds to these matters they could not see how these two interests could be reconciled, especially in view of recent differences. When the British colonial secretary, Lord John Russell, definitively refused the Lower Canada petition to make the governor accountable to the Legislative Assembly, Papineau in his own tormented way began to think of insurrection, something his Irish and more nationalist colleagues enthusiastically encouraged. In Upper Canada, after Mackenzie's direct appeal to Great Britain failed, after he had an election stolen from him by the governing party, and after having been repeatedly expelled from the assembly, his fevered mind also turned to thoughts of extra-parliamentary protest. In the fall of 1837 the leaders of the dissidents in Upper and Lower Canada made a desultory effort to coordinate their action. Armed men began to muster in rural communities east and northwest of Montreal. Insurrection broke out first in Lower Canada, followed a few weeks later by a rising in Upper Canada. On 23 November a band of Lower Canadian Patriotes ambushed a detachment of British troops in the Richelieu Valley. At this signal the Upper Canadian rebels descended upon Toronto from the north on 4 December.

When the first shots were fired, authority initially revealed itself to be indecisive and vulnerable. The governor of Upper Canada, for example, rendered his province virtually defenceless against a serious attack by sending all of his regular troops to Lower Canada to suppress the earlier outbreak. However, the general rising of the population expected by the rebels in response to their musterings and initial engagements did not occur in either colony. As a result, the Rebellion of 1837 turned into the American Revolution in reverse; authority triumphed and revolution was discredited. The forces of order quickly rallied. Moreover, the erratic behaviour of the two rebel leaders did nothing to advance their cause.

The Rebellion of 1837 turned into the American Revolution in reverse.

In Lower Canada when skirmishes turned to pitched battles on 28 November and 4 December, regular British troops ruthlessly cut the rebels to pieces. In this latter confrontation some 2,000 British troops confronted an undisciplined mob of 800 Patriotes, only half of whom were armed. After the first engagement 70 rebels sought refuge in a church, where they were gunned down or burned to death. The British then proceeded to torch buildings in the region. The Patriote Rebellion was serious and bloody, leaving hundreds dead and wounded, many villages destroyed, and more than 500 rebels confined in jail.

In Upper Canada the Rebellion quickly disintegrated. The march down Yonge Street between 4 and 7 December took on a tragicomic hue when militia and rebels both more or less ran away after firing their first shots. Another ineffectual rising broke out a few days later in the west of the province. Both insurrections in Upper Canada were suppressed not by regular British troops, but rather by the local militia rallying to the government side. Zealous militiamen arrested more than 700 suspects in Upper Canada, but bloodshed and property damage were minimal.

In 1837 the authorities decisively crushed the risings in Upper and Lower Canada, but military actions continued, some of them quite serious, for several years. Papineau and Mackenzie retreated across the border to the safety of the United States, from which they launched occasional raids into the Canadas. The Patriote movement soon split into radical and traditional factions. Robert Nelson, acting as leader of the more extreme Les Frères Chasseurs (Hunters' Lodges) wing, led a small force into Canada briefly in February 1838 to proclaim an independent, secular, democratic people's republic. Papineau brooded in Albany hoping for French or American intervention, all the while continuing to defend seigneurial tenure, an established Roman Catholic Church, and the French civil code. Mackenzie installed himself on Navy Island in the Niagara River from which his followers launched periodic raids into Upper Canada.

Thus in 1838 both the Lower and Upper Canadian Rebellions turned into a species of cross-border guerrilla warfare. The Upper and Lower Canadian dissidents were joined in their endeavours by groups of Irish Fenians—Irish resistors to imperial domination—striking out against Great Britain, US citizens who sympathized with the declared revolutionary aims of the rebels, and a small number of US vigilantes who imagined they might capture Canada for the republic on a freelance basis. These subsequent border incursions at Niagara, Windsor in the far West, and Prescott on the St Lawrence caused more damage and excitement in Upper Canada than had the earlier rebellions. Once again the militia mustered in force to drive out the invaders. In popular myth, the Rebellion became a replay in miniature of the War of 1812: an attempt to impose republicanism by invasion had been repelled by loyal Upper Canadian militia. In Lower Canada, these border raids, accompanied by promises to abolish seigneurial dues and claims that the US army would support the movement, ignited a serious popular rising on the south shore of the St Lawrence below Montreal in November 1838. The warehouses of English merchants and the Indian Reserves in the region provided the principal targets of this insurrection. This rising, like the one the previous year, was brutally suppressed. Skirmishes ended in Patriote defeats. Natives surrounded and captured some of the rebels. Insurgents melted away with the arrival of British troops after the promised arms, and US support failed to appear.

Reprisals followed as the British authorities determined to make examples of the more than 800 captured rebels. In 1838 in Lower Canada, British troops indiscriminately looted and burned Patriote farms. State trials condemned 99 rebels to death. Of these 12 were publicly hanged, 60 banished or transported to Australia, and in an act of counterbalancing leniency, the rest were released. Punishments in Upper Canada proved just as harsh. Two of the captured leaders of the 1837 insurrection were hanged, despite widespread sympathy for clemency. Following the invasions of 1838, nine of the leaders were executed for treason, and approximately 100 (most of them Americans) were exiled to the penal colonies of Australia. Mackenzie, Papineau, and the other rebel leaders in their American safe haven were barred from Canada on pain of death.

British troops and local militia readily contained the Rebellions of 1837–8. A truly popular rising might have succeeded, especially in Upper Canada after the British troops had been dispatched to the Lower colony. But the Rebellion received no popular support in Upper Canada. Rather the populace rallied to the government side. In Upper Canada the Rebellion attracted a disproportionate amount of support from residents of American origin. American immigrants accounted for 30 to 40 per cent of the identifiable participants in a colony where only 6 per cent of the residents had been born in the US. The militia mobilized with enthusiasm, especially when the Rebellion turned into an invasion, and in battle behaved admirably in beating off the American attackers and inflicting heavy casualties especially at the Prescott battle. In Lower Canada, there may have been more quiet sympathy for the rebels among the general population, but that did not turn into active support. The British garrison snuffed out the insurrection, not the local militia. The rebels in Lower Canada were more numerous and they put up a more vigorous armed resistance, but the insurrection did not spread beyond the region surrounding Montreal. Even there, it did not appear to have deep roots. In most encounters the rebels numbered in the hundreds not thousands.

The Rebellion of 1837 was a classic Canadian revolution. The poorly organized rising failed to arouse popular support; the forces of repression, authority, and loyalty prevailed. The vast majority of the population remained indifferent to the rebel appeal or believed that the issues could be better addressed through ordinary means within the existing political framework. In Canada revolutions fail as action, but triumph in recollection and history.

⌒

The border eventually quieted down. Mackenzie and Papineau languished unlamented in their American exile. However, the problem of Canadian government, which had caused the embarrassing violence in the first place, remained. The British sent out one of their brightest and most liberal-minded and troublesome reformers, Lord Durham, to study this question and propose a solution. In a brief tour of duty that lasted less than six months, Durham rushed quickly, confidently, and memorably to judgement. The problem in Lower Canada, he concluded, was essentially an ethnic conflict: 'I expected to find a contest between a government and a people: I found two nations warring in the bosom of a single state: I found a struggle not of principles, but of race'. He left no doubt as to where his sympathies lay in this struggle. He believed the French Canadians, in his regrettable phrase 'a people without a history and a culture', to be incorrigible, an obstacle to progress, and a security risk to British interests in North America. As for Upper Canada he found there a defective government out of step with the legitimate needs of the people. He condemned Family Compact rule and the attempt to impose an established Church upon a population for whom it was not suited. The political unrest and stunted economic growth of Upper Canada, he noted, presented a marked and melancholy contrast to neighbouring US states. Elite mismanagement had produced a comparative economic backwater in Upper Canada.

Lord Durham concluded that the only solution to the problem in Lower Canada was assimilation of the French population by an English majority. In his view, French Canadians would be swamped eventually. It would be better to end 'the vain endeavour to preserve a French-Canadian nationality in the midst of an Anglo-American colonies and states' in a brisk and orderly fashion. First, he recommended combining the two Canadas into one colony whose Legislative Assembly would immediately have an English majority. This would provide for a unified administration of the St Lawrence commercial corridor and represent the first step in the eventual amalgamation of all of the British North American colonies. Second, on the question of government, Durham recommended that the governor become responsible to the elected Legislative Assembly in most matters relating to domestic affairs. His report thus largely endorsed the 'responsible government' program that the moderate reformers had been advocating for some time.

The British government implemented most of Lord Durham's recommendations, particularly those pertaining to the subordination of the French Canadians. The Act of Union of 1840 joined the two newly named colonies, Canada East and Canada West, for administrative purposes. Since the Constitution of the former Lower Canada had been suspended, it entered the Union by administrative fiat; Upper Canada chose to join. Each received an equal number of representatives in the elective Legislative Assembly, even though Canada East's population was 30 per cent larger. French Canadians were thus underrepresented at the beginning. English became the only official language of government. The revenues of the two regions were merged into one consolidated revenue fund. This would, it was hoped, facilitate taxation and expenditures for the transportation improvements required to serve the mercantile growth agenda.

The British government did not accept Durham's endorsement of responsible government. Rather than delivering the British governor into the hands of the elected Legislative Assembly, the British government in effect decided to square this circle by giving the governor the means of producing an Assembly to his own liking. Armed with a combination of carrots and sticks, the governor became the de facto prime minister. The first governor under the Act of Union produced a working majority by flagrantly adjusting electoral boundaries to minimize French-Canadian influence, locating polling places in areas friendly to his administration, and intimidating opposition voters with British troops and paid thugs. The governor, who remained accountable to his superiors in Britain, could thus choose amenable advisors for his Executive Council who would obtain a majority in the Legislative Assembly.

A new generation of French-Canadian political leaders resisted the assimilationist agenda, but they choose to work within the system to change it. In doing so, they found common ground with some of the disaffected English-speaking reformers from Canada West. Under the heavy hand of assertive governors, a new bicultural reform alliance would gradually take shape. But for the time being, authority, manipulation, and intimidation would prevail.

In the aftermath of the Rebellion, Britain decided to attach Canada more firmly to it economically. Over the years a significant commodity trade had grown up between Canada and Britain. The initial shipment of furs down the St Lawrence had been replaced by a steadily growing volume of timber and wheat. The merchants of Montreal had long campaigned to improve the St Lawrence transportation system to increase the flow of trade. To accomplish this objective, the river below Montreal needed dredging, navigational aids, and port facilities. Above Montreal expensive canals were required to accommodate larger ships downbound carrying commodities, and upbound freighting merchandise. Better roads were needed to get the wheat, flour, and timber to the ports on the Great Lakes. With these improvements, the St Lawrence system could effectively compete with the canals of New York for the trade of the US Midwest. Under the Union, Britain endorsed this project of mercantile empire for the united Canadas. The governors arrived with British subsidies for canals, river works, and other transportation improvements. At the same time, the British government lowered the duties on Canadian wheat. On both sides of the Atlantic it was hoped that this combination of imperial preference and public works would integrate and stimulate the Canadian economy, settle its political affairs, and strengthen the bonds between Great Britain and its largest North American colony.

Exports from Canada to Britain reached a peak in the early 1840s. Businessmen invested in mills to process wheat into flour destined for British markets. In Atlantic Canada the decade was the golden age of 'wooden ships and iron men' as colonial ships and crews navigated sea lanes the world over, carrying the cargo of the British Empire. New Brunswick's exports of timber and lumber recovered in the early 1840s. In Newfoundland, fish production notched upward. Steamships, many of them owned by an entrepreneurial Nova Scotian, Samuel Cunard, reduced the transatlantic crossing to 13 days, tying Atlantic Canada even more closely into the British commercial nexus. To be sure there were problems to be overcome, and dark clouds on the economic horizon, but in the early 1840s the British Empire had become a functioning economic system for its North American colonies.

~

British North America was British by choice in the 1840s. Invasion had been repeatedly repulsed and rebellion decisively rejected. Prodded by an embarrassing revolt after years of relative neglect, the British government had bestirred itself to take steps that in its mind would ensure that it would remain so. A territory acquired by conquest had been incorporated into the British Empire— though not without some awkwardness and frequent changes of policy. British immigration to the North American colonies served to connect Canada culturally to Great Britain as well. The large Irish immigrant population was also primarily Protestant and thus firmly attached to British institutions. For those who viewed the growing political and military power of the United States as a threat, Great Britain was the ultimate protector. French-Canadian politicians as well as Upper Canadian reformers looked to British institutions and British constitutional practice in their conjoined campaign to acquire social equality and self-government. In 1846 a former Patriote rebel went so far as to predict that 'the last canon which is shot on this continent in defence of Great Britain will be fired by the hand of a French Canadian'. Native peoples looked to the Crown to respect their treaties and protect them from expanding settlement. It was thus entirely fitting when the chaos of a gold rush forced the British government to take over direct responsibility for government of the Hudson's Bay Company's domain on the West Coast that Queen Victoria should personally change the name of the proposed colony from Columbia to British Columbia.

After the American Revolution, a British North America, a loose collection of widely dispersed individual colonies within the British Empire, had risen on the northern borders of the United States. They persisted in their Britishness through invasion and rebellion, as an alternative to republicanism. Minorities, French and Native, struggled to preserve their communities by appealing to British ideals. Unquestionably many people chafed under some of the constraints of British imperialism and the benefits were inequitably distributed, but few British Americans could imagine a better alternative.

dominion limited

⌒

A handful of British American colonies coalesced by the early twentieth century into a recognizable country, Canada, painted red on the map, a huge expanse of territory north of the forty-ninth parallel extending from the Atlantic to the Pacific and north to the Arctic. The Dominion of Canada would play its role on the world stage, too, as a major trading partner, immigrant destination, as a combatant in the First World War, and a founding member of the League of Nations. Between the mid-nineteenth and mid-twentieth centuries, Canada would come to possess the attributes of nation-hood and become home to a recognizable people.

The conventional narrative of the history of the Americas in the nineteenth century is a story of progress from colony to inde-pendence and nationhood, usually through revolution or at least some heroic resistance. Canadian history would not follow that path. Rather, Canadians would choose something between inde-pendence and colonialism, preferring to expand the scope of autonomy within the framework of a modified Empire. In mod-ern times, this might mischievously be called sovereignty-associa-tion. Then it was called Dominion Status, something Canadians appeared to understand but others found confusing, even contra-dictory.

The colony-to-nation scenario did not quite work for Canada for several reasons. First, Canada had to be made up out of dis-parate and quite distant parts; the 'country' was not there to be found. Second, when the parts were assembled, the pieces did not fuse together into a larger alchemical whole. For various reasons, economic and social integration confronted a persistent regionalism that acted as a centrifugal force within the country. Thus the union would remain less than perfect. As for the course and direction of national emergence, revolution had been discredited, and republicanism bore the burden of association with invasion and conquest. Canadians would prefer an existential method of political evolution, within the British constitutional tradition, toward some vague and unspecified goal. Canadians might admire the United States and envy its economic performance; nonetheless, they felt the need to resist American cultural influences and politically define themselves negatively as 'not Americans'. Moreover, American history seemed to provide some lessons in what to avoid in the nation-building project.

The founders of the union, in Canadian language the Fathers of Confederation, would have preferred to style their country as a Kingdom because they no longer thought of it as a colony. The British found this pretentious and absurd. The founders then fell back to calling their country a Dominion, from Psalm 72 of praise to the King, 'And He shall have dominion from sea unto sea.' With typical condescension the British prime minister thought this silly but harmless. Queen Victoria, however, liked it. Canada would be a Dominion. But what *was* a Dominion? And what constitutional relationship would it have to Great Britain? These questions would take quite a long time to answer. Between the 1840s and 1930s Canadians established their Dominion; they filled out its boundaries to biblical proportions; they enshrined it in the statutes of Empire; at home, at work, and at war they expressed its character. But unambiguous unity and a singular identity eluded them. Canada remained a political expression and Canadians a confederation of peoples of 'limited identities'.

~

The journey from a cluster of colonies to Dominionhood begins not with a stirring manifesto on the part of the colonists yearning to be free, but rather a forthright declaration of independence of the mother country from its Empire. Canada was born of imperialism going into reverse. For largely domestic reasons, Great Britain abandoned mercantilism in the mid-1840s for free trade. Manchester School economic liberalism provided a theoretical justification. Mass demonstrations by the rising industrial classes for cheap food, and distress in Ireland gave the policy urgency. The growing influence of commerce and industry in the British Parliament eventually produced the legislative muscle to repeal the Corn Laws in 1846. These laws protected British agriculture against foreign competition and provided some incidental imperial preference for colonial producers. Dismantling these laws meant Britain would

Canada was born of imperialism going into reverse.

henceforth purchase its grain wherever it could be found most cheaply. It was believed that the elimination of these duties would lower the cost of food, thereby lowering labour costs, making British manufacturing exports even more competitive. Unilateral free trade would also seize the political high ground in a campaign to reduce foreign duties against British manufactures, thereby opening and expanding markets in which Britain had a comparative advantage. Brandishing the imperialism of free trade and its unrivalled industrial power, Great Britain could blast its way into world markets. Repeal of the Corn Laws was followed by similar reductions of duties on timber and hundreds of other products, and the repeal of the Navigation Acts that confined imperial trade to British or colonial cargo ships. The choice of free trade carried some logical consequences for Empire. Colonies were no longer considered primarily as captive markets for manufacturers or as preferred producers of commodities.

Free trade amounted to an economic abandonment of the Empire. The ideological equivalent, Little Englandism, soon followed. According to this view, colonies were actually considerable liabilities. They were expensive to administer, costly to defend, and they exposed Britain to needless foreign entanglements. Moreover, colonies were invariably troublesome, fractious encumbrances, destined for independence in any event. Better to be rid of them on good terms, sooner rather than later. Benjamin Disraeli, speaking of Newfoundland, bluntly summed up this position: 'These wretched colonies will all be independent too, in a few years, and are a millstone around our necks.'

Thus in the 1840s an economic revolution with far-reaching political implications occurred in Great Britain. This policy change had profound consequences for the British North American colonies whose administration, defence, trade, and economic prosperity had heretofore depended heavily upon Britain. Free trade changed everything. The constitutional complexities of making the governor responsible to the colonial legislature disappeared if Britain no longer had separate interests to protect against colonial interference. Under this new dispensation, Britain had every reason to encourage colonial self-rule in the hope that self-defence and fiscal self-sufficiency would accompany self-government. If colonies no longer enjoyed preference in British markets, and if Britain pursued its own self-interest economically, it followed that the colonies should in turn be able to make trading arrangements to suit their own needs. Small, scattered colonies should be encouraged to cooperate, perhaps unite, to create more viable political entities that could stand on their own in the world. While this revolution in British public policy presented an opportunity for some British American colonial politicians, it posed a worrisome threat to others.

By a happy coincidence, British American colonial politicians stood poised to demand self-government, or responsible government as they called it, at precisely the moment the British put themselves in a mind to give it. The breakthrough came first in Nova Scotia, but arrived with more éclat in the Canadas. The election of 1847 in Nova Scotia resulted in a majority for Joseph Howe, the charismatic popular tribune. When the Colonial Office instructed the governor to choose his council or cabinet from the political group that commanded a majority in the assembly, responsible government was achieved, as Howe boasted, 'without a blow struck or a pane of glass broken'. Governors could still reserve legislation for consideration, and the British Parliament could theoretically override it, but for all practical purposes Nova Scotia became self-governing in January 1848.

A good deal more than glass was put at risk by responsible government in the Canadas, however. Already during the mid-1840s constitutional reformers in the English-speaking region of Canada West had formed a working alliance with French-Canadian politicians from Canada East, seeking to regain the rights the French had lost under the Union. Much had been accomplished in opposition by their coordinated efforts. Constitutional reform would thus be accomplished under bicultural leadership, involving co-operation among English- and French-speaking interests, a fact that would have tremendous import for subsequent political developments. Together these two groups united to promote a new form of government and a new political agenda. But the road forward was not smooth or direct. Toryism was a popular ideology that enjoyed considerable electoral support; it stood in the way of reform just as it had in the 13 colonies before the

Revolution. Not until the election of 1848 did the combined Reform forces under the joint leadership of Robert Baldwin and Louis-Hippolyte La Fontaine obtain a solid majority in the Assembly. Soon after, the governor, Lord Elgin, following the policy established in Nova Scotia, called upon them to form a government.

But change had come too quickly for some. The new government, following hard on the heels of Britain's new economic policy, provoked a hostile reaction. Baldwin and La Fontaine had not only obtained responsible government, they had also put it promptly to use. The governor delivered the Speech from the Throne in French. Soon after taking office their government introduced and passed a bill compensating citizens for any property losses they may have incurred during the Rebellions of 1837–8 in Canada East (this matter had been settled for Canada West earlier). The most controversial provisions of the legislation allowed for payments to be made to both loyalists and former rebels. To those formerly in power, the world had gone mad. Treason was being rewarded, loyalism betrayed. When on 25 April 1849, the governor gave his assent to this incendiary piece of legislation rather than reserving it, an angry Tory mob expressed its displeasure by attacking his carriage in the streets of Montreal. In the ensuing riot, which destroyed La Fontaine's house, someone set fire to the Parliament Buildings. The first steps towards democracy in the Canadas literally turned to ashes.

Responsible government arrived more placidly in Prince Edward Island in 1851 and New Brunswick in 1854. New governors essentially imposed responsible government on legislatures that somewhat reluctantly assumed the financial burdens of public administration that went along with it. British administrators in Newfoundland experimented with a combined elected and appointed assembly before conceding a fully elected legislature in 1855. But there the governor retained considerable power. In the West, the much smaller colonies of Vancouver's Island and British Columbia remained under the direct control of appointed governors, though the Island colony received an elected assembly in 1856. Rupert's Land in the western interior had no formal government at all save the administration of the Hudson's Bay Company acting under its Charter from the Crown.

The British policy revolution forced some desperate colonists to consider previously unthinkable actions, partly out of frustration and partly because they could see no other way forward. For the merchants whose businesses had been nurtured under British mercantilism, free trade turned their world upside down. It seemed that all that had been invested in the St Lawrence route to Britain had been lost. A few months after the burning of the Parliament Buildings, the merchants of Montreal and Toronto, disoriented by the bewildering reversal of economic policy by Great Britain, issued a manifesto calling for annexation of Canada to the United States. Britain had abandoned its offspring; the United States would not trade with Canada on fair terms. In distress, the merchants believed that their economic survival depended upon Canada joining the United States.

The Reform alliance in the Canadas did not last. Neither did the apocalypse of annexation come to pass—the Americans were not interested in adding territory that would upset the delicate free soil–slave balance. Instead, a political realignment of cultural Conservatives in Canada East and moderate Conservatives in Canada West reestablished a measure of parliamentary equilibrium. This political realignment was driven in part by the rise of radical liberalism. In Canada East, French-Canadian radicals (Rouges) called for republican-style institutions. In Canada West, radical liberals (Clear Grits) also called for cheaper, more direct, American-style democracy but not republican government. Their mantra, 'rep by pop', a call for representation in the Assembly to be governed by population, became more strident and in the Canadian political context more divisive during the 1850s.

The Act of Union had set the representation of Canada East and Canada West in the assembly at 40 seats each. At the time this substantially overrepresented the population of Canada West. However, the population of the English-speaking West province expanded in the 1840s at roughly three times the rate of the East as a result of heavy immigration and the continuing exodus to New England of French Canadians. By the early 1850s the population of Canada West exceeded one million, about 100,000 more than in Canada East. In a decade the tables had been turned: on a population basis Canada West had become underrepresented in the Assembly relative to Canada East. With each passing year the disparity increased as Canada West grew at a considerably faster rate. English-speaking radical liberals thus fought to escape what they called 'French domination' through the instrument of representation of each province in accordance with its population. In doing so they steadily gained influence in rapidly growing Canada West, much to the dismay of the French-speaking majority in Canada East. Such a remedy, of course, was anathema to French Canada, whose defensive politicians found more congenial company among the moderate Conservatives of Canada West who seemed less doctrinaire about numerical representation and more tolerant of French institutions. Conservatives from the two regions and the two cultures thus established a *modus vivendi* upon which a relatively stable governing majority could be maintained throughout most of the 1850s.

After the combined policy and market jolts of the late 1840s, the economy rallied, spurred on by domestic demand, heavy immigration, and a growing continental reorientation of trade. High grain prices in Britain kept Canadian grain flowing down the St Lawrence even without British preferential tariffs. Forest products, mainly squared timber, continued to be shipped to Great Britain too, but the US market began to attract a larger proportion of this trade in the form of sawn lumber. To satisfy colonial desires to gain greater access to US markets, the British government negotiated a Reciprocity Agreement with the United States in 1854, which provided for effective free trade across the border in natural products such as lumber, minerals, wheat, flour, and other agricultural commodities. Producers and merchants thus received the economic benefits of association with the United States without the attendant political risks. Free trade in natural products gave a further boost to the economy, especially to the cross-border lumber and grain trades. Reciprocity stimulated the economies of the Atlantic colonies. Shipbuilding in New Brunswick reached new heights; Nova Scotia and Newfoundland increased their sales of fish products in the United States, at the cost of having to share their grounds with American fishers. Over the course of the 1850s total British North American exports increased almost three times. Within that period, exports to the United States increased by a factor of four.

British North America had entered a period of structural change.

Behind this rising tide of commodity exports the economy of British North America had entered a period of structural change. The colonial economy depended heavily upon exports, to be sure, but the vast majority of output was destined for domestic consumption. Agriculture, forestry, and fishing, taken together in the mid-1850s, continued to account for approximately 50 per cent of total output. Manufacturing, construction, and services accounted for roughly the other 50 per cent. Mills, workshops, and factories proliferated to supply the rapidly growing market with locally made manufactured goods. Indeed, in the late 1850s, the Canadian government even imposed a higher tariff on incoming manufactured goods to provide some incidental protection to this growing sector, much to the displeasure of British manufacturers. During this decade, railways hastened the growth and development of the colonial economy and governments did everything in their power to assist them. Railway construction provided a major investment stimulus, and by changing the time and regularity of travel the new railways served to integrate and expand markets. Industrialization affected the party system, a fact confirmed by a contemporary statesman's blunt admission: 'Railways are my politics.' Railway men seeking charters, subsidies, emergency loans, debt guarantees, and protective legislation paid attentive court to politicians from whom such blessings flowed. Political morality was not necessarily improved in the process.

A continued high birth rate of more than 45 births per 1,000 primarily explains most of the rapid increase in population. Renewed British immigration, much of it from Ireland as a result of the failure of the potato harvest, further accelerated population growth and introduced a combustible new ethnic element to the colonial cultural mix. Over a hundred thousand 'famine Irish', most of them Catholic, arrived in 1847. In the decade after 1851 approximately 350,000 immigrants poured into the Canadas, about 12 per cent of the total population. The Underground Railroad ferried fugitive slaves from the United States in increasing numbers north to freedom, but also to a largely segregated and confined life in Canada. However, an estimated 200,000 persons also quit Canada, mainly for the United States, leaving a net increase from immigration of about 150,000 for the decade. Immigration contributed significantly to the growing demand for goods and services and added the labour needed to lay and operate the new railways, and to build the houses, retail establishments, and manufacturing industries of the rising towns and cities.

The word *settlement,* commonly used to describe the peopling of the colonies, obscures the remarkable fluidity and mobility of a population constantly in motion. Over time the flow of people through towns, cities, and the countryside seeking better opportunities greatly exceeded the population stock that was resident at any given time. The new Irish immigrants, for the most part Catholic, poor, and unskilled, also changed the character of the population, especially in the industrial towns and cities. The coffin ships of the famine migration from Ireland to British North America deposited desperate cargoes of sick and hungry immigrants in the port cities. Assertive and unrepentant, this disadvantaged but rambunctious minority had to muscle its way into jobs, housing, pews, and leisure space. French Catholics resisted the intrusion of Irish Catholics into their churches. With each election, strike, and public celebration, the Irish made their presence felt. The Protestant Orange Order regularly challenged Catholic Irish 'Green' forces for control of the streets in these British colonial cities on St Patrick's Day, with typically violent consequences. Thus industrialization and immigration introduced new dimensions of religious and ethnic conflict into colonial societies already well endowed with mutual animosities.

◦—

Most of the British North American colonies had acquired self-government by the 1860s; many, too, experienced largely self-generating economic growth and developed strong trading ties with the United States. But none showed the anticipated interest in political independence. Quite the contrary. Except for the brief annexationist apostasy of 1849, Canadians remained resolutely British in their outlook and attachments. Loyal Canadians happily conferred on Queen Victoria the honour of selecting a permanent capital for their colony, though they were dismayed at her choice of Ottawa—a remote and disreputable lumber town. Beyond the obvious economic connections, they clung to Great Britain to bask in the reflected glory of the Empire. British North Americans paid close attention to British political and cultural trends. Ambitious colonial politicians sought knighthoods and careers in the imperial service. Colonists fought British wars vicariously through their newspapers, and adorned their squares with prizes from the Crimean War as if they had been there. French Canadians too had learned to embrace the British constitution that allowed them to enjoy their language, religion, and cultural distinctiveness now amid an English majority. La Fontaine, the old rebel, happily accepted a knighthood. If anything, British officials had to nudge the reluctant colonial governments to think more clearly about their long-term political prospects than they cared to do on their own. For British Americans the status quo seemed just fine. It must be said, they also attached themselves firmly to Great Britain for the protection the Empire afforded. And when the United States plunged into bloody civil war, in which both the British and British North Americans sympathized instinctively with the South, security became no mere academic matter.

In the forbidding shadow of the US Civil War, a movement for political union of the British North American colonies gained momentum. Impetus for the amalgamation of the small and scattered colonies into a larger territorial state came from three main sources: a long-standing general sentiment that union among the British states in North America, parallel to that of the United States, would eventually be a good thing; British Colonial Office encouragement to create more viable, self-sustaining political entities; and finally a well-founded concern for the defence of British North America as tensions between Britain and the North mounted during the conflict. Confederation was thus a plausible long-term objective; British policy was conducive, and the imminent US threat forced some common thinking among colonial politicians about their collective defence.

The immediate precipitating factor that propelled events from vague expressions of concern to concrete action was a political crisis in the Canadas in 1864 that forced constitutional reform to the top of the political agenda.

> *Thomas D'Arcy McGee, became the best-known hot gospeller of British North American union.*

Since the 1840s, colonial orators, in an occasional visionary mood, sometimes imagined the day when a continent-spanning union of British provinces might rise to rival the scope of the United States. However, no popular movement or political party made such a goal a top priority. It remained for the most part a 'some day it would be a good idea' after-dinner speech notion. The fiery former Irish nationalist journalist, orator, and politician Thomas D'Arcy McGee, became the best-known hot gospeller of British North American union. Borrowing rhetoric from his days as a Young Ireland activist, McGee in his speeches and newspaper articles envisioned a day when a New Nationality, loyal to Great Britain, united in a harmonious federal system, more tolerant of minorities and Catholics, would arise in Canada as a counterbalance to the United States.

In the late 1850s there was a brief flurry of interest in the idea in the Canadas, but the moment passed. Moreover, practical steps to improve communications among the colonies foundered. Canada had established its first railway connection with the Atlantic coast with an international line from Montreal through Maine to Portland. A plan for an intercolonial railway between Canada and the Maritimes lurched forward in the early 1860s, then derailed when politicians realized how much it would cost. A project intended to draw the colonies closer together collapsed in mutual recriminations and Maritime suspicion of Canadian sincerity.

Within the three Maritime colonies, New Brunswick, Nova Scotia, and Prince Edward Island, voices were sometimes heard advocating amalgamation into one colony, but general satisfaction with the status quo and seemingly insurmountable parochial concerns in each province always got in the way of substantial action. Enthusiasm for Maritime Union was probably limited to the three governors who, as outsiders and military men, felt the need to combine the resources of the colonies most urgently. The British Colonial Office, keen to reduce its obligations and minimize its defence liabilities, had instructed its governors to encourage such colonial initiatives whenever possible. The young and ambitious governor of New Brunswick eagerly promoted the idea. Without much enthusiasm the three Maritime governments, prodded by their British governors, agreed to meet in Charlottetown in the summer of 1864 to begin tentative exploration of the possibilities.

The looming threat of a war between Great Britain and the United States served to concentrate the colonial mind on matters long deferred. In the event of war, how could the British American colonies be defended and what would they be prepared to do to defend themselves? These were vexing questions with expensive answers. British policy had for some time been directed toward urging colonies to take on a great proportion of the costs of defence. British military authorities concluded that most of British North America could not be defended against a concerted US attack, especially from the huge battle-tested US standing army. However, fortifications in Montreal, Quebec, and Halifax could protect strategic sites until help might arrive. The colonists habitually looked to Britain to do most of the heavy lifting when it came to military matters. Perhaps realizing the futility of the task of self-defence, they were prepared only to undertake the minimum required. Tensions arising out of the Civil War put colonial politicians in a more receptive frame of mind to sharing costs in return for British protection. The British viewed the defence issue as a means of nudging the colonies towards greater co-operation on other common public purposes.

Events on the high seas brought Britain and the United States to the brink of war. Action by the North's navy enraged British opinion. US sailors intercepted a British vessel in neutral waters, taking two Confederate agents into custody. Until this incident could be defused diplomatically, war threatened. Then it was Britain's turn to infuriate the United States. Apparent British support for the Confederate side of the conflict raised the possibility of significant post-war retaliation by the North. Britain allowed two Confederate raiders to be fitted out in its ports; the raiders then went on to wreak havoc on the North's shipping before they could be destroyed. In the fall of 1864, Confederate guerrillas operating from Canada attacked a border community of St Albans in Vermont. After robbing the banks, setting fire to the town, and generally terrorizing the population, they fled back to Canada where a sympathetic magistrate refused to try them on a legal technicality. After the war, the president of the Confederacy, Jefferson Davis, went into comfortable exile in Montreal.

As British–US relations deteriorated, the British authorities moved troops into place to prepare for the defence of British North America. The international dangers and the defensive manoeuvres conditioned an apprehensive public to think harder about their potential common enemy. As a sign of things to come, soon after the St Albans debacle the United States served notice of cancellation of the Reciprocity Agreement and its desire to end the demilitarization of the Great Lakes. British North Americans realized they would not only have to make do in the future without favoured access to US markets, but also they would have to come to terms with an angry, triumphant, heavily armed, and deeply wounded neighbour.

In this threatening context, the internal politics of the Canadas became unmanageable. For some time it had been difficult to establish stable government. In a Legislative Assembly equally divided between the two Canadas, four main political groups representing different inclinations within each region vied with diminishing success to form a workable governing coalition. In Canada East, French conservatives (Bleus) led by Georges Cartier usually returned a majority of members, while French liberals (Rouges) received considerably less support. In Canada West, a growing Liberal majority led by the newspaperman George Brown, championing representation by population, usually outnumbered a centrist, governing party of moderate Conservatives led by John A. Macdonald. Typically the Canada East Bleus and the Canada West Conservatives could work together. However, the growing popularity of the Liberals in Canada West weakened that configuration by reducing Conservative strength. A government aligning the Canada East Rouge and the Canada West Liberals had first to overcome the ideological obstacle of representation by population and the electoral weakness of the Rouges in Canada East. Repeated elections produced essentially the same legislature, with enough loose fish and independents to destabilize whatever governing coalition might be cobbled together. Amid mounting frustration, conviction hardened that structural reform of some kind was needed to break the deadlock. Thus the local momentum towards greater British American union arose in part from desperation. Liberals from Canada West also deeply resented the way in which overrepresented French Canadians could dictate policies contrary to the wishes of the more numerous but underrepresented population of Canada West. A recent decision to establish a separate Catholic school system in the predominantly Protestant province served as the leading red flag exhibit of French domination.

Paradoxically, the movement towards a wider union of the British North American colonies stemmed in part from a desire on the part of the two Canadas to go their separate ways. In 1864, after repeated inconclusive elections and the routine collapse of short-lived governments, exhausted political antagonists as a last resort agreed to form a coalition of Canada West Liberals, Canada East Bleus, and English-speaking Conservatives from both regions. First, this Great Coalition, with Cartier, Brown, and Macdonald as its leading members, committed itself to resolving the constitutional question by exploring the possibility of a federation of all the British North American colonies, and then, in the event that option proved beyond reach, the creation of a federal system for the two Canadas alone. Second, it accepted representation by population as the principle governing membership in the new federal Parliament. Third, the Coalition vowed to take steps to acquire the Hudson's Bay Company's territories in the Northwest. Over the summer of 1864, the Canadian Coalition government developed a proposal for a federation, which it laid out before the delegates to a conference on Maritime Union in Charlottetown in late August

1864. Following the Maritimers' enthusiastic response, these general principles were worked up into 72 detailed resolutions, which were debated and approved at a constitutional conference held in Quebec in October.

Most delegates to the Quebec conference from both the Maritimes and Canada would have preferred to create a legislative union, like Great Britain, rather than a confederation. They feared federalism would eventually fail on account of the two levels of government and divided jurisdictions. They did not believe it to be a stable form of government and the civil war agonies of the world's leading federation gave them no reason to doubt their judgement. But legislative union, however desirable, lay beyond reach. Francophone Quebec would never accept being overwhelmed by an enlarged English majority. There were other complications too that required two levels of government. But if Canada must be a federation, it should be a highly centralized one—again the disintegration of the United States under the strain of states' rights provided an exemplary counterexample to avoid. According to the Quebec Resolutions, the federal government would be endowed with plenary authority to act in the name of peace, order, and good government; it would have a portfolio of enumerated powers covering all of the known important affairs of state, and it would be given residual powers granting it jurisdiction in unspecified matters, correcting a fatal defect in the US Constitution. The jurisdiction of the lower level of government would be strictly limited to local affairs sufficient for Quebecers to protect their culture, Upper Canadians to exercise local autonomy, and Maritimers to manage the affairs of their unincorporated municipalities.

Representation in the lower house in the federal Parliament would be based upon population. An appointed rather than elected upper house, however, would represent sectional interests. Here, too, the faulty American principle of equal representation for each colony was eschewed in favour of equality of representation for the three regions. Canada West, Canada East, and the Maritimes would each have 20 seats. In designing the new federal institutions the delegates had to tread lightly. As a Colonial Office official shrewdly observed: '[T]he great difficulty is to arrange for a real union of the five provinces . . . on terms which shall make the central or federal legislation really dominant, so as to make one body politic of the whole, and yet to provide security to French Canadians that this dominancy would not be used to swamp their religion and habits.'

A history student once declared on an examination that Confederation was the work of accountants. In fact, none of the Fathers of Confederation was an accountant. But this student intuitively grasped that an intricate and extremely clever financial substructure supported the general principles of the scheme. Perhaps, too, this response articulated an unstated belief that Confederation was more in the nature of a business arrangement between elites than a popular accord. Financially the federal government received the main sources of revenue: all forms of taxation and customs duties. For the surrender of these lucrative revenue sources and the confinement to direct levies and income from Crown Lands, the provinces would receive an annual subsidy from the federal government of 80 cents for each citizen. The federal government would take over all colonial debts. The colonies approached the union with different degrees of accumulated public debt. Some, such as the Canadas, had invested heavily in railroads; others, like Prince Edward Island, had little debt at all. To take into account the different levels of public indebtedness, the Canadian scheme charged interest to those governments on sums exceeding a certain level of debt allowance per capita and paid interest to those governments below that level. This was an only slightly veiled inducement to the Atlantic colonies. Further, the agreement called for the immediate construction of an intercolonial railway to provide a secure trade and communication link to underpin the union.

When the delegates, who had only just met and begun to get to know each other, looked up from the intricacies of draftsmanship, some of them began to glimpse the transcontinental possibilities of the country they were constructing. In the perambulations of the delegates around the Maritimes and the Canadas after these meetings, the general idea of Confederation acquired a larger public following. In a cheery post-prandial mood and in florid public speeches, the possibilities of a larger union generated some genuine excitement. But Confederation never became a popular crusade.

The possibilities of Confederation generated genuine excitement.

Canada was not created by a people blooded and bonded by revolution; nor were Canadians bound together by ancient ties of land, language, myth, shared antagonisms, and history. Most British Americans approached Confederation as a political arrangement to be viewed through the practical personal optic of regional or class interest. The proposal met a good deal of well-founded scepticism and outright hostility in some quarters, especially Quebec where promises of greater autonomy had to overcome nationalist fears of federal dominance. And Confederation had to overcome the inertia inherent in a more or less satisfactory status quo. As befits an arranged marriage, there was not much passion involved.

Understandably, the issue of representation in the upper and lower houses proved to be the most contentious aspect of the agreement for some of the smaller colonies, though the principle of equal representation for each province could not be readily defended in the dying stages and aftermath of the US Civil War. The minuscule 80-cent-a-head subsidy drew ridicule from some Maritime quarters, and the financial terms were deemed inadequate by anti-confederate accountants. The merchants of Newfoundland feared that the Canadian tariff, if applied to the new country, would put them out of business. So, Newfoundland backed out. Prince Edward Island rejected a proposal that did not recognize the stature of the province with adequate representation and failed to address the vexing land question directly. A general election in New Brunswick produced a new government opposed to Confederation for a host of local reasons. Finally, the redoubtable Joseph Howe issued a series of mocking articles, 'The Botheration Letters', that appeared to put paid to the scheme as far as Nova Scotians were concerned.

These setbacks notwithstanding, Confederation of four former colonies—Canada East, Canada West, Nova Scotia, and New Brunswick—did occur in 1867. How did the movement carry the day in the face of such opposition? In the first place, some of the alternative possibilities fell off the table. US refusal to reconsider its abrogation of the Reciprocity Agreement cut the ground from under some opponents. The status quo became less tenable. The British government strongly supported the proposals and instructed its governors to encourage the movement in any way possible. Some of the critics were brought around by the voice of authority and other inducements. Canadian politicians remained resolute and managed the ratification process adroitly. After lengthy debate the Canadian legislators approved the package by a vote of 91 to 33. This debate revealed considerable anxiety in French Canada about the degree of cultural autonomy that would be possible under such a centralized constitution; nevertheless, a considerable majority of the French members voted in favour.

The railway interests who stood to benefit from the scheme deployed their considerable powers of persuasion. Money from Canada bought elections when necessary in the Maritimes. Adversity stiffened the resolve of Confederation's proponents. They pressed harder instead of giving up. Irish nationalists based in the United States seized this moment of British weakness to launch a series of wild raids into Canada.[1] Though these had no official US approval and were beaten back with considerable effort, the excitement of these Fenian raids threw all Canadians into a collective defensive mode. In this highly charged atmosphere, Charles Tupper in Nova Scotia, and Leonard Tilley in New Brunswick when he returned to power after some heavy-handed interference by the governor, skillfully manoeuvred the Confederation proposals through their respective testy legislatures. By 1867, the four colonies agreed to join Confederation with provision for other colonies to be incorporated later. Following some last-minute tinkering at a conference in London, the British North America Act was passed by the House of Commons and the House of Lords, and received Royal Approval. On 1 July 1867 bonfires lit up the hills, church bells pealed, and dense columns of wordy editorial prose in the newspapers announced the birth of the Dominion of Canada led by its first prime minister, the newly knighted Sir John A. Macdonald.

⌐᠎⌐

The new country realized its territorial ambitions with remarkable speed thanks to considerable help from Great Britain. In 1870 the British government transferred the Northwest Territories formerly

---

1   A visitor to the National Museum of Ireland in Dublin could legitimately come away with the impression that some of the first shots in the Irish Revolution were delivered in the 'victory' of the Fenian forces over the British in the Battle of Ridgetown in the Niagara region of Canada in 1866.

the possession of the Hudson's Bay Company, to the jurisdiction of the new Dominion. A year later the West Coast colony of British Columbia, suffering through the detumescent phase of a gold rush, was persuaded to join the union with the promise of a transcontinental railway within 10 years. After bringing itself to the brink of bankruptcy with an ill-advised railway scheme, Prince Edward Island finally agreed to enter in 1873 after holding out for special terms. Finally, in 1880 Britain transferred to Canada all of the Arctic islands. Within little more than a decade of Confederation, Canada's boundaries had stretched to embrace a huge expanse of territory from Atlantic to Pacific and from the forty-ninth parallel to the North Pole. Only Newfoundland, isolated from continental concerns, self-absorbed, and reasonably content as a dependency within the British Empire, remained outside the Dominion.

But at the same time tensions boiled to the surface on the new body politic, revealing just how tentative and contingent the Confederation agreement remained. Dissatisfaction with the terms of Confederation persisted. The first provincial government of Nova Scotia was elected with the express purpose of repealing Confederation. This agitation weakened the fabric of the Dominion. Hard-pressed provincial governments chafed under the new financial arrangements and campaigned for better terms from the central government. Social conflict led to violence that cost Confederation one of its moving spirits. The Fenian Brotherhood assassinated the leading exponent of the New Canadian Nationality, Thomas D'Arcy McGee, in the streets of Ottawa to put an end to his damaging denunciations of Irish nationalism.

The greatest challenge to Confederation came from the West. The sudden transfer of authority in London from the Hudson's Bay Company to Canada without any consultation with local people provoked an open revolt in the West in the autumn of 1869. The years before the transfer had been difficult. With increased regularity the buffalo hunt, around which Métis life had been organized, failed. The paramilitary hunting expeditions ranged further afield, with diminishing results. The uncertain future of the buffalo hunt, compounded by changing labour requirements in the fur trade profoundly disturbed Métis life. A charismatic young Métis leader, Louis Riel, mobilized his people, who were also concerned about their uncertain title to their traditional lands, and organized a majority of the anxious local residents of the Red River colony to resist the Canadian takeover. The indigenous peoples of the West, who had different interests and concerns, did not participate. A provisional government under Riel's leadership drafted conditions on which the territory might be incorporated into the Dominion, terms that included security of land titles, provincial status, recognition of the French language, and separate Catholic schools. The federal government had no choice but to negotiate with the insurgents. Thus the province of Manitoba joined the union more or less on its own terms after achieving its demands through force of arms. The resistance enraged the small and somewhat obnoxious group of Canadian settlers in the region, who in their turn tried unsuccessfully to overthrow the provisional government. Riel ordered the execution of one of the most obstreperous counterrevolutionaries, a rash act that earned him a charge of murder, enraged public opinion in eastern Canada, and forced him to flee to the United States when British troops arrived in the colony in the spring of 1870 to restore order.

While Canadian expansion was contested in the West, and not completely accepted in some of the original colonies, the first few years of the young country proved disappointing in other respects. Throughout the 1870s emigration from Canada to the United States exceeded immigration to Canada. Contemporaries complained about a slowdown in the economy, a verdict confirmed by later macroeconomic estimates, but not to the level of 'depression' sometimes alleged. Real GDP levelled off while per capita income drifted downward throughout most of the decade before recovering near the end. The government of Britain, still the arbiter of Canada's foreign affairs, could not interest the United States in renewing the Reciprocity Agreement during talks in the early 1870s to clear up all outstanding Civil War issues. Moreover, in Britain's eagerness to reach an agreement, some other vital Canadian interests were sacrificed. In 1871, with what some thought indecent haste to escape North American entanglements, the British government withdrew its army from Canada, retaining only naval bases on the two coasts. Canada was now officially defenceless. Under the circumstances, the government of Canada may have overreached itself with railway promises.

The sensational discovery that the interests who had received the initial contract for the railway to the Pacific had financed the ruling party in a hotly contested general election created a scandal that brought down the government of the oft-inebriated Conservative Prime Minister John A. Macdonald. The new Liberal government imposed a regime of strict economy, and cut back on construction of the railway, choosing to build it in stages over a much longer period of time as a public work. This unilateral revision of the terms of union with British Columbia produced a fierce response on the part of the aggrieved province, appeals to Great Britain for redress, and more resentment at the grudging settlement. Nor was the new Liberal government any more successful than its ill-fated Conservative predecessor in its direct appeals to the United States to restore reciprocity. The triumphant northern US states preferred elevated tariffs to promote its own industrialization. Canada's first choice of an economic policy, free trade with its neighbour, thus remained beyond reach. Meanwhile the economy languished and the provinces complained. Undoubtedly a sense of country had begun to develop among some classes. A handful of poets, journalists, and historians formed a movement they called Canada First, to begin to instill a sense of national spirit. But at the same time the regional discontents that regularly flared up revealed the union still to be a business contract more than an affair of the heart.

In opposition, the disgraced John A. Macdonald recovered a good deal of his popularity. It probably was the case, as the legend would have it, that the country preferred John A. drunk to his opponents sober—especially after a steady diet of earnest, parsimonious Scots Liberals. Macdonald's Conservatives also developed an attractive new program of economic development that revived the party's fortunes. The Conservatives promised to accelerate the transcontinental railway project, encourage immigration, open the lands of the Prairie West to settlement, and institute an economic nationalist program of import-substitution industrialization. Back in power after the general election of 1878 the Conservatives hastened to introduce what they called a National Policy protective tariff to encourage infant industries. Macdonald and his minister of finance invited the manufacturers to tell them confidentially, in the plush confines of a hotel parlour, what they wanted, and they delivered the needful in the next budget. With this program the party gained the financial support of the business community and the electoral support of the rising urban working class, which it joined to strong support from French Quebec. After the failure of two previous economic regimes—the mercantilism of imperial preference and continental free trade in natural products under the Reciprocity Agreement—Canada embarked upon Macdonald's National Policy of tariff-protected industrialization and western development.

༄

Settling the West posed awkward challenges to the government. Canada had obtained the Northwest Territories from the Hudson's Bay Company through the good offices of the government of Great Britain in 1870. Acquisition, however, did not involve clear title. Nor was the West empty, as popular myth would have it; approximately 50,000 aboriginal peoples and Métis lived off its resources. Under the terms of the transfer to Canada, the policy of treaty-making to legitimize settlement laid down by the Royal Proclamation more than a century earlier had to be followed. In a bid to avoid the open warfare between settlers and Native peoples that characterized US western expansion, government agents in Canada began to negotiate a series of treaties with western tribes in 1871. By 1877 aboriginal title to most of the Prairie West had been extinguished in treaties numbered 1 through 7. Between 1899 and 1921, the North and Northwest Territories were surrendered in four more treaties. The terms of the agreements were roughly similar, though there is evidence that Native peoples shared information and learned to bargain for better terms in the later negotiations. They agreed to surrender all their rights to the land forever in return for exclusive Reserves of land for themselves, initial cash payments to each band member, and continuing annuities. Some of the later treaties included provisions for agricultural supplies, assistance in the event of famine, hunting rights on Crown Lands, and rudimentary medical services.

Why were the indigenous peoples prepared to enter into such agreements? They could see that the buffalo and other food resources were disappearing, and they knew their traditional way of life was passing. Settlers, traders, and missionaries grew more numerous with each season. One way or another, indigenous peoples would have to adjust to the changing environment and culture. Native leaders thus wanted to arrange a peaceful accommodation on the best terms possible to protect their people against the influx of surveyors, settlers, and whiskey traders. Native peoples also sought to avoid the bloodbath visited upon their southern brethren by negotiating with, rather than fighting against, the newcomers. The Canadian West wasn't won; it was traded.

Conflicting assumptions clouded the treaty-making process and bedeviled subsequent relationships between indigenous peoples and the government of Canada.

The Canadian West wasn't won; it was traded.

Native peoples struggled to survive as best they could while experiencing a major cultural upheaval. They may not have understood the full extent of the rights they surrendered or may have interpreted their meaning in a different way. Nevertheless, they believed the treaties to be a permanent foundation upon which continuing negotiations in the future could be based. With the cultural prejudices of the society they represented, Canadian government officials believed not only that the indigenous way of life was vanishing, but also that Native peoples themselves were doomed to extinction. They should, then, be assimilated as quickly as possible under the twin influences of the Bible and the plough. They should be encouraged to give up their nomadic existence, settle on their reserves, and become farmers.

The Indian Act of 1876 made indigenous peoples effective wards of the state. Treaties and regulations under the act confined them to limited Reserves. Government-appointed superintendents working with elected band councils took control of all aspects of Native life. Government regulations banned certain ceremonies considered disruptive, such as the sun dance on the Prairies and the potlatch on the West Coast. Government provided seeds, tools, and livestock in limited quantities and some minimal instruction to promote agricultural development on the Reserves. The health, welfare, educational, and spiritual services of the Christian missions played a central role in the process. Church-run 'industrial' schools strove to take the 'Indian' out of the children by removing them from the baneful influence of their communities, replacing indigenous languages with English, and teaching domestic skills to the girls and manual trades to the boys. Thus deracinated, the indigenous youth theoretically acquired the cultivated habits and economic skills deemed essential to enter the labour force. Native peoples believed the treaties formed the basis of their survival as a people. By contrast Canadian officials believed the treaties and the Indian Act to be instruments of acculturation and eventual assimilation. For them the future of the Native peoples lay as Canadian citizens, not a people apart.

To maintain law and order in the newly acquired West, Canada created an armed police force modelled on the Royal Irish Constabulary. The Royal North West Mounted Police, recruited from central Canadian volunteers, set out on a Great March to take up its duties on the Prairie in the summer of 1873. The arduous journey exacted a heavy toll from the largely inexperienced eastern troopers and their mounts. After losing their way several times on the trackless plains, the Mounties arrived at their destination, Fort Whoop-Up—whose liquor traffic they were ordered to suppress— greatly reduced in numbers, weakened by weather and discomfort, exhausted, and disoriented. Fortunately, none of the tough American whiskey traders stayed around to dispute their passage. Indeed the Mounties were compelled to seek supplies and help from the very traders they had been sent to police. Nevertheless, after this less-than-heroic entry onto the Great Plains, the Mounties gradually earned the respect and friendship of indigenous peoples, Métis, and incoming settlers for their tact, fair dealing, and dedication in the face of hardship. The Mounties quickly eliminated the liquor trade that regularly unleashed murderous havoc in Native communities, blocked unscrupulous fur traders infiltrating from the south, and curbed the lawlessness characteristic of the US western frontier. Their biggest test came in 1876 when thousands of Sioux warriors led by Sitting Bull fled to the Canadian Prairies following the defeat of General Custer at the Battle of Little Big Horn. The Sioux immigrants had to be protected against both Canadian Natives who resented their presence and American bounty hunters who tried to capture them in cross-border raids. All the while, the Mounties gently encouraged Sitting Bull and the Sioux to go back home—which they eventually did.

In going about their work the Mounties acquired a reputation for rectitude that remains to this day. Indeed the image of the resolute, straight-shooting, red-coated Mountie, magnified and projected around the world through American movies, has become an iconic symbol for Canada itself. Their trim red tunic, borrowed like many of their traditions from the British army, was adopted to impress and convey confidence to Native peoples. The first Mounties wore pillbox forage caps in their posts and wedge-shaped service caps in the field. For hot weather and dress occasions they were issued tropical white pith helmets. However, the men found the regulation headgear unsuited to western conditions, and in the 1890s they began informally to wear broad-brimmed felt hats in the American style to protect against sun and foul weather. The Stetson Brothers 'Boss of the Prairie' model became the hat of choice for most of the men. After the turn of the century this popular hat became regulation attire. Ironically, the distinguishing headgear of the Canadian Mounties came from the United States.

～

Gradually Canada began to exercise its nominal sovereignty over the West. Possession involved naming and knowing as well as legal authority. For that mission, the government of Canada dispatched a small army of surveyors and scientists westward. Employees of the Dominion Lands Survey superimposed the geometry of western civilization atop the rolling contours of the Prairie, laying out townships 36 sections square. Each section containing 640 acres (256 hectares) was further subdivided into four quarter-sections. As they marched westward with their transits and chains, the surveyors became enthusiastic promoters of the agricultural possibilities of the vast grassland. The land policy adopted by the Dominion closely followed that previously established in the United States. The even-numbered sections were thrown open to homesteaders who could acquire a 160-acre quarter-section for a minimal fee after three years' occupation. After 45 per cent of the surveyed lands had been set aside for homesteaders, 44 per cent was retained to support railways, 5 per cent to pay off the Hudson's Bay Company, and 6 per cent to finance school construction. Along with the surveyors, geologists scoured the Prairie and the front range of the Rocky Mountains for economic resources, especially coal and mineral deposits. Enthusiastic botanists, chancing upon the Prairie during a period of plentiful rainfall, pronounced it a virtual Garden of Eden. Scientific surveys, conducted at a time of both expansion and unusually good growing conditions banished the prior suspicion that large parts of the West might be desert and substantiated the belief that agriculture could flourish beyond the known fertile ranges even into the subarctic! These bulging scientific catalogues of resources gave wing to exaggerated hopes for the economic potential of the West.

The enthusiasm of the scientists and surveyors directly served the interests of the Dominion and the railway it now chartered to integrate and settle this vast domain. In 1880 the government contracted with a Montreal-based syndicate, heavily indebted to its New York and London partners, for the construction of a Canadian Pacific Railway (CPR). To support the construction of a railway so far in advance of actual commercial demand, the government provided extremely generous financial incentives. It gave to the syndicate the uncompleted portions of railway it owned in British Columbia and northern Ontario, worth $31 million, along with a subsidy of $25 million, more than 10 million hectares of prime Prairie land in alternate sections for about 39 kilometres on either side of the main line, a monopoly of railway traffic for 20 years, duty-free admission of equipment and construction materials, and a permanent tax exemption for its land and buildings. Encouraged by the surveyors and scientists the syndicate selected a southern route across the Prairies, occupying the strategic territory close to the border. The route of the CPR then went up the Bow River, across Kicking Horse Pass into the Columbia Valley, then into the Thompson and Fraser river territories further west. The railway selected a mainland terminus close to present-day Vancouver. However, the ultimate terminus, according to the agreement by which British Columbia entered Confederation, had to be Victoria. Thus the transcontinental railway continued on the other side of the Georgia Strait from Nanaimo down Vancouver Island to Victoria.

Driving a railway through Precambrian rock, across the bottomless bogs of northern Ontario, and over the steep mountain passes cost more than the promoters had anticipated. Acquisition of lines in eastern Canada and other ancillary projects ate into the proceeds.

Construction proved costly as well to the lives and limbs of the construction workers, especially the Chinese navvies imported to blast their way up the canyons and tunnel through the peaks of the western mountains. In British Columbia the contractors estimated accidents claimed the lives of three Chinese workers per mile of construction. Inevitably the money ran out before the railway was built. A financial crisis in 1883 extracted a grudging $22.5-million loan from an extremely reluctant Conservative government. Two more years of cost overruns on the mountain sections had the railway careening headlong towards bankruptcy. The government remained obdurate in the face of pitiful requests for further aid. A massive train wreck seemed inevitable when help appeared from an unexpected quarter. An armed insurrection of some Métis and Native peoples proved the value of a transcontinental railway for moving troops, thereby justifying further loans to speed its completion.

Following the dwindling buffalo herds, many of the Métis and Country Born of the Red River settlement had migrated toward the northwestern quadrant of the Prairies. Grouped in settlements along the North and South Saskatchewan rivers they feared that surveyors would ignore their titles and settlers would seize their land. The government paid little attention to their concerns. In frustration over land security, they invited Louis Riel to return to express their grievances to the federal government more forcefully. Indigenous peoples in the region had descended too into a desperate state. Following the settlement of Treaty Number 6, they had found they could not easily adjust to an agricultural way of life. The lands on their Reserves were not particularly well suited to farming, and Native peoples were denied access to the land they preferred. Moreover, the government refused to honour the famine-assistance provisions of their treaty when traditional food sources and farming failed. Independently, Native and Métis anger mounted.

When Ottawa ignored Riel's petition, he reverted to the script of 15 years before. In the early spring of 1885 he proclaimed a provisional government, his followers took up arms, and they routed a small detachment of the Royal North West Mounted Police sent to quell their rising. Native warriors then attacked an isolated settlement and killed nine civilians. However, retaliatory force could be moved more quickly into the theatre than had been the case in 1869, and this time there could be no doubt as to the legitimacy of the government of Canada's jurisdiction. Using the partially completed railway, the federal government dispatched a Canadian army of 3,000 troops westward. There they joined the Mounties and settler militias in a concerted campaign of repression. Riel, locked in religious ecstasy and convinced he was a prophet destined to found a reformed Roman Catholic state in the West, was of no tactical use in the conflict. His supporters, however, proved to be able fighters, as did the Native warriors. At first the combined rebel combatants fought the Canadian army to a standstill in ambushes, but eventually overwhelming force prevailed against the defensive lines of the Métis. Riel surrendered in mid-May; his senior collaborators fled to the United States.

The fighting claimed about 150 lives on both sides, though it could have been more deadly. Only a small minority of aboriginal peoples in the region actually joined the rising. This Rebellion of 1885, though it was relatively small and quickly suppressed, bore important consequences for those directly involved—and for Canadian politics. Afterwards, the government of Canada treated the Natives more harshly than the Métis. Hundreds were arrested and tried, 44 were convicted, 8 of whom were executed in the largest public hanging in Canadian history. The repression showed how dramatically power had shifted on the frontier. Indigenous peoples no longer posed a serious military threat. As for the Métis, never again would they exert any influence as an autonomous community in the Northwest; their power too had been broken. The government focussed its retributive efforts against their leader, Louis Riel, who was charged with high treason. Despite his erratic behaviour and religious delusions, which warranted excommunication from the Roman Catholic Church, he was nevertheless pronounced sane. The court doctors declared him fit to be tried, and when convicted by a jury of six Anglo-Canadians, also fit to be hanged.

The execution of Louis Riel on 16 November 1885 had much broader political consequences than the Rebellion. His hanging created a martyr for the Métis community and, by extension, French Canada. Over time this haunting figure of protest was embraced by the very forces he had fought, as a symbol of western discontent and alienation from the federation. Riel's hanging provoked an immediate angry outburst from French Quebec. French Canadians did not support the Rebellion while it was in progress. They did, however, view the execution of Riel as a vindictive political act, demanded by English Canada in retribution for the murder Riel committed in 1869. As such they regarded it as a further blow against French culture within Canada. Several French-Canadian ministers resigned the cabinet in protest. Within Quebec, Honoré Mercier led a proto-nationalist movement to power in the next provincial election to assert French-Canadian rights more forcefully within the federation.

Over time Riel became a symbol of western alienation.

For the next decade Canadians fell to intense bickering over provincial rights, religion, parochial schools, and language. The structure of the federation even began to show cracks at one of the points where earlier there seemed to be broad agreement. Ontario led the provinces in a movement to resist the centralized power of the federal government, in particular use of its power to disallow provincial legislation. Confederation, the provinces argued, had been a compact between colonies; therefore, the provinces should have a much greater say in the running of the country. The provinces did not have much success in their arguments with Ottawa; the courts, however, especially the final court of appeal, the Judicial Committee of the Privy Council in England, tended to side with the provinces in constitutional disputes, thus gradually enlarging the scope of provincial powers.

Feuding between ultramontane Catholicism and ultra-Protestantism tore the country apart along religious lines. In Quebec the Church hierarchy actually was more conservative and Catholic than the Pope; some extremists even imagined their mission to redeem Godless France. The phrase 'Toronto—the Belfast of Canada' errs only by suggesting the Irish were more vigilant in their defence against perceived Catholic aggression and more suspicious of papal interference in public policy. An uncontroversial restitution of property to the Jesuit Order in Quebec raised howls of protest in Protestant Ontario. New Brunswick abolished its Catholic schools, which had Catholics everywhere demanding the federal government disallow the legislation. The province of Manitoba repealed some of the institutions that had been set in place to protect the Métis people after Riel's rising in 1869. A recipient of heavy English-speaking immigration after 1869, Manitoba abolished French as an official language of the Legislature in 1890 and created a secular public school system that removed funding from French and Catholic schools. Quebec demanded federal remedial legislation to restore French rights. Temperance and prohibition advocates hounded politicians to curb the sale of liquor as an essential first step towards social redemption.

Religion offered solace, meaning to life, inspiration, comfort, and community. Church steeples, Gothic and Romanesque piles of masonary, and pealing bells proclaimed relative denominational dominion over cities, town, and country. But religion also divided Canadians, erecting invisible but virtually impenetrable social barriers between Catholics and Protestants and between both and the small but growing Jewish and Mennonite communities. Religion was a source of strength to society, a powerful institutional force, but as a breeder of suspicion, intolerance, and social dissension it was exceeded only by race.

All of this quarrelling took place against a background of disappointing economic performance. The previously strong growth of the economy, spurred by investment in railways, levelled off after 1885 and actually declined in the early 1890s. The exodus to New England and the US Midwest continued. For three consecutive decades from 1871 to 1901 emigration exceeded immigration as French and English Canadians left in droves for the industrial cities of the US north. The railway had been built, but the settlers had not come to Canada, and certainly not in the numbers expected. Farmers and urban consumers increasingly resented the tariffs that raised prices. Canadian growth lagged behind that of the United States, and far behind that of other settler societies such as Argentina and Australia. Corrosive religious and linguistic controversies, as they inevitably took on political form, rocked the ruling Conservatives. After the death of their wily old leader, John A. Macdonald, in 1891, the government gradually lost its grip on power and collapsed under a succession of lackluster prime ministers. After 30 years and under the pressure of accumulated grievances and sectarian feuds, Confederation appeared to be coming apart at the seams.

Then something quite remarkable happened. Canada became caught up in a whirlwind of economic, political and social change the like of which the world has rarely seen. Over the next generation a new country took shape within the skin of the old. The panels of the Transformation Mask flew open, revealing a new Canada to the world. The dramatic changes did not eliminate the old problems; rather they added complex new layers of social and political tensions that sometimes exacerbated and sometimes transcended the old scores. At the same time the extraordinary growth of the country and its sudden emergence as a significant state on the world stage imparted new integrative forces as well that served to contain this roiling social volatility. With a new power and self-confidence, Canadians could imagine a great future for their country— a sentiment nicely captured in the new Liberal prime minister's heady prediction: 'The nineteenth century was the century of the United States. I think we can claim that it is Canada that shall fill the twentieth century.' Not satisfied with this typically wordy political statement, public memory has edited this circumlocution to a more punchy: 'The twentieth century belongs to Canada.'

After 1896 the Canadian economy 'took off', to use an antiquated but compelling analogy. The search for the cause of this economic miracle has provided several generations of gainful employment to economic historians with intriguing, ingenious, but ultimately inconclusive results. Was it a general price rise resulting from an increased gold supply, some of it from the Klondike? Was it an export-led boom? Was it investment driven? Was it public policy? Was it the weather? All that can be said for certain is that simultaneously a lot of things fell into place and something like a virtuous circle of reinforcing interaction provided liftoff to a previously stagnant economy. For more than a decade, Canada experienced some of the highest levels of economic growth ever recorded in the developed world. After 1900 Canada grew twice as fast as the United States. The growth spiral was so sudden and so intense it has been likened by economists to a cyclone. Canada experienced simultaneously the full force of the first industrial revolution (textiles, iron, and steel) and the second industrial revolution (electro-chemical), accelerated by the rapid expansion of a highly productive agricultural sector, the rise of new resource industries, and a major investment boom augmented by heavy foreign investment. Steadily rising real income per capita strengthened the demand for goods and services and drew thousands of immigrants to the employment opportunities Canada presented in all sectors.

Suddenly Canada became a highly industrialized country. In Nova Scotia a sizable iron and steel industry arose based upon locally available supplies of coal and iron ore. Much of this steel went to produce ships, rails, and railway cars. In central Canada the iron and steel industry located along the Great Lakes transportation route, drawing upon US sources of coal and iron ore. Textile, clothing, and shoe factories proliferated in Quebec and the growing industrial towns of Ontario. An industrial corridor stretching from Montreal to Windsor grew up around the farm implements, transportation equipment, electrical, food and beverage, rubber, petroleum, and the infant automobile industries. Many of these industries were subsidiaries of US companies that established branch plants behind the tariff wall to serve the Canadian and sometimes the British imperial market. Canada's numerous waterpower sites gave rise to a technologically sophisticated hydroelectric industry supplying lighting and power to towns and cities, but also energy to the new electro-chemical industries such as carbide-, aluminum-, and nickel-refining. The

province of Ontario in particular benefited from this new industri-
alism and, to speed development even further, created a publicly
owned electrical system to ensure power would be provided to
turn the wheels of industry at the lowest possible cost. In the vast
northern forests, amply endowed with river systems, hydroelectric
sites, and transportation, a world-scale pulp and paper industry
appeared to feed the growing North American appetite for paper,
especially for newsprint. All across the country, gold, silver, copper, nickel, zinc, and coal mines extracted natural wealth from the
earth. On the West Coast the forest products industry gnawed its
way into a dense rain forest, serving export markets in the United
States and domestic construction on the Prairies. Pacific coastal
waters, teeming with salmon, supported a fishing industry much
of whose output was put up in canneries and shipped around the
world. The telephone network penetrated Canada as rapidly as it
did any place on the planet.

Canada's rapid economic growth was driven in large part by
an extraordinary investment boom. More than 20 per cent of
Canadian GNP was ploughed back into capital formation at this
time compared with a rate of about 8 per cent for the United States
and Great Britain. Moreover, not only could Canada draw upon its
own savings, but its opportunities attracted a huge wave of foreign
investment. Economists estimate over 40 per cent of gross domestic capital formation came from abroad, over 85 per cent of it from
Great Britain. Canada became one of the most favoured destinations for British, and to a lesser extent US, foreign investment. Of
course Canada had a well-developed branch banking system to
gather the savings of the population and to direct farm and commercial credit to profitable destinations. It also had a dynamic
insurance industry, aggressive trust companies, land and mortgage
lenders, and other financial intermediaries to channel savings into

productive investments in housing, farms, wholesale and retail establishments, factories, equipment, municipal and provincial works, power stations, transmission lines, and railways. The service sector itself, including financial services, became one of the fastest growing segments of the economy. Policy disagreements led to the construction of not just one but two new transcontinental railways. These railways and associated branch lines being laid across the country in the first two decades of the century were the most visible manifestation of this capital formation, and in retrospect perhaps the most excessive example. These railways, it was thought at the time, were desperately needed to move wheat east and goods and people west.

In a remarkably short period of time, homesteaders covered the surveyed grid of the western Prairies with wheat farms. Falling transportation costs, low interest rates, the development of dry farming techniques, improved strains of seed, and mobile labour made it possible for wheat to be raised in enormous quantities in this western interior and shipped to distant markets. Over a million farmers and their families flooded onto the Prairies in one almost instantaneous human wave. The 55,000 farms in 1901 increased to over 200,000 in a decade. Over 70 per cent of all Prairie lands ever claimed were occupied between 1901 and 1911. The federal government created two new provinces, Saskatchewan and Alberta, to accommodate the influx, though it retained control over their Crown Lands and natural resources to ensure development in the national interest.

An ocean of waving grain, about 60 per cent wheat and 40 per cent oats, stretching to the horizon, replaced the native grasses of the Prairies. Armies of agricultural workers migrated west each year to man the latest mechanized reapers and threshers to harvest the bountiful crop. Soon vast rivers of wheat and flour flowed through the system of elevators, mills, railways, canals, and steamships to North American and European markets. Net exports of wheat rose from 10 million bushels in 1896 to more than 145 million in 1914.

The growth and spread of wheat farming on the Prairies so astonished contemporaries and impressed economic historians subsequently that much of Canada's economic development has been attributed in one way or another to this wheat boom. According to this 'staple interpretation' of Canadian history, rising wheat exports attracted foreign capital and labour. Downstream linkages to processing and transportation industries spurred growth in those sectors. Upstream manufacturers and services expanded to supply the domestic needs of farmers. Railways and tariffs captured the benefits of this growing trade for Canada. Much of this is true, but not as much as once thought. Several generations of sustained revisionism by economic historians has diminished but not demolished the role of wheat as the motor of the Canadian economy. Even in this historiographical twilight, wheat retains a good deal of its explanatory potency. Perhaps just as important as its measurable influence, the golden growth of the West set aloft boundless optimism about the economic future of the Dominion.

෴

'The Last Best West', as the Canadian Prairie advertised itself, attracted an unprecedented number of immigrants. In the late 1890s about 50,000 immigrants landed in Canada each year. That number rose rapidly to over 250,000 in 1906 and then soared to over 400,000 in 1912, a record not equalled since. The Canadian population increased 34 per cent in the census decade following 1901, and almost half of that growth could be attributed to immigration. The foreign-born proportion of the population rose from around 13 per cent in 1901 to 22 per cent in 1911. Most of the new arrivals at the beginning came from either the United Kingdom or the United States. Black American immigrants were discouraged, though a small number persisted anyway. Very few immigrants came from French-speaking countries. Thus at first this incoming wave of humanity largely strengthened the English character of the country.

Over time, however, the origins of the migrants shifted. During the years of peak migration, more than 40 per cent of immigrants came from European countries, primarily Germany, Scandinavia, the Ukraine, the Austro-Hungarian Empire, Holland, Italy, Russia, Poland, Finland, and Belgium. A small, highly regulated and in some cases deeply resented trans-Pacific flow of immigrants from China, Japan, and the Indian subcontinent settled mainly in British Columbia. Immigration thus changed the linguistic and ethnic composition of Canada. A sizable and highly heterogeneous population of other non-English-speaking nationalities joined the existing British and French cultural mosaic. Large sections of the Prairies and whole city blocks filled up with ethnic, religious, racial minorities. Block settlements of Ukrainians, Jews, Mennonites, Hutterites, Doukhobors, Icelanders, and Slavs laid down a patchwork of non-English-speaking, self-reliant communities across the Prairies. In 1911, almost 50 per cent of the Prairie population originated outside of Canada. Most of the immigrants may have been bound for the free land of the West, but many, whether by choice or mischance, stayed in the cities and towns and found employment in the booming industrial, commercial, and construction sectors of Ontario and Quebec. The foreign-born portion of the population tended to be disproportionately urban compared to the native-born. Thus in less than a decade Canada's rapidly growing towns and cities also acquired a significant multicultural minority.

Ethnic change on this scale and over such a short interval inevitably caused trouble. Poverty, prejudice, and insecurity forced many newcomers into low-rent, polyglot, ethnic and racial ghettos in the main immigrant reception centres, Montreal, Toronto, Hamilton, Winnipeg, and Vancouver. Seen from the outside, the sudden appearance of these anti-communities presented a volcanic combination of misery, social disintegration, vice, even sedition. Some Canadians sought to speed the assimilation process; others fiercely resisted social change. Catholic welfare agencies ministered to the needs of some of the newcomers. A religious revival movement among some of the Protestant denominations, called the Social Gospel, which set social reform as the first step on the path of spiritual redemption, led the welfare campaign in English Canada to integrate these 'Strangers Within Our Gates' with settlement houses and other welfare activities. At the other extreme, racists and Nativist organizations hounded the newcomers, especially the visible minorities. Mobs attacked Chinese and Japanese communities in Vancouver; race hatred drove off a shipload of East Indian immigrants. Black settlers migrating north from the United States faced southern-style segregation. Everywhere Jews and eastern Europeans encountered discrimination in housing and employment. Even the English met open resentment for their haughty ways. Hostility forced the newcomers to band together, often using religious affiliations to build self-help societies, mutual-benefit organizations, and employment exchanges. With remarkable courage and determination immigrants clawed and elbowed their way into jobs, built small businesses, and with their sweat and sacrifice made Canada their home. As always migration was a two-way street for Canada; peak flows of immigration corresponded as well with peak flows of emigrants heading to the United States or recent immigrants returning home.

The rewards of rapid industrialization were not equally distributed by region or shared by all social classes. The Maritimes, for example, did not keep pace, as industry located or concentrated in the industrial corridor of the central provinces. Structural change in the economy favoured some occupations and drove others over the edge. Even as agriculture expanded in the West, rural poverty in the East began to push marginal farmers off the land, bright lights and higher wages pulled them to the city in a major rural–urban exodus. Women had always been part of the rural production process, though mechanization may have reduced their role in the late-nineteenth century. Soon unmarried women between the ages of 18 and 24 made up about 15 per cent of the wage labour force. They provided domestic service in bourgeois homes, and worked in shops, offices, schools, and hospitals, especially in textile towns and in the working-class districts of the cities.

The economy grew, but wages did not necessarily rise on their own. Workers had to fight for every penny of a raise, every hour of leisure, and steady, secure employment. Nor did rising wages always keep up with rising prices. The most effective trade unions turned away from European industrial unionism, political action, and socialist ideology, following instead the US-style 'bread-and-butter unionism' organized to advance the wages and working conditions of specific trades. Curiously, Canada's national federation of unions, the Trades and Labour Congress, consisted mainly of 'international' unions affiliated with their counterparts in the United States. The Canadian labour movement thus drew upon the resources and the managerial skills of its US counterpart. Labour militancy flared up, especially in the mine, mill, and rail towns of the regions but also in the factory towns and cities of the East. Strikes numbered between one and two hundred incidents a year mainly in the mining, manufacturing, and transportation sectors, rising and falling with the business cycle. To many observers, some violent confrontations raised the clear and present danger of a general class war. On 30 occasions the army had to be called out to maintain law and order, usually on the employers' terms. In response the government created a Department of Labour and introduced a mandatory mediation process to regulate the volatile industrial relations. Overall, despite residential segregation by income and class in many Canadian towns and cities, ethnic, linguistic, and religious pluralism militated against the consolidation of a lasting European-style working-class consciousness and solidarity.

Documenting, explaining, and even celebrating the many linguistic, ethnic, regional, racial, gender, and class differences that divided Canadians has been the major preoccupation of Canadian historians and other commentators in recent years. But a people is always more than the sum of its differences. Historians have been less adept at revealing the often-invisible web of compound identifiers that bound people together despite divisions. However slowly, institutions, associations, consumption, shared hopes, and collective activity knit Canadians together, sometimes unconsciously, into larger communities at the regional and national levels. Churches, voluntary associations, fraternal orders, men's and women's clubs, sports leagues, schools, missionary societies, militia regiments, lay fellowships, commercial networks, mail order catalogues, professional societies, branch banks, railway schedules, holidays, relatives back East or out West, brand names, trade union federations, children's careers, and especially newspapers built imagined communities extending well beyond the personal, familial, class, and local affiliations. All Canadians were not necessarily bound together in the same way or to the same degree. The web of integration was spun especially but not exclusively among the rising middle class of clerical, mercantile, professional, and skilled workers. Separate regional, religious, or cultural hierarchies were often linked at their apexes. French and English Canada were connected at the top rather than across all levels of the social order. Elites at the top of separate social pyramids arranged accommodation among groups. That model, rather than complete social integration, probably best captures the complexity of the evolving Canadian social mosaic. Perhaps the most visible institutions stretching filaments of attachment across the country were political parties.

⌒

The Liberal party under the adroit leadership of Wilfrid Laurier created a broad centrist coalition that governed Canada for a generation and laid the basis for a government party that held power for all but 30 years of the twentieth century. In Quebec, Laurier joined liberal progressives in a party with moderate Bleus gently dislodged from their former allegiance to the Conservative party. Outside of Quebec the Liberal party attracted strong support from farmers on account of its professed belief in lower tariffs. Recent immigrants rewarded the party in power with their votes. Urbane, statesman-like, articulate in both languages, Laurier developed a strong personal popularity in both English and French Canada. With such broad support the Liberals won substantial majorities in four consecutive general elections, 1896, 1900, 1904, and 1908. In power, Laurier brokered a compromise that calmed religious and linguistic tensions over the school question in Manitoba. The provincial government's insistence upon English-only schools had caused a crisis within the federation as Catholics and French-interest groups demanded the federal government use its power of disallowance to override this legislation. Laurier, with considerable help from the Papacy, managed to negotiate an agreement with the province that allowed French, Catholic schools under certain conditions that critics in Quebec could grudgingly accept.

The aggressive Liberal immigration policy and railway program contributed mightily to the economic boom. Labour legislation provided a fairly effective process to mediate industrial disputes. The Liberal party, of course, benefited from the general prosperity and expansionist temper. An awkward attempt to impose separate schools in the new provinces of Alberta and Saskatchewan, where they were not wanted, cost the government some defections. But for more than a decade, the Liberals managed to negotiate the swirling social, religious, and linguistic tensions of the country. Laurier personally embodied the bicultural ideal of what he called 'race fusion', which sought to transcend local differences to create a larger pan-Canadian nationality that respected both cultures.

The most divisive challenge confronting the government was the Empire. In a newly dangerous and competitive world, Britain had begun to revalue its Empire. In the new thinking, the Empire could be useful as a market for industrial goods, but more importantly as an instrument to augment the power of Britain in international relations. If all of the Empire could develop a coordinated defence policy under British direction, Britain's influence vis-à-vis its European rivals, France and Germany, could be substantially increased. Despite its growing economic power and political self-confidence, Canada remained a colony of Great Britain. The British government appointed the governor general (usually a second-tier British aristocrat); Britain conducted foreign relations on behalf of Canada; a British officer commanded the Canadian militia; and even though Canada possessed a Supreme Court, the final court of appeal remained a committee of the House of Lords in London, the Judicial Committee of the Privy Council.

A few Canadian intellectuals argued for independence, but

the looming presence of the giant next door tended to dampen enthusiasm for complete autonomy. Curiously Canada's national emergence at the beginning of the twentieth century led many Canadians to become more closely attached to Empire. If Canada had already become the 'Granary of Empire' surely one day this ascendant northern power would displace effete Britain itself as the emperor. For many Canadians, especially those of British background, the Empire was the best vehicle for an emerging country to express itself on the world stage. Working within a globe-girdling Empire, Canada could exert more influence than it could on its own. This way Canadians became vicarious imperialists; it was their Empire too, and they expected to inherit it. Thus imperialism, which took flight especially in English Canada, was a form of Canadian nationalism, an activist, outward-looking doctrine of assertion and involvement. By contrast, French Canadians tended to take

> *Canadians became vicarious imperialists; it was their Empire too, and they expected to inherit it.*

a different view. For them imperialism meant war, and war meant forcing young French Canadians into the army to fight Britain's wars in far-off places in which Canada had no direct interests. Nationalists in Quebec sought greater autonomy for Canada though not outright independence; they stressed the importance of putting Canadian interests first, and within that program the necessity of protecting French language and culture within Canadian institutions. An inarticulate silent majority in between seems to have developed a vague desire for slightly more independence within the Empire while avoiding costly commitments.

The Boer War in 1899 forced these questions onto the political agenda in an inescapable and urgent way. French Canada on the whole identified with the embattled Boers; English Canada supported the British retaliatory invasion. A behind-the-scenes conspiracy of the British governor general and the British general in command of the Canadian militia to manoeuvre Canada into full participation in the war almost brought down the government. Caught between imperialists on the one side and nationalists in his home province on the other, Laurier adopted the ludicrous compromise of equipping and transporting Canadian volunteers to South Africa, while Britain assumed responsibility for their command and maintenance in the field. As if to tie the bells on this jester's cap of a policy, the government solemnly declared this should not be considered a precedent for the future. Over 7,000 Canadian volunteers served in South Africa, about 250 of whom perished in the fighting. Not surprisingly, this crisis led to the appointment of a new governor general and, in due course, a Canadian commanding officer who reported only to the minister of defence. In imperial conferences the British pressed for closer imperial coordination of defence policy—to which Wilfrid Laurier politely but persistently resisted.

The naval crisis of 1908 re-opened these imperialist wounds. Germany's aggressive program of battleship construction threatened Britain's sacred doctrine of overwhelming mastery of the seas. To build the new capital ships needed to stay abreast in the arms race, Britain looked to its Empire for contributions. Many imperialists in Canada thought it Canada's duty to contribute a dreadnought or two as some of the other colonies were doing. At length the Liberals decided that Canada should establish its own navy, which in the event of an emergency, might be placed at Britain's disposal. Nationalists in Quebec could see no need for a Canadian navy at all, except perhaps to tempt Canada into imperialist wars on the high seas. Canada's decision to create a 'tinpot' navy satisfied no one. It alienated nationalists, offended imperialists, and as a self-defence force it served no practical purpose. In peacetime when it came to defence, Canadians could not, or would not, think clearly. On their own blessed continent, where they boasted endlessly about the longest undefended border in the world, they could see no need for defence. War was a European affectation; most Canadians thought the Europeans should do their own dirty work, the feverish imperialists notwithstanding. When it came to defence, less than the minimum was more than enough—an enduring theme in Canadian history.

As the Liberal ship of state foundered on these imperial reefs, a renewal of the Reciprocity Agreement with the United States offered hope of rescue. Farmers who sold their products on world markets deeply resented paying tariff-protected prices for their equipment, goods, and services. The Reciprocity Agreement of 1911, which held out the hope of a free trade in both natural products and manufactured goods, rewarded their faith. At the same time, however, it profoundly disturbed the railroad, banking, manufacturing, and commercial interests who had built up extensive east–west trading channels behind the comforting tariff wall. They defected in droves from the Liberal party in the general election called to endorse the treaty and threw their considerable muscle behind the Conservative opposition. The defeat of the government instilled in the disillusioned farmers an abiding conviction that 'the interests' controlled the political parties. If they wanted legislation favourable to their welfare they would have to take direct action themselves as a group and perhaps change the political system itself. The new government of Robert Borden allied ultra-imperialists and high-tariff Conservatives in English Canada with anti-imperialist nationalists in Quebec—not a particularly stable compound. As expected, the new government did not ratify the Reciprocity Agreement, but surprisingly it could not get a $35-million contribution to the British navy through Parliament with its Liberal-dominated Senate. Canada stumbled towards Armageddon with a battered government, an army of 3,000, and a navy consisting of two obsolete British destroyers.

◌

Britain's declaration of war against Germany and the Austro-Hungarian Empire on 4 September 1914 automatically included Canada. The prime minister, on vacation, learned that his country was at war from the newspapers. Canadians answered the call to arms en masse as if their own country had been attacked. High levels of unemployment, the thrill of adventure, and the large number of young, recent British immigrants explain much of the early success of recruitment for the Canadian Expeditionary Force. But all classes and regions of the country displayed a patriotic willingness to volunteer. French Canada rushed to the colours to defend both Britain and France. Japanese, Black, and Native volunteers demanded places alongside their fellow Canadians at the front. Many hoped to earn respect as soldiers on foreign soil that would subsequently convert to respect as full citizens at home. Over the course of the four years of combat Canada put an army of almost 500,000 men and women on the ground overseas with another 100,000 or so serving at home. In a country fully employed in the production of food and munitions for Europe, remarkably one-third of the eligible manpower enlisted. Over 2,000 nurses went overseas to care for the sick and wounded. Artists too contributed. An innovative program of artistic documentation produced a moving permanent record of the Canadian contribution. When the call to duty came, Canadians instinctively and overwhelmingly responded—at least for the first three years.

Canadian troops fought more or less continuously from their arrival in Flanders in the spring of 1915 to the final days of the advance along the Canal du Nord in the fall of 1918. In their first taste of combat, Canadian troops held the line against a ferocious German gas attack at Ypres. At the Battle of the Somme in 1916, Canadians acquired a fearsome reputation as assault troops. But Canada's finest hour came at the Battle of Vimy Ridge in 1917. Advancing behind a creeping artillery barrage, Canadian troops took a strategic height that other forces had failed to capture. Canadian airmen gained renown as skilled and deadly fighter pilots duelling with the likes of the Red Baron. On the ground, in the trenches and mud Canadian infantrymen earned a reputation for bravery, endurance, disciplined assault, and ruthlessness with overzealous officers. Continuous fighting, especially on the attack, exacted a murderous toll.

Numbers can never tell the full story, but they are nevertheless chilling. Combat claimed close to 60,000 Canadian lives. Many thousands more limped home maimed or psychologically damaged. Half of the Royal Newfoundland Regiment suffered casualties on the first day of the battle at Beaumont Hamel on the Somme. Death visited every community, in some places every street, in the country. The war memorial in the tiny hamlet close to where I write—still strewn with floral tributes a century later—simply and solemnly records that 42 young men went off to fight in France, 13 failed to return. A country the size of Canada could not sustain this level of carnage for long. Nor did the youth of the country have the stomach for fighting as the long lists of dead and wounded filled columns of newsprint every day and shell-shocked veterans returned changed men. Moreover, farmers and their sons did their patriotic duty growing the bumper crops needed to feed war-torn Europe; female and male munitions workers in the cities toiled overtime forging the shells urgently needed at the front. In 1917, with no end to the war in sight, with generals demanding more reinforcements, and the flow of volunteers drying up, the government of Canada imposed conscription to draft non-essential workers to fight. It was a desperate measure that tore the country apart.

To ensure maximum war effort, the state assumed responsibilities, resources, and a commanding role in the economy and society that were inconceivable in peacetime. The state took responsibility for moving western grain to European markets in an orderly fashion. Government controllers took command of the production and allocation of strategic commodities, transportation, fuel, and power. Two of the new transcontinental railroads, already faltering before the war, were nationalized to save them from bankruptcy and merged with the existing government railway to create a publicly owned Canadian National Railway (CNR) system. A public body, the Imperial Munitions Board, directed the production of *matériel* in Canada. Public debt increased tenfold to finance the war. Having conscripted manpower, the government also confiscated capital by imposing an income tax and a business-profits tax for the duration of the war. In this respect the war has never ended.

Total war demanded something of everyone. It heightened idealism, made sacrifice noble, and made cynical acts seem patriotic. One by one the provincial governments—with the merciful exception of Quebec—banned liquor sales to conserve grain for food, not alcohol, and men for the army rather than the saloon. Mothers of soldiers received the vote federally in 1917, after the widespread but not universal introduction of provincial female suffrage following Manitoba's lead in 1916. These women, and later all female British subjects, received the vote on the reasonable expectation that the mothers of soldiers would vote to conscript other mothers' sons. They did. Prohibition, female suffrage, and a host of other measures of social reform that had not made much headway before the war advanced during it on the premise that they would be needed to create a land fit for heroes.

All did not go smoothly. Scandals involving ministerial misconduct, patronage in the issuing of war contracts, war profiteering, and the supply of troops with defective weapons rocked the government from time to time. Accidents brought the war close to home. In December 1917 a collision between two ships in Halifax harbour, one loaded with munitions, triggered the largest manmade explosion experienced before Hiroshima. The blast, tidal wave, and ensuing firestorm levelled the north end of the city, damaged 12,000 buildings, killed 1,600 people, wounded another 9,000, and left thousands homeless.

Across the country, manpower shortages eventually changed the nature of Canadian politics. The Conservative government could not prosecute the war to the hilt on its own. When Prime Minister Borden approached Laurier to form a national government, Laurier refused on the grounds that conscription would inevitably pit English against French. He was right. Borden nevertheless found enough support among other members of the Liberal party to create a Union government in 1917 and appeal to the country in a wartime general election for a mandate to prosecute the war effort to the full. A certain amount of idealism suffused this end-of-politics-as-usual measure. But the resulting election divided Canada almost exactly along linguistic lines. Union government was in effect English government, the majority dictating to the minority. Volunteerism in French Quebec had fallen off in part because of recruiting incompetence, understandable war weariness, but also because of overt anti-French measures taken in other provinces. Conscription was the ultimate blow.

By 1917, having contributed so heavily to the war effort and suffered so many losses, Canada sought greater influence over the direction of the war. Britain at first refused. Borden and some of the other Dominion prime ministers took the position that if Britain needed more help it should give the Dominions greater responsibility. In desperate need of full Dominion help, the new Lloyd George government in Britain eventually conceded the point by establishing an imperial war cabinet made up of senior British ministers and the Dominion prime ministers. In the later stages of the war, this body played a major role in deciding strategy and mobilizing resources. The Canadian imperialists' ambition of taking charge at the centre seemed to have been fulfilled, though at a terrible cost. Canada demanded and received representation at the post-war peace conference in Paris. The major powers looked down their noses at what they considered a British attempt to stack the conference with puppet states, but they had to admit that the Dominions deserved places at the table much more than some of the more operatic European principalities that were automatically represented. Borden's main contribution was to represent the Empire on a committee struck to draw the boundary between Greece and Albania. Nations are made of such mundane things. Canada signed the peace treaty in its own right, though under the British signature.

～

The Great War enhanced Canada's national stature abroad, but ripped apart the social fabric at home. Returning soldiers inadvertently carried the deadly Spanish Influenza with them. The resulting epidemic killed almost as many young people at home as the war did abroad. The flu epidemic also spread fear and uncertainty at a time of growing civil unrest. When the war ended in Europe, rebellion broke out in Canada's cities and mining towns. Wartime inflation had driven up prices; wages failed to keep pace. Union membership consequently soared during the final stages of the war as workers organized to recover their lost standard of living and perhaps gain a little. In the most tumultuous year, 1919, more than 450 strikes broke out across the country. Heightened conventional union activity occurred against an international and domestic background that coloured these incidents with a startling red hue: the Russian Revolution abroad and the rise of the radical One Big Union movement advocating a General Strike at home.

In the spring of 1919 a strike of metalworkers in Winnipeg drew other unions out in sympathy. Without much forethought a General Strike broke out. When the strike committee appeared to take control over essential services for humanitarian reasons, anxious authorities detected the hand of Red Revolution. The closest thing to open class warfare took shape in Winnipeg with the returned war veterans playing an ambiguous wild-card role in the affair. When workers in other cities struck in sympathy,

Canadian farmers had been raising hell as well as wheat.

the spectre of the General Strike spread beyond Winnipeg. The menace of revolution elicited sharp and swift repressive measures by the state, whose legitimate authority had been challenged. The Royal Canadian Mounted Police and special citizens committees, with the army in reserve, confronted strikers in the streets; police arrested the leaders on charges of sedition, 'foreign agitators' were deported under hastily revised provisions of the Criminal Code, and spies were set on the labour movement. Within a year, extreme labour militancy had been tamed, in part by repression but largely by the onset of a sharp post-war recession and the need to incorporate more then 300,000 returned veterans into the labour force. The General Strike set back the organized labour movement in Canada by a generation.

Out on the range roads and the back concessions, Canadian

farmers had been raising hell as well as wheat. However, they staged their revolt at the ballot box and were thus a much more formidable force to contend with. Farmers deeply resented having their sons conscripted for war when bumper crops demanded all the labour available to harvest it for a hungry Europe. As independent producers, they had to sell the crops in a world market where prices rose and fell with supply and demand. At home, they had to buy consistently high-priced equipment and goods within a tariff-protected regime. The services they depended upon to get their crops to market—elevator companies, railroads, grain companies, and banks—were all oligopolistic organizations charging inordinate fees. It was futile to look to the traditional political parties for solutions to these problems because they were beholden to these big interests. Agricultural grievances boiled over during tough times on the farm. The rural urban exodus continued; and farmers' self-esteem eroded with the diminishing rural population.

Farmers were no longer the majority and their influence was on the decline. Indeed the 1921 census year recorded for the first time more urban than rural Canadians. The farmers entered politics directly with a broad program that addressed specific regional grievances, but also a series of structural reforms intended to purge the political system, loosen the grip of party discipline, and make representatives more directly accountable to their electorate. Farmers' parties exerted their power first at the provincial level, in Ontario, Alberta, and Manitoba. In the general election of 1921, the Progressives, as they called themselves, elected more than 60 members, enough to form the official opposition.

The incumbent Conservatives became a magnet for all of the pent-up antagonism of the war. Quebec, which could never forgive them for the crime of conscription, voted solidly Liberal as did most of the Maritimes. The Liberal party, with its base in Quebec, elected the largest number of members, but not enough to form a majority government. Under their new leader, William Lyon Mackenzie King, the Liberals nevertheless formed a government in a loose and somewhat disorderly arrangement with some of the Progressives. A wily Mackenzie King, the grandson of the hoary old rebel, with his Harvard PhD, political experience, and training in industrial relations, stole just enough of the farmers' program to win enough of them over to gain their provisional support. He also befuddled them with complicated parliamentary manoeuvres and, when scandal threatened his government, he managed to cloud the situation by turning it into a legalistic constitutional conflict in which, with wounded righteousness, he seized the moral high ground. The Progressives contributed to their own demise by fighting among themselves over whether it would be better to strive for root-and-branch structural change or the achievement of immediate objectives. Amid all of these expressions of class and regional discontent, the Maritime provinces insisted that the federal government raise tariffs and lower freight rates to spur lagging local economic development. King, for all his faults, cautiously if unimaginatively managed the political agenda and maintained power throughout the decade—save for a brief comic interlude in 1925 when the overeager opposition briefly formed a government.

Much of the inflated idealism that marked the end of the war dissipated during the 1920s. Women won the vote, but the New Jerusalem of moral rejuvenation failed to appear. Women as voters did not appear to differ much from men. Though Canadian feminists famously succeeded in having the courts recognize that the word *person* included rather than excluded women, very few women were elected to the provincial legislatures or the House of Commons. Nor did prohibition deliver the promised moral millennium. Indeed, it seemed to have the opposite, corrupting effect.

The manufacture and export of liquor were not prohibited. Rum-running to slake the American thirst for Canadian whiskey provided men with fast boats and light consciences abundant opportunities for adventuresome, lucrative, late-night, outdoor employment. Since liquor could only be obtained in Canada with a medical prescription, prohibition effectively turned doctors and pharmacists into bootleggers. Returned soldiers, whose salvation it was intended to ensure, demanded their customary drink. Bit by bit provincial regulation by liquor control boards replaced prohibition and the beer parlour replaced the bar as the purveyor of milder forms of alcohol and centres of largely male sociability.

A dramatic economic revival after 1922 and especially after 1925 contributed to this sense of 'business as usual'. By 1928 grain exports to Europe exceeded wartime levels, soothing sensibilities on the farm. On the resource frontier a booming pulp and paper industry overtook wheat as the leading exporter. Mining, heavy investment in hydroelectric facilities, US direct investment in branch plants, and the rise of the auto industry in central Canada contributed mightily to the expansion. But growth was uneven. Once again the Martime provinces did not participate in the general expansion of manufacturing. Per capita income levels in the Atlantic region remained significantly below the national average.

⌒

Electoral fortunes rose and fell in the 1920s exclusively on domestic issues. Nevertheless foreign policy, about which no one seemed to care a whit, was the one domain in which Canada did achieve something of significance. One of the lessons that might have been taken from the war was that Canada, by virtue of its size and power, could exercise much greater influence than was previously thought, within the Empire and in the international community. Canadian Conservatives emerged from their experience in London and Paris with this inclination and a general willingness to say 'ready, aye, ready' when Britain called. That was not the lesson subsequent Liberal governments, with their base of support in Quebec, and the majority of English Canadians preferred to take. Instead, Canadians believed they lived in a fireproof house, in the memorable if mistaken phrase of a French-Canadian minister, far from the flammable materials of Europe. They did not, therefore, see the need for expensive fire insurance. Canada, therefore, had no need of entangling alliances.

As for conflicts in other parts of the world, Canada would not be bound by the policies of Britain; it would make up its own mind over whether and what it might contribute when the time came. Though Canada was a founding member of the League of Nations, it expended its greatest effort attempting to eviscerate Article X, the collective security clause, on the presumption it would commit Canada in advance to participation in unwelcome foreign wars in which it had no direct interest. At successive imperial conferences, Canada insisted upon local autonomy in foreign policy. Canada established its own Ministry of External Affairs, negotiated a fisheries treaty with the United States without British mediation, and eventually established its own embassies abroad— first, of course, in Washington. Canada adamantly refused to be drawn in by British attempts to establish common imperial foreign policies. The fussy, prematurely aged, bachelor prime minister, Mackenzie King, took that refusal one step further by insisting Canada should not even be consulted about foreign affairs for fear consultation should imply responsibility to act subsequently upon the advice given.

Canada sought equality with Great Britain but not, paradoxically, independence. At the 1926 Imperial Conference, the South African delegation drafted a definition of Dominion Status that served in effect as a quasi-declaration of Dominion independence, except that Mackenzie King insisted the word *independent* be removed from the text so that the emphasis fell on 'allegiance'. The Balfour Declaration, as it came to be known, defined the Dominions, in a run-on sentence every Canadian schoolchild once knew by heart as 'autonomous communities within the British Empire, equal in status, in no way subordinate to one another in any respect of their domestic or external affairs, though united by a common allegiance to the Crown, and freely associated as members of the British Commonwealth of Nations'. This declaration received legal expression in the 1931 Statute of Westminster. The

The Dominions achieved autonomy by civilized negotiation— not revolution.

Dominions were extremely proud of this accomplishment, an achievement of autonomy by a civilized process of negotiation rather than revolution, which resulted in continuing ties of allegiance through a common sovereign. Other countries, nevertheless, found this all very odd. Britain still appointed the Canadian governor general and supplied its final court of appeal, and the key document of the Canadian constitution remained a British statute that could only be amended by an act of the British Parliament. In those key respects Canada remained a legal dependency.

෴

Mackenzie King was not in power in 1931 to savour this moment of constitutional obfuscation on a truly Kingsian scale. The Liberals had been decisively defeated in the general election of 1930 and the Conservatives had returned to power under R.B. Bennett, a rotund, readily caricatured, corporate lawyer. It was a good election to lose. A worldwide economic collapse hit Canada with particular ferocity. If the Canadian government was obsessed with limiting its political dependence upon Great Britain, the Great Depression in it own grim way revealed the extent of Canada's new economic dependence on the United States.

A sharp monetary contraction in the United States to rein in the roaring stock market started a calamitous chain of unintended events. The gold standard that locked monetary regimes together around fixed exchange rates transmitted this US domestic measure to the major economies of the world that were still burdened with post-war reparations payments and debt. To maintain the value of their currencies, countries had to raise interest rates and curb imports. Investment in all sectors plummeted; commodity prices went into free fall; unemployment rose; consumption fell. In a highly interconnected world, this downward spiral, once it had begun, became self-reinforcing. The United States and Canada were the two countries to experience the steepest and the deepest contractions in national income; industrial production collapsed to barely 50 per cent of previous levels. For Canada, heavily dependent both upon capital imports and a few commodity exports, the effects of plunging newsprint, wheat, flour, and metals exports ripped through the rest of the economy. Plants closed or operated at well below capacity. The only bright spot was the gold mining sector, which boomed. As a result the gold barons swaggered about with the arrogance of the one-eyed in the land of the blind.

The 1930s earned the sobriquet 'Dirty' in every respect. Farmers and blue-collar workers bore the brunt of the recession. About 33 per cent of Canadian workers lost their jobs. Farmers, who couldn't sell their wheat, lost their farms to the banks. A record drought cruelly exaggerated the rural distress; Prairie farms literally blew away in suffocating dust storms. The hardest hit regions of the country were the West where farmers had expanded into marginal land, and the resource towns when the sole-employer mines and mills shut down. At the lowest point 15 per cent of the population, more than 1.5 million people, depended upon relief for survival. It was an economic shock the like of which the world, but especially Canada, had never seen and, one hopes, will never see again.

The Bennett government reeled under these unprecedented blows, at first not knowing what to do. What role should government play in such a situation? This was uncharted territory where old beliefs did not provide much guidance. The government increased welfare payments and public works expenditures; then, when relief costs began to spiral out of control, anxiety over fiscal responsibility compelled the Conservative government to cut back. Canadian governments went into the Depression heavily indebted—the federal government for the war and railways; the provincial governments for roads, hospitals, schools, power plants, and so on. Much of Canada's industrial expansion in the 1920s had been financed with debt. These fixed payments weighed heavily upon the public and private sectors. On the monetary front, Canada remained hamstrung until Britain abandoned the gold standard, freeing Canada to do the same. When the United States raised its tariffs to record levels, the Conservatives hoped to encourage recovery by negotiating preferential trade agreements within the Commonwealth. In due course, the government began to address some of the underlying issues, creating the Bank of Canada to manage monetary policy, a grain board to coordinate the export of wheat, and a farm rehabilitation program to relieve distress in some of the hardest hit drought areas.

Fear drove public policy as much as did reason and compassion. Deportations of immigrants who had become public charges rose dramatically. Remote relief camps were built to occupy the idle hands of unemployed, single, young men. Political repression resumed. Police rounded up the leaders of the Communist party on the grounds that their protest demonstrations were aimed at overthrowing the government. Convicted, they were jailed in Kingston Penitentiary. Late in his term Bennett seemed to experience an ideological conversion, copying a page from Roosevelt's New Deal book. Bennett's New Deal called for major government intervention in the economy to provide health and unemployment insurance; regulation of employment, wages, and prices; and extended farm relief. This abrupt change in course seemed to lack conviction; more troubling, it also appeared to violate the Constitution, trenching as it did upon exclusive provincial responsibilities. Voters threw out the Conservatives in the 1935 general election, and that great survivor of Canadian politics, Mackenzie King, returned for the third time.

The crisis not only exposed Canada's dependence upon external markets, but also revealed gaping regional disparities that destabilized the federation. Not all regions of Canada shared in the general prosperity of the 1920s; similarly the pain of the crisis seemed to be concentrated mainly in the commodity-producing regions of the West. Income per capita varied significantly across the vast geographical extent of Canada, in good times and in bad. But some regions, Ontario in particular, seemed to do better all of the time. Not only was growth uneven and the benefits unequally shared, but fiscal capacity and government responsibility seemed to have come unbalanced within the federation. Provincial jurisdiction over health, education, welfare, transportation, property, and civil rights, which at the time of Confederation had been minor responsibilities, had risen to become the most important areas of public policy and the most costly government expenditures. Judicial interpretation of the British North America Act had further strengthened provincial powers at the expense of the federal government.

The Depression dramatically showed that the provinces had most of the expensive responsibilities, but that the federal government had the major revenues. Some of the western provinces teetered on the edge of insolvency. The colony of Newfoundland actually did go bankrupt and had to surrender its responsible government to a British financial commission.

Provincial premiers emerged in the 1930s as major political figures, often consolidating their hold on local power with attacks on the federal government. In British Columbia and Ontario, premiers struck a populist pose while pursuing quite conventional policies. In Quebec, a socially conservative political regime wrapped itself in nationalist rhetoric. Desperate circumstances justified new ways of thinking. In Alberta, a political and religious revival movement took up the gospel of Social Credit and stormed into power, promising to pay out a social dividend to each citizen with a view to inflating the economy. Communist militants in the Workers' Unity League organized industrial unions rather than craft unions. On the right fascist movements intimidated minorities, especially in Montreal. The Ku Klux Klan experienced a revival on the Prairies and in Ontario. Federally, a small-business splinter party flourished briefly on animosity directed against the large, retail corporations. In 1933, farmers' organizations, labour representatives, and some urban intellectuals established a socialist party, the Co-operative Commonwealth Federation, dedicated to the eradication of capitalism by democratic means and its replacement with a co-operative, state-regulated economy. Fear and suffering heightened suspicions, exaggerated ethnic hatred, and prompted fundamental rethinking of political arrangements in some quarters.

In general, it must be said, the vast majority of Canadians did not seem much interested in political experimentation. Amid the social and economic uncertainty, they preferred the tried and true, the safe and old. Mackenzie King's avuncular, suspicious, hyper-cautious outlook was more attuned to Canadian sensibilities than more aggressive or ideological modes. He happily watched as the courts struck down the New Deal legislation as ultra vires of the federal government. As for the provinces, he did nothing by setting a large royal commission to work studying the question of federalism. The Liberals did have recourse to their reflex policy under such circumstances, seeking freer trade with the United States with some success. But Liberal suspicion of European-style statist government precluded any major policy innovations. Mercifully, the economy slowly and with faltering steps began to recover. By 1939, national income and employment had almost returned to 1929 levels.

There were no more enthusiastic appeasers than Canadians.

However, as the economy brightened, the world slowly descended into a maelstrom. Throughout the 1930s, Canadian governments, both Conservative and Liberal, maintained their resolute focus on questions of national unity. Canada must not be seen to commit itself in advance to any policy that might require force whether within the Commonwealth or the League. Canada's refusal to countenance sanctions against Japan for its invasion of Manchuria in 1931 elicited a note of thanks from the Japanese ambassador to Ottawa. When the Canadian representative to the League of Nations supported the imposition of economic sanctions on Italy for its invasion of Ethiopia in 1935, the Canadian government repudiated his actions. Canadians feared what they saw happening in Europe, but could not imagine anything they could do about it. There were no more enthusiastic appeasers than Canadians. Mackenzie King's consultation with the spirit world deluded him into undertaking what he imagined to be a mission of peace to Germany in 1937. Like so many others he was completely taken in by Hitler, whom he likened in his diary, following an interview with the man, to Joan of Arc. Yet in a typically roundabout way King did tell Hitler something he would not say out loud to the Canadian people and only hinted at in private to the British prime minister. If Great Britain were attacked by another European power, he told Hitler, Canada would be compelled to come to her aid. With exasperating punctiliousness, Canada carefully avoided undertaking any international commitments for fear they might end in the country being torn apart again by conscription.

It is tempting in retrospect to write the 1930s off as a low, dishonest decade in which no nation particularly distinguished itself, least of all Canada with its obsession with autonomy, isolationism, and national unity. This natural tendency to moralize should be balanced, however, by a candid appraisal of what more heroic policies might have accomplished internationally and domestically and, above all, by an appreciation of what Canada subsequently did when its moral duty became clear.

⌒

By the end of the 1930s the Dominion of Canada had filled itself out from sea to sea, and risen to become a major economic power. Its economic and political institutions had been badly shaken by the Great War and the Great Depression but had also demonstrated considerable resilience. However, regional disparity and federal–provincial conflict had frayed the fabric considerably. Over the years Canada had gradually moved away from Great Britain and closer to the United States economically, both as a source of investment and as a trading partner. Paralyzed by domestic concerns Canada insisted upon staying on the sidelines in international affairs. Those were issues on which Parliament must decide on a case-by-case basis. Self-satisfied isolationism and racism prevented Canada from even recognizing its humanitarian obligations. Throughout 1938–9 Canadian immigration authorities in Europe routinely rejected Jewish refugee claims; in May 1939, Canada turned away a boatload of desperate Jewish refugees from its waters (as did most of the countries of the hemisphere, including the United States).

Sometime in the aftermath of the First World War the country in its collective imagination had drifted from being a British possession to thinking of itself as an autonomous, self-conscious Dominion. The moment of separation cannot be identified—it was more a mood shift than an event—but if a precise date for the tipping point must be specified, 22 May 1919 should suffice. That day the Canadian House of Commons petitioned the King to cease granting royal honours to Canadians. The major politicians in Canada in the late-nineteenth and early twentieth centuries, including Sir John A. Macdonald, Sir Wilfrid Laurier, and Sir Robert Borden, thought of themselves as British subjects and readily accepted knighthoods. Significantly Mackenzie King, Canada's longest serving twentieth-century prime minister, did not. That his one-term successor R.B. Bennett retired to England to live out his life a viscount is usually taken as a further sign of how far out of touch Bennett was with his own people. Alone among the states of the Commonwealth, Canada adopted a self-denying ordinance towards royal titles consistent with its autonomous and increasingly populist ethos.

Canada had asserted its autonomy from Great Britain in many ways but it had purposefully not declared its independence. Mackenzie King understood that what Canadians wanted most out of the British connection was royalty, even in its then somewhat tarnished state. A degree of vestigial legal dependence was important to maintain this emotional connection that commanded immense political force. Canada even played a small role in the abdication crisis. The British prime minister had to tell the crestfallen King Edward that his matrimonial plans not only faced insurmountable constitutional obstacles, but also that the Dominions, Canada foremost among them, would not have an American divorcee as their Queen.[2]

In the summer of 1939, Mackenzie King achieved the crowning glory of his long, drawn-out campaign of detaching Canada from British political influence by paradoxically putting the new King and Queen on display on a cross-country tour of Canada. The prime minister attended to even the tiniest detail of the tour to ensure, in the words of his biographer, that all arrangements were consistent with Canada's autonomous status and that no hint of colonial inferiority should intrude. The shy, chain-smoking, stammering King George VI and his steely wife came to shore up imperial unity at a time of international crisis. They received an ecstatic reception at all their stops from coast to coast. Mackenzie King fastened himself terrier-like to Their Majesties to bask in their reflected glory, but also to show that the prime minister of Canada had the sole authority to present the King and Queen to Canadians. The sweet, perverse pleasure of Dominion Status was something Canadians could only fully enjoy in acts of royal homage.

---

2   Ironically one of the few monuments to the abdicated monarch stands in
    Toronto, where a luxury hotel opened in the mid-1930s still bears his name,
    the King Edward.

distinct society

$\sim$

If a Rip Van Winkle had fallen asleep during the Royal Tour of 1939 and come to in contemporary Canada, he would be forgiven if he imagined he had awakened in another country. His eyes and ears would tell him that this Canada consisted of an entirely new people; the country had a new flag, a new Constitution, and it operated within a new Empire. During his slumbers the society, the state, and the external relations of Canada had changed completely.

In less than a lifetime, Canada had experienced something akin to a social revolution. The world had moved to Canada. Immigration had turned a largely white settler Dominion into a multicultural, multiracial society. Native peoples too, after a century on the margins, had acquired a renewed presence in the social mosaic. French and English now were both official languages. More than a pretense had been made of providing public services in both languages, and for high office, bilingualism had become a requirement. French remained the predominant language in Quebec, and English in what was now called the rest of Canada, but many other languages flourished in the neighbourhoods of both regions. Women constituted almost half of the wage labour force and were prominent in the arts, media, professions, and public affairs. They enjoyed legal equality with men and claimed economic equality. Not only had the relationship between the sexes changed; so too had the nature of sex itself. Sexual practices deemed criminal in 1939 were now legal, and the practitioners were protected against discrimination. The institution of marriage itself had been transformed. Fewer people married; common law relationships were more common; far more marriages ended in divorce. Society may not have been turned upside down, but it had been vigorously shaken.

The economy too had been transformed. Canada, once defined by its open space and its West, had become one of the most highly urbanized countries in the world with more than 80 per cent of the population resident in its largest centres. Most of the factories had disappeared, and so had most of the working class and the farmers. Canada no longer made things or grew things the way it once had; most Canadians worked in the service or knowledge sectors. Canadians had been so rich for so long that the Depression was a distant memory. This wealth and opportunity, notwithstanding enduring inequalities, acted as a magnet to the world. The population had tripled, but the economy had grown much faster. Real GNP in 2000 was more than 10 times larger than 1939.

Something like a political-constitutional revolution had also taken place—but without the revolution part. The state had swollen in size; it had also changed as to kind. Huge government bureaucracies at the federal, provincial, and municipal levels assumed responsibility, and certainly were held accountable, for the economy, social security, public health, welfare, transportation, education, and recreation; in short, bread and circuses and almost everything in between. Rip certainly would have noticed this when it came time to pay his taxes. Since the state in its various forms accounted for more than 50 per cent of GNP, he now would have to work well into June to begin earning money to keep for himself. The state engulfed the citizen with its services—that was a big change from the 1930s when the reasons for the state staying out of private affairs were more compelling than interventionist arguments.

The nature of citizenship itself had changed. A new Constitution had been proclaimed, with an attached Charter of Rights and Freedoms. Together these two documents transformed the relationship of the citizen and the state. Citizens were now endowed with rights that were constitutionally protected against violations by fellow citizens and also by the state. The state might be pervasive, but there were constitutional constraints on its conduct. Parliament was no longer sovereign; or rather it had to share sovereignty with the Charter. Moreover, this new regime of 'rights' elevated the Courts to virtual equality with Parliament as interpreters of public policy.

But if the state sector was vast and pervasive, levying taxes on a scale unprecedented in the 1930s, at the same time the country seemed more fragile as a political entity. Canada seemed perpetually to be on the brink of splitting apart. The federation had become more decentralized as provinces rivalled the federal government. At times Quebec seemed determined to separate from the rest of Canada, though this prospect waxed and waned with the electoral outcome of the long-running debate between independentists and federalists within the province of Quebec. Canada as a political entity had seemed so definite and assured in 1939; some 60 years later it appeared to be in a state of continuous negotiation.

In the interim, Canada changed empires and adopted a completely different view of its external obligations. Britain had virtually disappeared from Canadian life, and conversely Canada from British consciousness. Constitutionally, Canada remained a monarchy. But the Queen's visit in 2002 scarcely attracted the attention, crowds, or excitement that the 1939 visit had. British prime ministers travelling to Washington no longer made the obligatory stopover in Ottawa, acknowledging Canada's linchpin role in the three-way relationship. For most Canadians, Britain had become just another European country. By contrast, the United States had been transformed from the large isolationist country-next-door into a global superpower. Canada, a small country on its northern edge, had been overwhelmed, some might say absorbed, by the rising giant. As a counterbalance, Canada strove in any number of international organizations to establish an independent foreign policy separate from that of its neighbour. Yet in so many ways Canada was dependent upon the United States for much of its defence, and most obviously its economic well-being. Canada depended upon the huge flows of trade and investment across the Canada–US border, much of it between US corporations with plants on both sides. Informally, and then formally in free-trade agreements, the two economies had become organically integrated in a way the Canadian and British economies never had been. In commercial and foreign-policy terms Canada had been swept up into a new, undeclared but equally domineering and threatening American empire. But history would not repeat itself. Canada sought to establish its separate identity in this new dispensation through action rather than inaction. In the post-war world, it put aside its previous fear of overseas commitments. Canadian troops at the end of the twentieth century—many of them French Canadians and under French-Canadian command—were on the ground in Africa, Europe, and Asia.

Looking backward from the present, the not-so-distant past of the late 1930s seems like a foreign country. In a lifetime Canada would undergo fundamental changes in its societal, governmental, and imperial relations as dramatic as any of those it had previously experienced. In the process Canada became a distinct society, different from what it had formerly been, differentiated from other countries, and composed internally of distinct collectivities. How did Canadians get here from there? This latest metamorphosis began in war, but progressed even more profoundly in peace.

～

As a measure of Canadian self-absorption, the one week that it took to recall Parliament and to complete the debate following the British declaration of war against the Axis on 3 September 1939 has been looked upon universally as a triumph of responsible government, a confirmation of Dominion status, and a signifier of sovereignty gained, rather than a dereliction of duty. Eventually, the Canadian Parliament duly voted to go to war in Britain's defence with only a few dissenting voices from the socialist left and isolationist Quebec. Canada's aversion to defence spending and its refusal to entertain any consideration of contingency planning with Great Britain during the 1930s meant that Canada declared war without any clear idea of how it would wage it, and with a regular army of fewer than 5,000 men. There was no popular enthusiasm for the war in any part of Canada. Indeed, at the time some officials speculated that had a plebiscite been held, there was no certainty that a majority of the population would support going to war.

There was no popular enthusiasm for the war in any part of Canada.

Canada had a clearer notion of what it hoped to avoid than what it hoped to do. Canada went to war, voluntarily but without much enthusiasm, because Great Britain was at war. The lessons of the First World War loomed large, especially in the mind of the prime minister. On that account Mackenzie King, in his speech in the war debate, made an uncharacteristically unqualified declaration: that his administration would not impose conscription for overseas service. By keeping combat commitments to a minimum, Canadians would avoid the terrible internal troubles over conscription that destabilized the country in the First World War. The government also intended a 'pay as you go' war to avoid disruptive inflation. Canada could best contribute, it was widely believed, by defending itself, and perhaps Newfoundland and the West Indies as well, and by serving as an arsenal, training ground, and supply depot for the Allied cause. That at least was the vague plan going into war. The British saw it as a cynical scheme to make the war benefit Canada.

As it turned out, Canada did play a remarkably important role in arming and feeding Great Britain, but the notion of a 'limited liability' war did not survive the fall of France in the late spring of 1940. The British Commonwealth Air Training Program, negotiated with considerable acrimony in the fall of 1939, represented Canada's fondest hope for the war. Britain, Canada, and the Dominions agreed to build and equip airfields all across Canada where Commonwealth and Allied aircrews would be trained. More than 100,000 pilots and navigators, almost half the total Allied airmen, learned to fly in Canada's wide-open spaces during the course of the war. This program also provided a tremendous stimulus to the Canadian economy, particularly to the aviation industry, which had to build and service the aircraft and the construction sector that laid down the runways and threw up the hangars and barracks at top speed. In a similar fashion Canada expected to provide munitions, equipment, medical supplies, and food under contract to Great Britain. All of this would eventually transpire; Canadian guns, tanks, reconnaissance aircraft, heavy bombers, flour, bacon, ham, and butter would flow across the Atlantic in the massive convoys that became Britain's lifeline. The only problem was that Britain was 'broke'—in the words of its ambassador to Washington—and could not afford to pay for any of it. With France out of the war and the United States neutral, Canada became Britain's most important ally and supplier. Far from profiting from the war, Canada had to give, and give heavily. It gave Britain a billion dollars in 1940, then a second billion in 1942. All told the war cost Canada $18 billion, almost $4 billion of which constituted aid to Great Britain. Whatever Britain may have thought of this, the aid constituted a rather dramatic and well-timed return on its colonial investment.

Canada's extraordinary war effort and its direct aid to Great Britain paradoxically drew Canada closer to the United States. Soon after the German victory over Denmark, Holland, Belgium, and France, as the United States prepared for a possible invasion and surrender of Great Britain, the president of the United States, Franklin Delano Roosevelt, initiated a meeting with his old friend Mackenzie King, the prime minister of Canada, at the border town of Ogdensburg. There the two agreed to establish a Permanent Joint Board of Defence to coordinate military planning on the continent. With Britain beleaguered, Canada in effect sought and received the protection of the United States. But from a Canadian perspective the Ogdensburg Agreement represented an even more fundamental shift in policy than the change in hegemony. After only six months of war, Canada had gone further with the United States on the subject of joint hemispheric defence than it ever had been prepared to go with Britain on the coordination of imperial defence. As of 1940, Canada and the United States had entered a mutual defence alliance that would set the pattern for relations between the two countries for the rest of the century.

The logic of economics as well as the strategic situation drove the two countries closer together. In the pre-war era Canada's surplus of exports over imports to Great Britain had paid its current account deficit with the United States. With Great Britain now out of the picture, and Canada needing more parts and equipment from the United States, a way had to be found for Canada to earn US dollars; otherwise Canada, too, would soon be bankrupt. Once again the United States proved an accommodating partner. Meeting again at the president's Hudson Valley home of Hyde Park on 7 April 1941, King and Roosevelt readily agreed on a defence purchasing agreement that gave Canada all the dollars it needed to buy essential military supplies from the United States. As long as the United States remained neutral, Canada occupied a strategic position as an interlocutor and negotiator between the United States and Great Britain. That changed, however, when the United States entered the war after Pearl Harbour. The Great Powers—Britain and the United States—dealt with each other directly, leaving Canada very much on the sidelines, a neglected and out-of-sorts junior ally. US entry into the war, however, brought a flood of US dollars into Canada for the construction of pipelines, highways, and defence works in the Northwest to protect against further Japanese attacks. This solved Canada's dollar crisis, stimulated the economy further, and provided some of the reserves necessary to finance aid to Britain. As the US war machine geared up for combat in both the Pacific and the European theatres, it dwarfed the Canadian contribution. Despite the joy at the United States weighing in with all its might, Canadians would never forget that for 18 months Britain and the Commonwealth fought alone. During the course of the war, Canada passed from being a partner in British defence, to being a strategic link between Britain and the United States, to becoming a military and economic satellite of the United States.

Early in the war when Britain asked for military assistance, the Canadian government authorized the recruitment of one division of ground troops for Europe and another for home defence. During the crisis of 1940, when the fate of Britain hung in the balance, the public mood in Canada changed from caution to hawk-ish determination. It is difficult in retrospect to recapture this fateful moment in history, influenced as we are by knowledge of the eventual victory. A visit to the War Cabinet Rooms in Whitehall, from which Churchill and his general staff directed the Battle of Britain, offers a bracing reminder of what was, and what might have been. Britons were forced into such circumstances because they were losing. We too easily forget that for five fateful days in April, the British government debated in coded language the possibility of negotiating a separate peace. The maverick Churchill, who insisted on fighting to the last gasp, prevailed over the patrician Lord Halifax, who saw some merit in sparing the country a certain ruinous bloodbath if at all possible. Britain would fight on against all odds with the much-despised Churchill at the helm. For Canada, British surrender was a possibility too horrible even to contemplate. Tentative

Churchill warmed to the prickly and difficult Canadian prime minister.

inquiries from the United States as to the disposition of the British fleet in the event of surrender, however, concentrated the Canadian government's mind on the enormity of the task ahead. To its credit the government threw caution to the wind in 1940 and began the total mobilization of Canadian human resources and *matériel* for the war. Old scores and prejudices were set aside for the duration. Churchill, whom Mackenzie King thought to be 'the most dangerous man I have ever known', rose considerably in his estimation. For his part, Churchill warmed to the prickly and difficult Canadian prime minister, whom he had been in the habit of referring to as 'the little son of a bitch'.

The vanguard of the 1st Division of Canadian troops had arrived in Britain in December 1939, only three months after the declaration of war. Many more waves of men and equipment followed. Canada eventually sent more than 500,000 soldiers and 210,000 airmen to defend Britain. A Canadian fighter squadron would arrive in time to engage the enemy in the final stages of the Battle of Britain. The high proportion of Canadian aircrews in the RAF Bomber Command caused some disquiet among the British commanders. And this massive invasion of mainly young Canadian men with lots of time on their hands led to some friction with the local population, but more often to mutually agreeable fraternization. By the end of the war, Canadian soldiers and airmen had married about 45,000 British women. These unions produced more than 20,000 children by the end of 1946. Most of these war brides returned to Canada with their husbands. More Canadians returned from war than went.

During the Second World War, Canada would mobilize over a million men and women, 99 per cent of them volunteers. The army, air force, navy, and home defence called upon fully 40 per cent of the eligible population aged 18 to 45 in a society experiencing full employment. Without giving it much thought, when Britain asked for help, Canada also sent 2,000 troops to reinforce the garrison of Hong Kong. The Canadian navy's four destroyers were deployed in British waters and put under British command. On the North American side of the Atlantic, the navy rapidly equipped itself for convoy escort duty. In their new-found enthusiasm to pitch in, Canada's generals and politicians perhaps showed too great an eagerness for action. The Hong Kong expedition ended in disaster with the capture of the colony by the Japanese on Christmas Day 1941. And Canadians, eager for combat, willingly volunteered for the ill-conceived Dieppe Raid in April 1942. A sortie intended ostensibly to test German defences, the Dieppe debacle ended with two-thirds of the invaders either killed or captured. The raid taught the Allies many valuable but costly lessons; it also allowed Churchill to show Stalin that the western front could not be opened just yet.

On the North Atlantic, the hastily trained and poorly equipped Canadian navy proved incapable of guarding the convoys all the way to Ireland and had to be replaced east of Newfoundland by the Royal navy. German submarines and Japanese battleships rudely brought the war to the very doorstep of the supposedly fireproof house. German torpedoes sank cargo ships and Canadian escort vessels in the St Lawrence River and in the approaches to Halifax harbour. The Battle of the Atlantic and the Aleutian campaign brought the grim menace of war home to Canada and led to the indiscriminate internment here of Japanese, German, and Italian immigrants deemed a threat to security. However, these early setbacks and palpable threats to homeland security steeled Canadian resolve.

Canada's 210,000 airmen and approximately 100,000 sailors saw action throughout the entire war. Canada's 500,000 soldiers, up to now mostly cooped up in England, itched to get into combat. Canadian politicians, Mackenzie King included, authorized the splitting of the first Canadian army in order that Canada could participate in the summer 1943 invasion of Sicily. From that point on, Canadian troops would remain in continuous engagement with the enemy until the end of the war. Through 1943–4 the Canadian 1st Division would fight alongside British and American forces from the toe up the entire boot of Italy. Canadians attacked with great valour at heavily defended Ortona in December. They fought their way north, driving the retreating Germans across the Arno in the fall of 1944. The Italian campaign cost 26,000 casualties including almost 6,000 fatalities. On D-Day, 6 June 1944, Canadian soldiers swept ashore at Juno Beach in Normandy against fierce resistance. They gained their beachhead at heavy cost, then fought their way inland to a deadly encounter with the German army at the Battle of the Falaise Gap. Reunited with the returning Italian Division, the combined Canadian army moved north to secure the Scheldt estuary and liberate Holland. In these post D-Day operations Canadian troops suffered more than 44,000 casualties; 11,000 officers and men died in combat. Meanwhile in the air, Canadian crews in the British air force and the Canadian air force continued the strategic night bombing of Germany and provided close air support for the invading Allied army. A total of 42,000 Canadians perished in battle during the Second World War, 55 per cent in the army, 41 per cent in the air force, and 4 per cent in the navy.

Maintaining an armed force of this size and experiencing losses on this scale inevitably raised the most feared consequence of war: conscription of manpower for overseas service. The issue would provoke several major crises, and at one point threaten to bring down the government, but the Second World War would not see a repetition of the bitter divisiveness of the First World War. Mackenzie King managed the issue as if he had been saving up all of his shrewdness and ruthless decisiveness for this moment. As we have seen, King began the war with a forthright promise not to impose conscription for overseas service. Early in the war, however, his government did introduce manpower registration and conscription for home defence.

Mackenzie King handled the politics of war masterfully. When the government of Ontario passed a resolution in the spring of 1940 regretting the weak federal war effort, he seized the opportunity to call a snap election. The five-year term of his government was expiring; he could happily blame the wartime election on his critics. The overwhelming majority he won silenced his political enemies and spiked the guns of the opposition for the duration. In 1942, as pressure mounted to field a much larger army, the King government held a nationwide plebiscite asking the people of Canada if the government should be released from its pledge of no conscription for overseas service. The country voted 64 per cent in favour and 36 per cent against. However, as might have been predicted, the vote revealed a deeply divided country. In Ontario, 84 per cent voted yes, while in Quebec, 73 per cent voted no. The federal government thus had a mandate to introduce conscription, but with its power base in Quebec it also had very good reasons not to. Mackenzie King, to the frustration of many of his ministers, held off, refusing to introduce such a divisive policy without a pressing need.

The casualties encountered during the invasion of Europe, and the projections for even greater losses in the fighting that lay ahead, would force the issue—but not until 1944. Still, the wily prime minister wriggled evasively, refusing to surrender to the pressure. In the face of a looming cabinet revolt, he ruthlessly fired his popular minister of defence, parachuting into the portfolio a general who promised to find the necessary volunteers. These efforts failed, as did the general's political ambitions. The insistence of the commanders on the ground in Europe that they desperately needed reinforcements, and mounting popular pressure in Canada that every part of the country should be seen to do its bit, finally forced Mackenzie King to admit that conscription was necessary. About 58,000 home defence troops were transferred to active duty, 13,000 of whom were sent overseas. Fortunately for the government, the war came to an end before extensive drafts were required. Slippery and distrusted though he might be, even by his ministers, Mackenzie King managed to smother an explosive issue with his political manoeuvring. His ability to blunt and complicate issues, his legendary procrastination, and, as the poet said, his frustrating ability 'to do nothing by halves that could be done by quarters', served him and the country well in a time of war. The government managed the conscription issue. It was not an elegant or even an honourable performance, but it worked.

The war also engendered an important transformation of the Canadian state. The pre-war state in Canada was a puny affair compared to what would follow. In 1939, the Canadian government spent slightly less than 11 per cent of Gross National Expenditure. A civil service of only 45,000 managed the country's business affairs, about one-quarter of them worked for the Post Office. As government commandeered larger proportions of manpower and output for the war effort, the scale of the state expanded enormously. Government spending soared to over $5 billion in 1943, an almost tenfold increase over pre-war levels. The war effort at its height in 1943 consumed 45 per cent of Gross National Product.

Under the War Measures Act the federal government took command of the economy. Foreign exchange transactions were regulated, prices controlled, and strategic materials channelled into the war effort by 'dollar-a-year men' seconded from industry. The newly created Department of Munitions and Supply directed the conversion and extraordinary expansion of Canadian industry for war production. Massive private and public investment—the government built about 100 plants on its own—doubled Canadian manufacturing output during the war. A Grain Board oversaw a tripling of Canadian wheat exports to Great Britain—though overall the agricultural sector did not expand relative to others. War accelerated the structural transformation from agriculture to manufacturing and services that had been under way for some time. Remarkably the government paid for this in large part out of current expenditures. That meant, of course, a dramatic increase in taxation and a wholesale invasion of provincial revenue sources. Inevitably, though, the public debt ballooned. A disciplined expansion of the money supply by the Bank of Canada, and wage and price controls kept inflation in the 5 per cent range. The state emerged from the war not only much bigger, commanding unprecedented resources, with a much larger influence over the whole economy because of its size, but also with enhanced prestige and legitimacy. Ottawa's mandarins, wielding new development plans and with new tools at their disposal, gained enormous influence vis-à-vis the private sector. If the state had managed the war effort so effectively, surely it could also be constructively mobilized for the peace as well.

$\backsim$

The war brought a welcome and abrupt end to the Great Depression. Military recruitment and the boom in war industries expanded and transformed the labour force and began a process of social change that had profound long-run consequences. There simply were not enough men to fight, farm, and forge weapons. Women, who had always been a significant minority of the workforce, greatly expanded their participation rates and the range of their employment. Areas of work in heavy manufacturing and transportation previously closed to women opened up, as the surviving photographs of women riveting in aircraft plants and oiling mammoth steam engines attest. The armed forces took on about 50,000 women in combat support roles. The urgent needs of war overcame prejudices against middle-class, married women working outside the home. About 1.2 million women, or about 33 per cent of the female working-age population, joined the wage labour force during the war, demonstrating quite decisively that women were both willing and capable of working across a much wider spectrum of employment than had previously been thought. Organized labour, too, achieved a new level of recognition and legitimacy in policy considerations. Acute labour shortages enhanced the bargaining power of unions. Union membership, strikes, and labour stoppages mainly to achieve union recognition increased dramatically during the first years of the war. In 1943, to head off a crisis, the state and labour negotiated a tacit 'social contract'. The government conceded a much broader range of collective bargaining rights to unions in return for labour peace. Government control of inflation through its disciplined monetary policy, rationing of commodities, and price controls minimized the problem of falling real wages, thereby removing one of labour's main irritants. Labour found government mediation and conciliation activities to be more sympathetic than in pre-war times.

Wartime conditions rapidly advanced the development of social policy in Canada. With full employment it became possible to conceive of a scheme of contributory unemployment insurance. In the massive dislocation of the 1930s, any such scheme had seemed far too costly to manage. With the approval of the provinces, the government of Canada instituted an unemployment insurance system in 1940. This was not the first step towards the development of a welfare state—that honour probably belongs to the veterans' programs and 'mother's allowances' of the 1920s— but it did represent a major step towards the redefinition of the state as the provider of social security across a broad spectrum of the population. The corollary, of course, was that the state assumed greater responsibility for the management and performance of the economy, though that would not be marked with a major piece of legislation. During the war, economic planners acquired valuable experience with growth and stabilization policies. They emerged from the war believing that full employment could be sustained through proper macroeconomic management and that they had the knowledge and the tools to do the job.

In the midst of war, driven in part by the rapid increase in popularity of social democratic political parties, the heretofore hesitant Liberal government embarked upon some quite advanced planning for the post-war era. The constitutional objections to federal action in this jurisdiction were removed in a curious but typically Canadian way. A wide-ranging royal commission review of federal–provincial relations had recommended early in the war that the federal government be given larger scope in taxation and that in return it should assume provincial debts and pay unconditional grants, adjusted according to fiscal need, to sustain the provinces' responsibilities. Most of the poorer provinces favoured this scheme; the richer provinces, led by Ontario, strongly objected to what they interpreted rather rudely as a federal tax grab and invasion of their jurisdiction. The federal–provincial conference in 1941 to implement this plan broke up amid bitter recriminations. The federal government, however, simply took over a host of taxing powers as a war measure, paying 'rent' to the provinces to maintain government activities. This ad hoc system, begun in war, continued with some adjustment and considerable griping on the part of the provinces into the post-war era. The federal government also found a way to exercise its influence even within areas of exclusive provincial jurisdiction, also without significant constitutional revision. Ottawa simply used its unqualified power to spend for any public purpose, to create programs on its own, and to enter into joint shared-cost programs initiated by Ottawa with the provinces.

> *Ontario strongly objected to what they interpreted rather rudely as a federal tax grab.*

Now that Ottawa had money, as a result of higher taxes and a rapidly growing economy, it could think of entertaining the kind of social programs that attracted voters towards the social democratic party. With the election of a socialist government in Saskatchewan, and the sudden rise of the Co-operative Commonwealth Federation (CCF) in opinion polls at the federal level, the obstacles to assertive federal intervention in the social policy arena melted away. The federal government, with its much expanded taxing, spending, and bureaucratic capabilities, promised a host of post-war social programs directed towards promoting economic and social development. If it could wage the war, it could also enhance social security and economic well-being. In addition to the unemployment insurance scheme already implemented, the government promised an ambitious program of post-war reconstruction: a social housing program to alleviate an acute shortage; children's allowances to mothers to provide a minimum level of family support and to stimulate the demand of goods and services to head off an anticipated post-war recession; old age pensions to address the poverty of the elderly; and public health insurance. Not all of these would be instituted immediately—though the politically attractive 'baby bonus' was quickly launched—but the war certainly prefigured the full flowering of the welfare state in Canada in the decades that followed.

Canada went into the war a small, laissez-faire, moderately conservative state and emerged with a commitment to a full-scale welfare state under Keynesian economic management. The war gave the government the capability, the leadership legitimacy, and a sweeping social and economic policy agenda, and largely cleared away the constitutional obstacles previously in the way. Mackenzie King's late and somewhat unconvincing conversion to state intervention nevertheless came at the right time. It was no small achievement, given the accumulation of hopes and grievances during the war, that his government was re-elected in June 1945.

◌◞

The horrendous explosion of two atomic bombs that hastened the unconditional surrender of Japan in August 1945 also signalled the dawn of a brave new, and frighteningly unfamiliar world for Canada. In the past the British Empire and then the Commonwealth had been the essential context within which Canada engaged the world. The war bankrupted Great Britain, destroyed much of its industry, and stripped away its Empire. Britain remained a Great Power, but in much straitened circumstances. Indeed in the immediate post-war period, Canadian financial aid was necessary as well to keep the British economy afloat. To a large degree, the relationship between the imperial and the colonial powers had reversed. Canada had asserted its effective independence from Britain, a policy symbolically acknowledged in 1946 when, by law, Canadians became Canadian citizens rather than British subjects. With Britain much diminished in the world, Canada stood on its own, but it now did so next door to a political and economic superpower armed with nuclear weapons.

During the war, when the United States remained neutral, Canada briefly played a role as a strategic link between the United States and Great Britain. But once the United States entered the war, Canada's role disappeared; it was no longer much consulted and its co-operation was taken for granted. Roosevelt and Churchill met twice at Quebec during the war to plan strategy, occasions in which Mackenzie King was much in evidence, bustling about and posing in pictures giving the impression that Canada retained its linchpin role. But he was more hotelier than host; Canada had no effective voice in Allied strategy. Even the British began to worry late in the war about their place in a post-war world dominated by the United States, and they floated the old idea of Commonwealth unity on foreign policy as a counterweight. But the Canadians, sensing a resurrection of British domination, quickly scotched that notion. In this new dispensation, Canada preferred to establish its political autonomy vis-à-vis the United States and assert its interests in the wider world through multilateral organizations. Through these, it was hoped, middle powers like Canada could achieve status and standing in international affairs commensurate with their contributions.

As the government of Canada embarked upon its post-war domestic social agenda, it thus made some fundamental changes in its external policy in a much-changed world. As the Canadian people readjusted to civilian life after the Depression and war, they too made personal choices with equally profound long-range consequences. These public and private choices accelerated the transformation of the Canadian nation.

In the post-war regime, the government of Canada abandoned the isolationism and protectionism that had characterized the inter-war era and made a choice for an active internationalism on both the political and economic fronts. Canada could best promote its interests, protect its citizens, and contribute to international security by committing itself with other nations to a collective security regime and to the construction of the institutions deemed necessary to stabilize international relations, expand trade, and stabilize monetary affairs. Canada raised its international profile by greatly increasing the number of diplomatic missions abroad and playing an energetic role in the talks leading up to the founding of the United Nations and in the drafting of its Charter. Canada's previous position that Parliament would have to decide on each case of international intervention was replaced by a firm commitment to the principle of collective security in which international organizations would decide matters of peace and war. In economic affairs, Canada also adopted an internationalist approach. As a major exporting nation, Canada reasoned that it stood to benefit from a gradual liberalization of trade and stabilization of international monetary relations. At the Bretton Woods conference in 1944, Canada participated in the creation of the International Monetary Fund, the International Bank for Reconstruction and Development, and a system of fixed exchange rates tied to the US dollar. An international trade organization did not emerge from that meeting, but Canada supported the later creation of the General Agreement on Tariffs and Trade aimed at reducing barriers to international trade.

⌒

Canada opened its doors to immigration as a humanitarian measure to alleviate suffering and to expand the Canadian economy. More than 100,000 displaced persons from Europe were admitted. Canadian policy-makers also sought, through immigration, to obtain the skilled workers needed to sustain its program of industrialization and expand the productive labour force through immigration. Canada undertook aggressive efforts to recruit skilled immigrants abroad, especially in northwestern Europe and the United Kingdom. Immigration in the late 1940s returned to levels not seen since the 1920s, and in the 1950s an average of about 150,000 immigrants annually sought new homes in Canada. Heavy immigration in turn created a large domestic constituency favouring further immigration.

The government of Canada explicitly linked its immigration policy to what it termed 'the absorptive capacity' of the Canadian economy. The open door remained closed to those who might change the fundamental composition of the Canadian population. Canada retained its race-based policy of discouraging, if not excluding, non-white immigrants. A fundamental contradiction lay at the root of Canadian policy. At the international level Canada reluctantly subscribed to a rights-based, antidiscriminatory regime represented by the United Nations Universal Declaration of Human Rights, yet it practised systematic racial discrimination in its own immigration policies. Eventually, these contradictions would have to be resolved. In the meantime, even a restrictive immigration program had begun to change the ethnic composition of Canada. In the first decade after the war, about 30 per cent of Canada's immigrants came from Britain, another 30 per cent or so from northeastern Europe, especially Germany, the Netherlands, Belgium, Austria, and Sweden, and about 35 per cent from central, eastern and southern Europe, in particular Italy, Portugal, Spain, and Greece. Asian immigration was restricted to less than 5 per cent of the total. Thus after the war the non-English, non-French proportion of the population increased, reasserting the multicultural dimension of Canadian society.

The intimate private choices of millions of Canadians, however, had much more influence over the growth of the population than did immigration. The marriage rate, which had fallen off dramatically during the Depression, spiked just before the outbreak of war and during its early stages as couples seized what they believed to be their last chance to unite. Marriage rates fell off significantly as the fighting dragged on. However, when the men and women returned from war, a burst of new marriages (counterbalanced in part by a corresponding uptick in divorces) and a resumption of deferred conjugal relations resulted in a sudden increase in the birth rate. The crude birth rate rose sharply and stayed elevated. In the 1930s, Canadian families produced an average of 230,000 babies each year; after the war, that number rose to over 350,000. Moreover, with a higher proportion of the population married, with marriages occurring somewhat earlier, and with couples choosing (or accepting their fate) to have more children over the course of their marriage, the 'baby boom' that began in 1946 continued unabated into the 1950s. Fertility rates peaked in 1958–9 at 54 per cent above pre-war levels.

All regions of the country experienced this increase, though curiously Quebec seems to have been less sharply affected than other provinces. This sudden and sustained burst of fertility produced a huge bulge at the bottom of the Canadian age–sex pyramid, which, over time, would gradually move up through the age cohorts. A sudden drop in fertility rates in the 1960s as a result of improved and legalized birth control methods and changing family preferences accentuated the bulge by constricting the cohorts that followed. The baby boom, like the legendary pig in the python, would move inexorably forward in time with rip-

> *The baby boom was like the legendary pig in the python.*

pling economic, social, cultural, and political consequences. Provincial governments in particular initially faced the challenge of housing these growing families, and doubling the number of hospitals and schools. As the baby boomers aged, these swollen demographics would subsequently strain the capacity of higher education, the economy, and, much later, pensions, and health and social services.

Domestic optimism founded upon one of the most remarkable and extended periods of economic expansion in Canadian history explains the extended reign of the baby boom—which lasted much longer in Canada than most other countries. For two decades after the Second World War, Canadian economic growth averaged more than 5 per cent compounded annually. There were some ups and downs of course—0 per cent growth in 1954 and over 9 per cent in 1958—but the prosperity was widely shared as wages and salaries rose across the board in real terms.

Many factors contributed to this strong post-war economic growth, but two in particular stand out: expansion of Canada's natural-resource export industries, and a rapid increase of investment and demand occasioned by Canada's rapidly growing population. Traditional sectors—forest products and mining—expanded to serve mainly US markets. New resource industries flourished as well: mines in northern Ontario and Saskatchewan produced uranium to fuel nuclear reactors and arm American atomic bombs. Canada's abundant and cheap hydroelectricity drew bauxite ores from the Caribbean and elsewhere to electrolytic refiners in Quebec and later British Columbia, where it was turned into aluminum. The most spectacular development in the resource sector, though, occurred in 1947 with the discovery of a major oil field just south of Edmonton. The subsequent rapid expansion of the oil and gas sector in Alberta with its associated refining, pipeline, and distribution activities stimulated the economic growth and development especially of western Canada. As usual, growth on the resource frontier was uneven. Coal mining in eastern and western Canada experienced adjustment problems as oil and the diesel engine displaced coal and steam as the main motive power on the railways. Oil, too, made inroads in home heating. The agricultural sector increased its production of wheat, meat, and dairy products, but with much less labour and far more capital than before. As the service, manufacturing, and resource sectors expanded, agricultural labour as a proportion of the total labour force fell from about 20 per cent at the end of the war to around 10 per cent in the 1960s. Growth in rural Canada was thus much less marked than that of the towns and cities.

The rise of an affluent, child-centred, consumer society provided an additional impetus to economic growth. The increasing number of families and their growing size created a powerful demand for houses, consumer goods, consumer durables such as furniture, stoves, and refrigerators, and with the new-found affluence, an irresistible desire for that ultimate symbol of North American freedom: the automobile. Abundant spaces combined with a taste for single-family garden homes sent Canadian towns and cities sprawling into vast suburbs. With so many mothers at home raising children, the proportion of women in the labour force declined temporarily.

Sustained consumer demand stimulated heavy capital investment in manufacturing and distribution, much of it foreign investment, mainly from the United States, in manufacturing and resources. The auto sector, for example, consisted almost entirely of US subsidiaries. All levels of government invested heavily in housing, hospitals, schools, utilities, infrastructure, and, of course, roads to carry the growing number of automobiles. Provincial governments assumed control of hydroelectric systems and took on other public sector 'province-building' schemes. Public and private investment, expanding employment, increasing per capita incomes, expanding demand for consumer goods and especially consumer durables, created a virtuous circle of growth feeding more growth.

This more or less unbroken era of prosperity also financed a rich flowering of Canadian cultural activities and an expansion of leisure. Gradually, too, a new urban sensibility began to emerge in Canada's most rapidly growing metropolitan areas. Subways, modernist architecture, theatres, art galleries, symphony orchestras, sports, media, and entertainment became as Canadian as forests, lakes, wheat fields, and banks.

Canada's new-found wealth may have been broadly based, but

it was not evenly shared. Indigenous peoples on their Reserves and in the North did not benefit. The increasing scale and capital intensity of agriculture drove many people off their farms. Fallout from immigration and urban migration expanded the pools of wretched urban poverty. Nevertheless across the vast majority of the population the standard of living improved dramatically during the 1950s.

༄—

All of this took place in the shadow of nuclear war. A good case can be made that the Cold War broke out in Canada in late 1945 when a notorious Soviet code clerk Igor Guzenko defected, carrying with him abundant evidence of Soviet espionage in Canada and elsewhere. Soviet spy rings acquired nuclear secrets in the United States and Great Britain and soon an expansive Soviet Union possessed atomic and then thermonuclear weapons. At first, Europe was the front line in this struggle between the nuclear superpowers. An airlift by the United States and Great Britain kept the beleaguered western sectors of Berlin alive in 1949 in the face of a Soviet ground blockade. Communist takeovers threatened in a number of unstable countries. In the suppressed but potentially lethal conflict between the Communist Soviet Union and the West, the Canadians identified overwhelmingly with the anti-Communist containment doctrine of the United States. With the United Nations immobilized, Canada participated actively in the formation of the North Atlantic Treaty Organization (NATO) in 1949, sending ground troops and air force personnel overseas to defend western Europe. Canada hoped that this European North Atlantic alliance would in some respects provide a counterweight against overwhelming US influence in foreign relations. When the United States led a UN force into Korea in 1950 to repel Soviet-supported aggression from North Korea and then China, Canada too sent a significant military contingent to prevent another Communist takeover in Southeast Asia.

With the advent of long-range strategic bombers, Canada itself became the trans-polar front line in any all-out conflict between the United States and the Soviet Union. During the early 1950s with Canadian approval, the United States built a ring of radar stations in the North to provide early warning of any attack. To ensure coordinated hemispheric defence Canada and the United States created the North American Air Defence Command (NORAD) in 1957 to detect and jointly intercept an airborne attack. In self-defence, and fully sharing the US ideological alarm at the rise of an expansionist nuclear armed Soviet regime, Canada willingly entered military alliances, allowed its forces to come under foreign command, sent troops abroad to distant theatres of combat, and gave the United States considerable liberties within its borders. Under the threat of nuclear war and without much anxiety, the niceties of sovereignty were set to one side.

Canada remained very much a junior partner in this North American alliance. Its technological and military capabilities paled by comparison with those of the United States. Canada had been a participant in some of the wartime nuclear research, but it had not been involved in the ultimate construction of nuclear weapons. Nor did it proceed to make or acquire its own. Rather Canada directed its nuclear program exclusively towards peaceful medical- and power-production purposes. Canada's small size and its lack of nuclear weapons kept it in the political minor leagues in its relations with the United States. However, Canada had a strategic location, it was a source of a host of important materials needed by the US arsenal, and of course, it was a region in which a significant proportion of US international corporate assets were located. Canada was important to the United States despite itself.

The Cold War may have thrown Canada into the arms of the United States, but bonds of trade, investment, and above all Canadian enthusiasm for American material goods and popular culture, ensured that it would be a mutual embrace.

After 1945 Canada gradually cut many of its formal ties with Great Britain. In a 1949 referendum, the British dependency of Newfoundland voted narrowly to join Canada as a tenth province. Many Newfoundlanders sentimentally preferred Dominion status of their own, which they could not afford, and Britain was determined to be rid of its anachronistic North American colonial encumbrance. Canada's social programs, especially unemployment insurance, the baby bonus, and federal grants to provincial governments enticed a majority of voters. In 1949, Canada fished, filling out its territorial boundaries with the acquisition of Newfoundland, and Britain cut bait.

The few remaining formal ties between Canada and Great Britain also dropped away at this time. Canada ended legal appeals to the Judicial Committee of the Privy Council in Britain in 1949. The Supreme Court, which had been in existence since the 1870s, finally became the highest court of appeal for Canadian cases. The Queen acquiesced too in 1952 to the appointment of a Canadian governor general. Her representative in Canada would no longer be a British aristocrat or a British general who had commanded Canadian troops in combat, but rather a distinguished Canadian citizen selected by the government of Canada. Indeed, only the Queen herself, the Union Jack on the Canadian Ensign flag, and the curious situation that the major document of the Canadian Constitution, the British North America Act, remained a British statute that could be amended only by the British Parliament, remained as links to the old Empire. Canadians professed interest in the British Commonwealth of Nations, and there remained a good deal of sentimental attachment to things British—especially royalty—among recent British immigrants and older English-speaking Canadians. But economically and politically Canada had clearly drifted away from British influence.

The extent of that detachment could be measured in 1956 when Britain, France, and Israel invaded Egypt to protest the nationalization of the Suez Canal. The United States took a dim view of this operation. At the United Nations a worthwhile Canadian initiative, a multinational peacekeeping force, provided the diplomatic middle ground that defused the crisis. It won a Nobel Peace Prize for the Canadian minister of external affairs, Lester Pearson. It also earned Canada the resentment of the government of Great Britain. From Britain's perspective Suez signalled that Canada had moved inescapably into the American orbit. And so it had.

⌒

Late in the 1950s the Liberal dynasty, established by Wilfrid Laurier and neurotically maintained by his long-running successor, Mackenzie King, stumbled uncharacteristically, and the government changed hands. In a carefully managed succession King had followed Laurier; then Louis St Laurent, a Quebec lawyer, replaced King in 1948. The Liberal party established itself as the governing party of the century by maintaining a solid hold on Quebec and gathering enough seats in the rest of the country to form a government. As long as the opposition could not break into Quebec in a major way, this formula worked magically. The Liberal party nurtured this outcome by kindling unhappy memories of the Conservative's past hostility to Quebec and by alternating the apostolic succession between English and French leaders. Louis St Laurent, a gentle but somewhat distant and austere figure, dubbed by the press 'Uncle Louis', presided over a government of managers, men in grey suits and snap-brimmed fedoras who rode the club cars between Ottawa, Montreal, and Toronto. The electorate eventually tired of them, especially when the impatient managers overstepped the boundaries of acceptable behaviour, ramming a controversial pipeline bill through Parliament with closure, the forced end to debate. However right or capable the Liberals might be, they needed to be taught a lesson. Gradually that indefinable but ineluctable mood settled in over many parts of the country. It was time for a change.

The Conservative party for once offered a striking alternative, something completely different. John Diefenbaker, a country lawyer from northern Saskatchewan, had wrenched the party out of the hands of the businessmen from Montreal's St James Street and Toronto's Bay Street who had run it for many years. A theatrical orator of the old school, a Prairie populist who cast himself as the protector of the little man against the interests, John Diefenbaker expanded the Conservative party's popularity beyond its usual constituencies. Diefenbaker tapped into deep-rooted anxieties about the extent of US dominance and the steady erosion of the country's British heritage. He promised to divert more trade to Great Britain, professed a mawkish loyalty to the Crown, and offered Canadians a vague vision of alternative, more self-directed economic development in the North. But he attracted voters more by his style than his substance.

Diefenbaker was in some ways a throwback to an earlier era and at the same time a modern figure, made for the media. On the hustings he was a strange but compelling man, with his wavy lightning-bolt hair, rheumy eyes, and hawklike facial features. As he jabbed his finger in accusation, growled in admonition, then shook his head in judgement, his ample jowls would waggle. Palms on his hips, elbows splayed out holding back the invisible lawyer's gown, puffed up like a peacock, he would tear into his opponents, to the delight of the crowd, taunt them like a bear baiter, and, when he had made a particularly malicious debating point, he would burst into a great Cheshire-cat grin, his full rack of prominent teeth gleaming in exclamation. As a self-portrayed outsider he flayed his political opponents, displaying an unerring instinct for the jugular. The haughty presumptuousness and sputtering rage of the Liberals provided him with an abundance of plump targets. A raucous, gaudy, exotic bird in a parliamentary aviary of grey sparrows, Diefenbaker arrived as a gift to cartoonists and comedians, and made himself a much-loved figure on the side streets and back concessions of the country.

In the 1957 general election the Conservatives won enough seats to form a minority government. After the Liberals had anointed a successor to Uncle Louis, Lester Pearson, and then incautiously

> *Diefenbaker arrived as a gift to cartoonists and comedians.*

demanded that the Conservatives relinquish power to the party with the hereditary right to govern, Diefenbaker gleefully called an election in 1958 and won in a landslide, piling up the largest majority in Canadian history to that time. Diefenbaker and the Conservatives seized control, determined to take government in a different direction. Diefenbaker was good at the grand gesture. He appointed the first female Cabinet minister; he passed a Bill of Rights applicable to federal fields of jurisdiction. It was routine administration and crisis management that exposed his weaknesses. Inevitably too the media turned against him. The electric presence all too easily came across as self-parody.

His government was not helped by a mild recession, a sudden rise in unemployment, and a jolting devaluation of the Canadian dollar. From today's vantage point we may look wistfully back at a

92-cent dollar, but then, mocked as a 'Diefenbuck', it was regarded as shocking evidence of economic mismanagement. The government got into an unseemly spat with the governor of the Bank of Canada over his tight monetary policy. As the title of a popular journalistic account of the administration declared, Diefenbaker acted as a classic *Renegade in Power*.[1]

The qualities that made him an outstanding leader of the opposition did not serve him well as prime minister. He was suspicious of the civil servants, did not wholly trust his ministers, tried to make all the key decisions himself, and then procrastinated. Ultimately, foreign policy failures fatally wounded the Diefenbaker administration. With no great subtlety the Diefenbaker government had sought to distance itself from the United States and assert an independent Canadian point of view. This was a harmless instinct on ordinary occasions. However, when Canada was seen to fall out of step with the United States in a moment of extreme crisis, dire consequences ensued. In the early 1960s, the US tried and failed to invade Cuba; then the Soviet union was found to be surreptitiously preparing to install intercontinental ballistic missiles there. With the world to the brink of nuclear war, the Diefenbaker government had the temerity to hesitate in the mobilization of its armed forces, suggesting that it did not fully share the US view of the situation. The military made preparations anyway. Mercifully, the apocalypse was avoided. But the US administration deeply resented what it interpreted as Canadian insubordination.

However justified the response, it also troubled the Canadian people who were for the most part in the thrall of the United States

---

1   Diefenbaker exacted a cruel revenge upon the author, a swashbuckling ladies man of middle-European origin, dismissing him as 'the bouncing Czech'.

and saw the crisis through the eyes of the US media. What appeared then as Canadian obstinacy became unbearable as Diefenbaker's defence policy descended into farce. The Diefenbaker government had willingly entered a military alliance with the United States, permitted overflights by US military aircraft, allowed US radar station and military installations onto Canadian soil, and accepted US missile batteries. Canada too had cancelled its indigenous interceptor aircraft program, relying henceforth on US military procurement as an economy measure. The missiles located in north-central Canada required nuclear armament to be effective against massed Soviet bombers. But when the time came to commission them, Diefenbaker refused to accept nuclear tips or give the US control over them. The missiles sat, pointed harmlessly at the sky, with sandbags in place of nose cones. Already in a minority position following a disastrous general election in 1962, the Diefenbaker government collapsed. A modest revival of Liberal electoral fortunes in the general election of 1964 put it out of its misery.

Lester Pearson's Liberals could not muster enough support, however, to form a majority government. The sudden rise and persistence of third parties prevented the Liberals from gaining full control over the House of Commons: on the right a low-tax, anti-statist Social Credit party attracted support in British Columbia, Alberta, and surprisingly, rural Quebec, and on the left a social democratic party (the descendant of the CCF) with a formal link to the labour movement, reorganized under the name the New Democratic Party, gained popularity among the fishermen, loggers, and farmers of the West, and the urban industrial workers of the East. Across the aisle John Diefenbaker continued as leader of the Progressive Conservative opposition, embarrassing the Liberal government at every opportunity—and there were many indiscretions great and small upon which he gleefully pounced.

Forced onto the defensive by Conservative accusations of impropriety, the Liberals exposed a racy scandal of their own to besmirch the reputation of the Opposition. While the Conservatives had been in power, a courtly, French-Canadian cabinet minister with a distinguished war record had kept a mistress, a husky voiced, full-figured German lady of a certain age. As the extent of the cabinet minister's official duties left her with considerable time on her hands, she began seeing a handsome young military attaché, who happened to be Russian. The spectacle of a Russian spy and a minister of the Crown sleeping with the same woman at the very least raised security issues that the previous government had studiously ignored. What state secrets might have been divulged in her pillow talk? The press and tabloid television roared into full-throttle indignation at each salacious revelation, quite satisfied with themselves that they had manufactured a sex and security scandal to rival that of the British.

Diefenbaker, however, lingered in politics like a bad smell in the basement, resented even among his own party. But as long as he stayed, his loyal following in the Conservative party, combined with the regional appeal of third parties, denied the Liberals a majority. Then when the Liberals finally won a majority, Diefenbaker's presence polarized politics and poisoned the atmosphere in the House of Commons. The sour wrangling of grumpy old men, bitter warriors incapable of putting each other away, to a certain extent discredited politics. A diffident, perennially frustrated Lester Pearson lacked the kill instinct or the political skill to deliver the stiletto blow; that was left to the treachery of Diefenbaker's own party. These were not the worst of times, but they weren't good.

An alternative politics found its expression in the streets as the vanguard of the baby boomers came of age. The vacuous noise of the House of Commons contrasted with the sacrifice and idealism of the civil rights movement and the campaign to prevent nuclear war with which Canadian youth strongly identified. The Kennedy era, ended with an assassin's bullet, made Canadian politics seem parochial. The shallow film-set sordidness of the so-called Camelot only showed up later, but that would not have made much difference at the time. The bright lights of pop culture, sport, sex, drugs, and rock and roll cast the moral censoriousness of previous generations into an outer darkness. Youth created an extra-parliamentary politics of its own.

Yet quite a lot of important public work got done amid all the parliamentary bickering. Canadian immigration policy was reformed in 1962, replacing cultural absorptive capacity with selection criteria based upon labour force skills. In theory, and in large measure in practice, Canada adopted a race-blind immigration policy. Since the door remained open, and the sources of immigration had shifted from Europe to Asia, this policy would have enormous social implications for the future. In 1965, Canada and the United States negotiated an Auto Pact in their most important mutual industry. The US companies in Canada agreed as a minimum to make as many cars in Canada as were sold in Canada. Meanwhile, the big three US automakers and their customers across the continent benefited from the economies of scale of a North American market in parts and manufacturing. The Auto Pact underpinned an important engine of Canadian economic growth and accelerated the trend towards continental economic integration.

On the foundation of a rapidly growing economy, federal and provincial governments expanded the scope of the welfare state. Many provincial governments in the late 1950s had introduced partial hospital insurance programs. In 1962 the social democratic government of Saskatchewan, under the leadership of Tommy Douglas, launched a program of socialized medicine in the province over the objection of striking doctors. The Diefenbaker government appointed a royal commission to investigate the possibility of establishing a comprehensive medical insurance scheme for all of Canada. It fell to his Liberal successors to implement Mr. Justice Emmet Hall's report that endorsed that project. In 1966 the Liberal minister of health, Judy LaMarsh, negotiated a federal–provincial agreement that established nationwide contributory Medicare. By the early 1970s socialized medicine was looked upon as the crown jewel of the Canadian welfare state. A contributory pension plan raised huge sums for social investment in hospitals, schools, roads, and higher education, while at the same time supplementing other old age security policies. Within a generation Canadians would regard these social programs as one of the defining characteristics of their nation and consider them a 'sacred trust' not to be meddled with.

Canada also re-branded itself with a new symbol. The government adopted a new and distinctive red Maple Leaf flag after a prolonged and exceedingly bitter parliamentary battle almost everyone now forgets. A characteristic Canadian maple-leaf image with which all Canadians might identify replaced a British symbol, the Ensign. Legislation caught up with social change. The minister of justice reformed the Criminal Code, in the process legalizing abortion and the dissemination of birth control information, and decriminalizing homosexuality with the famous justification that the state had no business in the bedrooms of the nation.

Tensions and anxieties remained in Canada–US relations. Apprehension about overwhelming US economic and political influence on the Canadian side, especially high levels of foreign investment, raised the spectre of Canada becoming a de facto colony of the United States. A nationalist minister of finance vainly attempted to stem the flow of US ownership of Canadian industry, but his fumbling efforts, and the strength of his continentalist opponents within the government, led to an ignominious retreat. The United States too harboured its grievances. While Canada squared itself with the United States on the strategic nuclear arms issue, Prime Minister Lester Pearson, the confirmed internationalist, and a majority of Canadians could not align themselves wholly with the escalating US engagement with a communist revolution in Vietnam. Canadians learned that the Quiet Diplomacy they had hoped would permit them to exercise influence with the United States did not always work. When Pearson issued a mild criticism of US policy during a speech in Philadelphia, the president of the United States stunned him with a harangue afterwards at Camp David. In the kind of diplomatic language apparently

> *Canadians learned that Quiet Diplomacy did not always work.*

preferred in Texas, Lyndon Johnson accused Lester Pearson of 'pissing on his rug'.

⌒

A revolution at home, albeit a quiet one in Quebec, posed the greatest challenge to the government of Canada throughout the 1960s. For most of the century, Quebec had been passively self-absorbed, a traditional agricultural-forestry and growing urban-industrial society centred around the Catholic Church. Political elites brokered relations with business and with the federal government, both of which operated in English. Canada, as a result, was a country of 'two solitudes', in the apt phrase of a novelist, a French minority focussed upon its own affairs within Quebec and an English majority largely indifferent to this self-sufficient French enclave. The rise of the welfare state, especially promoted by a centralizing federal government, and an integrated national, even continental, economy, upset this tacit political arrangement. French-speaking Canadians also became increasingly conscious of gross social inequalities. As the media, work, and bureaucracy drew them into contact with a wider world, they bristled at the knowledge that they were second-class citizens in their own country—economically disadvantaged, a political minority, unable to conduct business in their own language even at home in Quebec. Quebecers particularly resented the anachronistic persistence of monarchial symbols, which they interpreted as signs of colonial domination. They also resisted interference by the federal government in their own affairs. During the 1950s a conservative, moderately nationalist, anti-statist Union Nationale provincial government in Quebec simply refused to participate in federal programs for highways, higher education, and a host of other measures. It simply didn't take the money offered. That, of course, would not last long.

In its search for greater autonomy, a new government of Quebec, elected in 1960, shifted from a policy of defensive reaction and isolation within the federation to aggressive constitutional challenges to the status quo. The election of the provincial Liberal party under Jean Lesage inaugurated a six-year period of rapid change that an anonymous newspaper headline writer at the time described as a Quiet Revolution. It was quiet because no shots were fired and much of the insurgency took place in federal–provincial conferences, but no less revolutionary on that account. Almost overnight, Quebec society, culture, and politics experienced an exhilarating revival. The revolution had three main targets: the Catholic Church, the English economic elite, and the federal government. Secularization, economic and social modernization, and greater political autonomy were the primary goals of the movement. The provincial Liberals shared the interventionist, welfare-state ideology of the federal government. However, they wanted to go one step further, using the provincial rather than the federal state as the instrument to modernize the society, liberate its people economically, and 'catch up' with the rest of the country. The provincial government did not see the need for federal direction; indeed it believed the province was able to design and deliver its own programs if the federal government would give it the room to tax and spend as it saw fit. A new, self-confident, assertive nationalism inspired a generation of well-educated Quebecers to be 'masters in their own house'. To realize this objective Quebecers believed the terms and conditions of Confederation would have to be fundamentally changed.

Once in office the provincial Liberal government assumed responsibility for education, health, and some social services, displacing the Catholic Church. In a deeply symbolic move, the Lesage government seized the commanding heights of the provincial economy from English capitalists by nationalizing the large, private hydroelectric companies. French Canadians thus took charge of the largest, most technologically sophisticated organization in the province and set about running it in French. As the federal government proposed new social policies dealing with health, pensions, and education, the Quebec government demanded the right to opt out, but insisted upon compensation in return to fund programs of its own design. The Quiet Revolution transformed Quebec society, unleashed a new culturally vibrant nationalist spirit, and posed a major challenge to the constitutional status quo. Even when the old Union Nationale party defeated the Liberals in 1966, the new government of Premier Daniel Johnston showed itself to be just as nationalist as its predecessor. Indeed, his political manifesto, entitled in English *Equality or Independence,* bluntly and succinctly encapsulated Quebec's goal and levelled a powerful challenge to the federal government and the rest of the country.

On the margins of this nationalist revival within Quebec, there were disturbing signs of real revolutionary activity. A fringe terrorist group, the Front de libération du Québec (FLQ), borrowing freely from the rhetoric and tactics of a well-known Algerian guerrilla movement, took to bombing symbols of English domination—post boxes bearing royal insignia and monuments—and more troubling, robbing banks and munitions depots. The FLQ fought not only for the self-determination of Quebec, but also for a social revolution within Quebec itself. Voices calling for separation and complete independence, though still on the political fringe, were accorded a more sympathetic hearing in Quebec. In bewilderment, the rest of the country wondered aloud what Quebec wanted, fearing that the end game of greater autonomy would be an independent Quebec. Quebec had awakened as if from a long sleep, and citizens of the country, of English, French, and other origins, worried about some of the nightmarish possibilities. In the face of this challenge, Lester Pearson's government did what Canadian governments usually do in such situations; it struck the Royal Commission on Bilingualism and Biculturalism to investigate the situation, condition public opinion with its hearings and studies, recommend action that might be taken to make French-speaking Quebecers full partners in Canadian society, and in the meantime, buy time.

These anxieties over the federation and Canada's subordinate position in the new world order inserted a discordant note into the highly orchestrated celebration of the Centennial of Confederation in 1967. The federal government used the occasion to cultivate a broader Canadian national spirit. In the place of British honours,

Canada established its own three-tiered Order of Canada to recognize significant individual achievements. At the popular level a Centennial Train roamed the country carrying displays of notable achievements in Canadian history and technology. The federal government shared the funding of community-sponsored projects—hockey rinks, curling arenas, civic centres, parks, and monuments—in towns and cities all across the country. In Ottawa the government built the National Arts Centre as a lasting legacy of the Centennial and a showcase for the Canadian performing arts. A revival of popular interest in Canadian history and literature provided a needed boost to Canadian publishing and the cultural industries generally. In Montreal a glittering World's Fair, Expo '67, put Canadian design and technological prowess on display. Crowds flocked to the Expo site to experience the visual and aural spectacle of the strikingly modernist vision of Man and His World. Tingling to the popular anthems of nationalism, Canadians imagined what a modern and sophisticated people they were becoming in the eyes of the world.

While Expo was intended to point the way toward the future, in some ways it and the Centennial gestured backwards to an old Canada that was passing. The celebration of Canadian nationalism during the Centennial also revealed some embarrassing cracks in the façade of national unity. The Centennial Train was a throwback to an earlier era when railroads mattered. Most of the festivities involved English and French; indigenous peoples and Canadians of other origins seemed left out. However modern Man and His World might be in style, in language it denied the aspirations of the increasingly vocal women of the country. About this time the proportion of women in the labour force surpassed that of the Second World War. As part of an international movement Canadian women too demanded equality of opportunity, equal pay for work of equal value, and greater political representation so that women's issues would form a larger part of the national agenda. That same year the Royal Commission on the Status of Women would address this compelling demand for equity. In retrospect we can see more clearly that socially, at least, the Centennial was the last hurrah of the old Canada.

Politically, too, it marked the passing of an era, as separatism was openly espoused. In 1967, René Lévesque, the popular former minister who had overseen the nationalization of the Quebec hydroelectric industry, left the Liberal party to form a new political movement dedicated to Quebec sovereignty. Then the visit of General Charles De Gaulle to Canada dramatically drew world attention to Canada's internal difficulties. Arriving on a French battleship in Quebec, De Gaulle set off in a motorcade along the historic route from Quebec City to Montreal through teeming, cheering crowds. Once in Montreal, on the balcony of the city hall, whether on the spur of the moment or with a calculated eye to a future with France standing beside an independent Quebec, De Gaulle uttered the immortal words that still resonate in Canadian popular memory: 'Vive le Québec'—with a pause for dramatic effect, and then a rolling, roaring—'Vive le Québec libre!' For some Quebec nationalists these words from the mouth of the president of France represented international recognition of their political struggle. For a majority of Canadians these shocking words, spoken to a free and democratic people by a man whose country had twice been liberated at some considerable sacrifice by Canadian arms, were the height of gall. Apparently bemused by the fury he had stirred up De Gaulle cut short his tour without going to Ottawa for a state visit. He retreat-

Socially, the Centennial was the last hurrah of the old Canada.

ed to his battleship quite pleased with himself—before the government of Canada kicked him out.

<o—

These were the extraordinary circumstances within which Pierre Elliott Trudeau rose to become leader of the federal Liberal party and prime minister of Canada in 1968. Trudeau had been one of three prominent Quebecers whom Lester Pearson had brought into his government to help it respond to French-Canadian aspirations. As minister of justice he had been responsible for the reform of the Criminal Code, and at Pearson's right hand during several federal–provincial conferences he had challenged the premier of Quebec. In various essays as an academic, Trudeau had composed a classical liberal critique of nationalism; in the cockpit of Quebec politics he had developed a personal dislike of many French-Canadian nationalists. As minister of justice Trudeau had the primary responsibility of formulating the federal government's response to the constitutional challenge posed by the province of Quebec. At a tumultuous leadership convention in the spring of 1968, the Liberal party characteristically elected to follow an English-Canadian leader with a French Canadian, and to reach out to a new generation of Canadians by choosing Trudeau, a relative outsider. He eschewed the old-fashioned politics of buying people with their own money; instead he promised a 'Just Society', a vague but noble-sounding goal that resonated with the women, French Canadians across the country, and the idealistic baby boomers just coming of age. A well-travelled, cosmopolitan intellectual, Trudeau was also a handsome bachelor who attracted beautiful women. Fluently bilingual, and above all cool, he offered Canadians an image of themselves not as they were but as they wanted to be. He appealed to some Quebecers because he was one of them; it must be said too that his popularity among some

English Canadians rested upon the belief that the bilingual minister of justice who had dared confront the premier of Quebec would also put Quebec in its place. For most people, Trudeau seemed to promise a welcome renewal of the country. In the ensuing general election, in which popular excitement about the new prime minister approached pop-star proportions and was dubbed Trudeaumania, Trudeau and the Liberal party won an overwhelming majority centred on Quebec and Ontario.

Trudeau set in motion federal–provincial dialogue aimed at reforming the Canadian Constitution to address some long-standing jurisdictional issues within the federation and in particular to respond to the demands of Quebec. Other provinces shared many of Quebec's concerns, but the province of Quebec would not commit itself to a consistent final position, lending support to the suspicion that its end game was not constitutional reform but rather ultimate independence. In these seemingly interminable discussions, Trudeau refused to follow the former government's policy of making an exception for Quebec by steadily conceding jurisdiction and taxing powers. This could only end in his mind in the creation of a special status for the province of Quebec. Some people thought special status might cure Canada's debilitating constitutional paralysis. Trudeau disagreed. Quebec exceptionalism, he believed, would lead to the gradual erosion of the federation. It would enhance the status of Quebec to the point that independence was but a small remaining step. In the pure logic of federalism, the more authority French Canadians had within their special province of Quebec, the less authority they could exercise within the government of Canada. He sought instead to answer the prospect of a French-Canadian retreat into

Excitement about the new prime minister approached pop-star proportions.

an autonomous, fortress called Quebec by making Canada a place where all Canadians, French Canadians included, might feel at home. If governments served Canadians in their own language, provided equal career opportunities for English- and French-speaking citizens, and created federal institutions that all Canadians would respect, Quebec could be a province like the others and Quebecers in turn could express themselves and realize their economic and political ambitions within the much wider boundaries of Canada. Trudeau thus offered an alternative to the evolving vision of a separate French-Canadian nation: a bilingual, bicultural Canada. The Official Languages Act passed in 1969 created a bilingual public service, and compelled the government of Canada to provide services in French across Canada where the number of French citizens so warranted.

Trudeau held out the hope that Canada could be saved, but only by undergoing a fundamental transformation. Subsequently, all prime ministers would be bilingual; capability in both languages became a requirement for high office and senior appointments in the public service. French language schools flourished, and enrolment in French immersion education programs increased dramatically among the urban English-speaking population. Trudeau's vision appealed to many French Canadians inside and outside Quebec; younger, urban English Canadians responded with enthusiasm to the idealism of national renewal and to the French language as never before. But for died-in-the-wool French-Canadian nationalists within the province of Quebec, Trudeau's pan-Canadian vision represented a dangerous delusion.

The FLQ struck with fiendish cleverness. Their targets were English domination and the bourgeoisie of Quebec. In the fall of 1970, in what came to be known as the October Crisis, terrorists kidnapped the British consul in Montreal, James Cross. Soon afterwards they abducted Pierre Laporte, minister of labour in the recently elected provincial Liberal government. These ruthless attacks and the chilling communiqués from the kidnappers instilled widespread panic. Both the old and experienced mayor of Montreal, Jean Drapeau, and the young and untried new premier of Quebec, Robert Bourassa, flinched. Amid chaos and confusion within their administrations, they jointly called upon the federal government to intervene to restore order and public confidence. Prime Minister Trudeau grasped the only antiterrorist weapons he had at his disposal, the War Measures Act and the army. The former, which could only be proclaimed in the event of war or real or apprehended insurrection, suspended the constitution and civil liberties. Tanks and troops began patrolling the streets of Montreal and federal installations in Ottawa.

These were blunt instruments but they worked. Using the War Measures Act, police rounded up hundreds of suspected FLQ sympathizers and held them without charges. Only in hindsight did it become clear that only a few dozen militants were involved. Nonetheless, for about a month the shadowy FLQ held the government of Canada hostage as a massive security operation combed Quebec. The government took the now-familiar hard line that it would not negotiate with terrorists. The grim discovery of the garrotted body of Pierre Laporte in the trunk of a car shook that resolve. The October Crisis ended as one group of kidnappers subsequently negotiated safe passage to Cuba in return for the life of the captive James Cross. The other FLQ cell, responsible for the murder of Pierre Laporte, was eventually located and brought to justice. But the whole grisly crisis represented a loss of innocence for a people who had fondly imagined they inhabited a peaceable kingdom. Moreover, in the classic mode of guerrilla theatre the FLQ strike discredited federalism by casting the federal government in the role of military occupier of Quebec and defender of the British. The indiscriminate arrests aimed at denying the FLQ support, which detained many prominent Quebec artists and intellectuals, caused a harsh backlash against the federal government and stripped Pierre Elliott Trudeau of his mantle as a civil libertarian.

In the background, partly screened by the electrifying flow of current events, some fundamental economic and social changes had been set in motion that would have a profound impact on the future of Canada. After 1965, when as usual about 75 per cent of immigrants arriving in Canada came from the United Kingdom, Europe, and the United States (about 10,000 of whom were young men evading the military draft for service in Vietnam), the origins of immigrants to Canada began to change. Over the next decade, the proportion of immigrants from Asia, the West Indies, and other parts of the world increased from 25 per cent to over 50 per cent of the total. The significance, of course, is that previously immigration had been linguistically plural but primarily white. During the 1970s, immigration to Canada originated in primarily non-white countries, a trend that would become more pronounced during the remainder of the century. Large and well-organized communities of visible minorities from Hong Kong, India, Pakistan, Vietnam, the West Indies, and Central and South America sprang up, especially in the cities. Immigration tested the tolerance of Canadians in new ways; the lessons of the US civil rights movement, with which Canadians had vicariously sympathized, now had to be learned and applied at home. Immigrants, older communities, and more recent arrivals demanded recognition of their contribution to the country alongside that of what was referred to at the time as the two 'founding peoples'. A policy of bilingualism and biculturalism had to be adjusted to one of bilingualism and multiculturalism to accommodate the increasing cultural and racial diversity of the country.

The female labour force participation rate continued to rise; so too did women's demand for equality. In 1966 women made up just over 30 per cent of the Canadian labour force; by the end of the 1970s the rate had risen to about 40 per cent. The Royal Commission on the Status of Women, reporting in 1970, rested its case for the full participation of women in the economic, social, and political life of the country upon the United Nations Universal Declaration of Human Rights. Equality between the sexes demanded a fundamental redrafting of laws, social programs, and employment practices that directly or indirectly discriminated against women. Canada had the benefit too of the demonstration effect and powerful media presence of the US women's movement. Women's organizations proved increasingly effective advocates in the political arena; women by their presence, persistence, and performance gained much greater recognition in the professions, higher education, business, and the arts.

A third equity issue crowded its way onto the political agenda. It echoed the cries for racial and sexual equality but took a quite different form. A population explosion in the Native communities of Canada had reversed a long-term trend of numerical decline. Natives had migrated in large numbers to the cities, especially in the West. However, poverty and extreme forms of social disintegration continued to plague indigenous peoples in both their urban enclaves and their rural Reserves. The distress of Canada's Native peoples had begun to attract international attention. Other countries regarded Canadian lectures on apartheid, racism, and human rights abuses as the height of hypocrisy in light of the plight of aboriginal peoples within Canada itself. The 'third world' within Canada was not going to go away and could no longer be ignored. In the late 1960s, the federal government, which had responsibility for Native affairs, broadly concluded that the best way to improve the welfare of indigenous peoples would be to make them full citizens of the society and address their economic and social problems within existing public policies. This classical liberal, individualistic approach of making them citizens galvanized Native organizations across the country.

The political revival of Native Canadians began with this struggle to have their collective rights recognized. In language shrewdly calculated to get attention in the ongoing debate between the two nations of English and French Canada, indigenous peoples began referring to themselves as First Nations. Native peoples as well as Quebecers became more assertive about their rights. They rested their claim to decent living standards and political autonomy upon prior occupation and principles enshrined in treaties that could

Indigenous peoples began referring to themselves as First Nations.

not be extinguished. These treaties confirmed their historical nationality as a people and laid down permanent terms and conditions between governments that must be fully honoured. Moreover, indigenous groups demanded compensation for lands—about one-half of Canadian territory—that they claimed had simply been taken without treaties. First Nations' leaders followed the logic of treaty rights more than human rights; they sought not to be citizens like the others, but rather to be separate self-governing peoples with a claim to fair dealing and well-being based upon their ownership of land, resources, and the terms of their treaties. First Nations' protests effectively blocked construction of a pipeline to the North and set in train land-claims negotiations with the federal government that continue to this day. In

1973, the Supreme Court formally recognized Native treaty rights, a judgement that elevated treaties subsequently to the level of fundamental constitutional documents alongside the British North America Act.

The long period of growth and prosperity upon which the welfare state and rising standard of living rested came to an abrupt end sometime around 1973. Growth rates that had routinely averaged 5 per cent during the 1950s and 1960s fell off to less than 3 per cent in the 1970s. Unemployment rates soared just as the baby boomers flooded onto the labour market. Prices, which ordinarily rose less than 3 per cent per year, ballooned upwards by 11 per cent in 1973. Inflation would remain at dangerously high levels for almost a decade. In the 1970s the economy sputtered and then entered a long period of stagnation.

The causes of this slowdown in growth, both domestic (political instability, demography, policy choices) and international (oil shocks, US monetary policy, war), can be identified with some precision. But a mystery remains. Productivity, which had driven improvements in living standards for several decades, began to decline all over the western world. The rapid rise of the labour-intensive service sector is suspected, but not yet proven. A much weaker, slower growing, and unstable economy thus had to sustain expensive health, education, and social security programs inherited from the past, as well as to sustain hopes for equity and social betterment in the future. No major welfare state proposals would be adopted after the 1960s, though some would be amended and improved. After 1974 the federal budget, which had been in balance for many years, plunged into ever deeper annual deficits. Both the federal and the provincial governments began borrowing from the future to pay their current obligations. The 1970s ushered in an intense period of economic, social, and political confrontation during which an old Canada began to transform itself anew.

Politically Prime Minister Trudeau's passions were constitutional reform and foreign policy. However, his constitutional initiative ran into a dead end when, after agreement at a federal–provincial conference in Victoria in 1971, the province of Quebec backed out. That effectively shelved the issue for a decade. The provinces blamed the federal government for the failure, citing federal insistence it should set standards for national social policy and Trudeau's dismissive, sometimes insulting negotiating manner. Others blamed the deadlock on excessive provincial demands and Quebec's refusal to be pinned down in any agreement. In foreign policy Trudeau hoped to find a new course for Canada between the assertive middle-power internationalism of the Pearson era and colonial clientage to US interests. His proposed independent foreign policy for Canada, a 'Third Way' based upon closer ties with Europe, Asia, and the Third World, seemed to fly in the face of the realities of Canada's geographical proximity to and close economic integration with the United States.

While Trudeau indulged his political passions without much success and concentrated on improving federal decision-making capability, he was condemned to grapple with urgent economic issues for which he displayed little aptitude. Selling Canadian wheat bored him. When President Nixon, in the face of rising unemployment and balance-of-payment deficits, devalued the US dollar and imposed a 10-per-cent import surtax, Canada had to beg an exemption based upon its supposed special relationship with the US. With visible reluctance in the face of pressure from economic nationalists Trudeau's government examined the question of high levels of foreign investment and then introduced a regulatory screening mechanism. On his watch, the federal government bought out one of the smaller European-owned oil companies in the overwhelmingly foreign-owned strategic sector, and used it to build a state-owned integrated oil company, Petro-Canada. But Trudeau showed only slightly less disdain for economic nationalism than he did for cultural and political nationalism.

When the Organization of Petroleum Exporting Countries (OPEC) cut back production and jacked up prices, Canada responded by maintaining a domestic price much lower than world prices and imposing an export tax on shipments to the US. Since Canada produced significant quantities of oil and gas in the West, which supplied most domestic requirements west of the Ottawa River and significant exports to the United States (which was paying world prices), federal policy protected eastern consumers at the expense of western producers. The proceeds of the export tax in effect paid for the higher cost imports for Atlantic Canada and Quebec. The oil shocks of the 1970s thus opened another deep rift within Confederation between the oil-producing provinces of the West, mainly Alberta, and the East. Federal policies in effect internalized the international struggle between oil-importing and oil-exporting countries in the form of federal–provincial conflict. The West had long felt alienated from a political union dominated by eastern interests; Canadian energy policy heightened western anger. Meanwhile higher energy prices, as they rippled through the Canadian economy, not only created a new East–West, producer–consumer tension within the federation, but also sent prices and wages into a frantic upward spiral. After campaigning against wage and price controls as a solution to this problem, Trudeau imposed just such a temporary remedy. He had begun to look like a politician, just like the others.

Then in 1976 Trudeau suffered his most embarrassing setback, on his own home turf, as the province of Quebec elected a Parti Québécois (PQ) government dedicated to the separation of Quebec. The insouciant charm of the popular and charismatic premier, René Lévesque, combined with his blithe assertion that Canada would have to negotiate a continuing economic association with an independent Quebec, made the bitter pill of separatism much easier for Quebecers to swallow. The Lévesque government promptly passed a language bill that made French the language of business and government in Quebec, compelled immigrants to attend French schools, and made French the dominant language on all signs. The PQ election, however, initiated a major exodus of anxious English Quebecers and worried businesses out of Quebec, primarily to Toronto.

With a separatist government ruling Quebec, the West thoroughly disgruntled, and the East just gruntled, the economy in a mess, the deficit rising, and the dollar falling, the Liberal government wilted under mounting grievances. The bruised provincial premiers sniped away at Trudeau at every opportunity. In only a few years, Trudeau fell from pop-star adulation to being many people's favourite political punching bag. If Pierre Elliott Trudeau had retired from public life after his defeat in the 1978 general election, he would likely have gone down in history as one of Canada's less distinguished prime ministers, perhaps even as a failure. He would likely have been judged to have delivered much less than he promised and be remembered more for his style than his accomplishments. But that did not happen.

⁓

The minority Progressive Conservative government led by a young bilingual western Canadian, Joe Clark, lasted only 12 months. Clark's more accommodating 'community of communities' federalism made no more headway with the provinces towards breaking the constitutional log-jam than had Trudeau's harder line. On energy policy the government wavered between East and West. Then when Lévesque promised a referendum on separation, many people became anxious that Joe Clark might lack the experience and toughness required to debate the separatists and to convince Quebecers of the advantages of remaining in Canada. Clark's minority government, behaving as if it had a majority, fell over a measure to increase gasoline taxes. In the ensuing general election in 1980 Pierre Elliott Trudeau and the Liberal party returned to power to face the greatest political crisis in the history of Confederation.

The referendum of 1980 did not ask Quebecers if they wished to separate. Rather the question posed was designed to secure the maximum number of affirmative responses. Quebecers, when polled, have never been in favour of outright independence or separatism. So Lévesque's referendum asked Quebecers if they wished to give the government a mandate to negotiate an agreement with the government of Canada intended to create a sovereign Quebec within a restructured Confederation. The referendum campaign brought the two powerful gladiators of Canadian politics, Trudeau and Lévesque, into head-to-head confrontation. Lévesque played upon the humiliations and frustrations experienced by Quebecers since the conquest and promised that sovereignty-association would free the two founding peoples to pursue their own destinies within their own governments without dysfunctional interference with one another. Trudeau defended federalism, his own version of Quebec within Canada, and he promised to bring home and revise the Constitution during his term of office. When the votes were counted the 'no' votes outnumbered the 'yes' votes by a ratio of 60 to 40. Political scientists stirring the entrails have determined that the Native, English, and ethnic voters in Quebec voted almost unanimously no; similarly they have calculated that 52 per cent of French-speaking voters also rejected authorizing sovereignty-association negotiations. The first round in this high-stakes political bout had gone to federalism. But Trudeau now had to deliver on his promises of constitutional reform to satisfy Quebecers' aspirations for a renewed federalism.

Constitutional reform advanced in several stages. The government developed its proposals; Parliament examined them. Federal–provincial talks, with Quebec absent, led to an impasse. The federal government consulted the Supreme Court as to whether it might proceed unilaterally without provincial consent. The Court in one of its finer fence-sitting moments answered both yes and no. The federal government went back to the provinces, and this time Quebec participated. In these talks, provincial opposition to the federal proposals shifted as Quebec appeared to be playing a separate game. At a dramatic midnight meeting, the federal government accepted some important amendments to its proposal that shored up provincial rights. Quebec, having been outmanoeuvred by the federal government and perhaps abandoned by some of its erstwhile provincial allies, refused to agree. But having previously given up its right of veto in these talks, Quebec was powerless. Sufficient provincial approval had been gathered to bring about the necessary changes.

Parliament and the provincial legislatures gave their assent, and the British House of Commons was petitioned to change the terms of the British North America Act accordingly and send it to Canada. Canadians called this 'patriation', the bringing home of a piece of British legislation that had never been home in the first place. On 17 April 1982, the Queen herself gave Royal Assent to the new Canadian Constitution. When she put down her pen after signing the document at a windblown outdoor ceremony on

Parliament Hill she must have realized that she personally was the only formal link remaining between Canada and Great Britain.

Whole books could be written about each stage of the process. What can be usefully said in a paragraph? First of all Trudeau insisted that bringing the Constitution home with an amending formula was not enough; it would also have to contain an entrenched bill of rights. That was not negotiable. The provinces generally agreed on an amending formula, but resisted a bill of rights, which they rightly believed would intrude upon their unlimited freedom of action within their areas of exclusive jurisdiction. They conceded the principle of the need for a bill of rights, recognizing its broad popularity, but sought to mitigate its application as far as each province was concerned. On this narrow bit of shared ground an agreement was struck. A bill of rights would be entrenched, but any legislature could prevent its application to specific pieces of legislation for five years by invoking what was referred to as a 'notwithstanding clause'. In effect provinces could act, the bill of rights notwithstanding, for a period of five years. Provinces could behave unconstitutionally, but they had to seek explicit legislative, and ultimately voter, approval. Once it became clear that a bill of rights would be included in the revised Constitution everyone wanted to be part of it. First Nations peoples, women, gays and lesbians, and disabled people all insisted that their inherent human rights be enshrined in the Constitution and protected. Lastly it must be said that this was Trudeau's finest hour. The Canadian Charter of Rights and Freedoms was his idea; he drove the process forward, overcoming obstacles and creating political momentum. He cajoled the premiers, cleverly split their ranks, brought them together again, and compromised just enough and just at the critical moment to get essential agreement. He debated his opponents with passion, overwhelmed opposition with the power of his intellect, and when the game called for decisive measures he manoeuvred Lévesque into a no-win position, and then pulled the trap. Instead of crowing over his accomplishment, he stood back and let his creation take greater shape as others signed on. For his vision, negotiating skill, and decisive leadership at a critical moment, he will be remembered along with Macdonald, Laurier, and King as one of Canada's greatest prime ministers.

∽

Trudeau's Charter changed Canada forever. Though people did not fully realize it at the time, the Charter raised the Courts to the same level as Parliament as lawmakers. The Charter created a new national institutional framework based upon law and the Courts to which Canadians looked for justice and protection from arbitrary government. Trudeau created what subsequently came to be called 'Charter Canadians', a new generation of citizens who possessed fundamental rights that overrode parliamentary sovereignty, and who looked to Ottawa and federal institutions to protect those rights. He complemented a language of powers in the Constitution with a discourse of rights. This was a considerable accomplishment.

Trudeau's Charter changed Canada forever.

The rest was anticlimax, and to a certain extent counterproductive. The 1981 National Energy Program (NEP) responded to yet another quantum leap in world oil prices following the Iran–Iraq war. The government agreed to an increase in domestic oil prices, but still held them below world levels. It restricted exports and imposed a tax to capture the majority of the rents that would have accrued under the higher-price scenario to the oil companies and the producing provinces, mainly Alberta. With the proceeds, the federal government provided handsome incentives to expand oil exploration and production on northern frontier fields and offshore in Eastern Canada. It would be a considerable understatement to say that the government of Alberta deeply resented federal intrusion into what it considered its exclusive right to regulate the oil and gas industry on its Crown Lands. Alberta regarded the federal tax as nothing short of theft of provincial treasure, and retaliated in various ways; western separatist organizations flourished, and for a time angry rhetoric ('Let the eastern bastards freeze to death in the dark' was the most frequently heard example) divided the regions of the country. Soon afterwards oil prices fell and the whole process had to be put in reverse. Oil exploration in the West virtually shut down; the western economy plunged into recession. The NEP was now held responsible for the bankruptcy and unemployment of thousands of workers in the oil and gas industry. A sharp continental recession and oil price declines must also share the blame for a good deal of the misery that befell the oil and gas industry, but the NEP and Trudeau were more accessible targets.

The most lasting legacy of the NEP, apart from its contribution of a new sense of western alienation, was the promotion of a great deal of rethinking of party organization and political structures. To this point constitutional reform had been largely driven by the Quebec problem. The West, particularly Alberta, saw policies like the NEP as indicators that the federal government was not really acting as a national government, but rather as the government of the eastern provinces. Federal institutions would need to be redesigned. The NEP replaced the railroads as the all-purpose explanation of western ills. Western alienation in turn gave rise to a new Alberta-based populist protest movement, leading up to the Reform party, determined to redesign Canadian federalism to give more power to the West.

In the foreign policy area, Trudeau went on a farewell tour. With the Reagan White House promoting a new Star Wars intercontinental ballistic missile defence system, which in turn threatened to destabilize the strategic balance, Trudeau set out on what some likened to a children's crusade against nuclear war. His campaign fit nicely with a Canadian vision of itself as, if not a peaceable kingdom, then one that promoted peace. Trudeau had long been sceptical of the extent of Soviet hostile intentions, and he had come to distrust the judgement of the hawkish Reagan administration. Canadians too had come to admire Trudeau as a representative on the world stage. At the meetings of the heads of state of the leading industrial countries (the G7) he seemed more articulate and thoughtful than many leaders. Margaret Thatcher in Britain and Ronald Reagan in the United States may have thought of him as a pain in the ass, but he demonstrated that at the very least he was their intellectual peer and that he too had a view of the world that seemed to resonate at home and also with the Germans, the French, and occasionally the Japanese. In the end Trudeau's crusade came to nothing—as did Star Wars. The Americans, however, harboured only faintly disguised displeasure at a junior partner breaking ranks over a vital strategic issue.

Trudeau took a famous walk in the snow one February evening in 1984 and announced his resignation the next day. His successor had to carry quite a bit of heavy baggage. Many Quebecers had emerged from the constitutional negotiations bruised and angry; western alienation had reached new heights with the NEP. A severe economic recession in 1981–2 had not been forgotten. Not surprisingly, the Conservative party, under a smooth, mellifluous, fluently bilingual Quebec lawyer of Irish extraction, Brian Mulroney, swept to power in the general election of 1984. In the largest majority in Canadian history, Mulroney overwhelmed the Liberals even in their former stronghold of Quebec, where he had recruited many former Union Nationale supporters and prominent separatists as candidates. Mulroney came to power promising to mend the tattered relationship with the United States, remove irritants in the federal–provincial relationship, put the government financial house in order, and bring the government of Quebec into the Constitution as a willing partner in Confederation. His government of two terms made substantial efforts on each of these matters. In doing so, however, it also raised a hornet's nest of opposition that shattered the promised era of harmony.

With his broad smile and ingratiating ways, Mulroney set himself the task of mending fences with the Reagan White House. His attentive courtship convinced the Americans that Canada was back onside. At an extraordinary 'summit' at Quebec City in 1988, the Canada–US friendship reached new heights of amity and a new low in excruciating embarrassment as a baritone Brian Mulroney persuaded the old trooper Ronald Reagan to join him on stage to croon 'When Irish Eyes Are Smiling'. The Conservative government concluded, following the recommendations of a massive royal commission report on Canadian economic policy, that the best way to improve Canadian economic performance would be to pursue more extensive formal economic integration with the United States. Thus teams of negotiators from both sides eventually produced a Free Trade Agreement (FTA), a massive technical document that removed most of the few remaining tariffs between the two countries and established complicated rules for resolving trade disputes. The Free Trade Agreement set off an intensive, highly emotional debate in which one side preached the benefits of free trade and the need to make Canadian industry more competitive and the other pointed to the one-sided nature of the deal and the loss of protection for distinctive Canadian institutions. The Free Trade Agreement was easily passed by the US Senate and the House of Commons; Mulroney stacked the Senate to secure final parliamentary approval, and in a subsequent general election his government was handily re-elected, though with a reduced majority.

The Free Trade Agreement never lived up to either the high hopes or apocalyptic fears claimed for it. The adjustment process was masked on both sides of the border by the onset of a sharp and wrenching economic recession in the early 1990s and a slow recovery thereafter. Economic growth in Canada was slower after the agreement than before. Prior to the agreement the two economies had already been thoroughly intertwined; more than 85 per cent of Canada–US trade crossed the borders freely. In that respect, the FTA only recognized de jure something that had existed de facto for many years. The agreement was more symbolic than substantial in that it acknowledged Canada's final surrender to the continental economic embrace. In 1989, the Canada–US trade accord was rolled into a broader North American Free Trade Agreement (NAFTA) that also included Mexico.

Following the logic of the Free Trade Agreement, the Conservatives systematically dismantled residual elements of Liberal economic nationalism, cancelling the NEP, for example, and ending the review of foreign investment. Public opinion reacted sharply when the Conservatives appeared to undermine the 'sacred trust' of social programs, in this case pensions, and the government promptly changed direction. The institutions of the welfare state were seemingly above politics. However, Mulroney and the large Quebec contingent within his caucus were particularly determined to reverse some aspects of the constitutional settlement. Quebec, even under the management of the Liberal 'federalist' government, still smarted over what it considered Trudeau's coup d'état. Quebec had been left out. It had not signed the new Constitution and would not do so until the province's conditions were met. Under the cover of bringing Quebec into the Constitution and meeting Quebec's demands, Mulroney set about undoing much of what Trudeau had accomplished. Trudeau's classic liberalism, enshrined in the Canada Act and the Charter, ensured a federal government capable of legislating for and being respected by all Canadians in all parts of the country. All provinces possessed similar powers and jurisdictions. The Charter established rights above legislature. It also protected minority language rights. Quebec's declared conditions for signing challenged many of these fundamental principles. Mulroney began a series of discussions with provincial leaders aimed at reaching a settlement on this touchy matter. For a time Canadians had a new indoor winter sport to rival hockey: televised federal–provincial conferences.

Meeting at the prime minister's Gatineau Hills retreat in 1987, the federal government and the provinces negotiated the Meech Lake Accord. This agreement called for an amendment to the Canada Act requiring that the courts interpret the constitution as recognizing Quebec as a distinct society with a French-speaking majority, and that the Parliament and legislatures of Canada should preserve this fundamental characteristic of Canada. It also gave the legislature of Quebec a special responsibility 'to preserve and promote the distinct identity of Quebec'. The agreement required approval of almost all Canadian provincial legislatures to take effect.

The Meech Lake Accord unleashed a fierce debate within the country. Many Quebec nationalists claimed it did not go far enough towards meeting Quebec's legitimate demands. Elsewhere the Accord was regarded as a fairly straightforward statement of the obvious fact that Quebec was not a province like the others; it had special characteristics that set it apart and that properly required constitutional protection. But across the country many voices rose in protest, seeing the deceptively simple language as a complete reversal of the Trudeau legacy by giving Quebec a special role, above the Canada Act and the Charter, to promote 'the distinct identity of Quebec'. This it seemed was an invitation to permanent opting out, and continued step-by-step movement towards independence. Trudeau broke his self-imposed silence to perform a devastating dissection of the Accord before a parliamentary committee. For a time all dinner parties in the country resembled seminars in constitutional law. Eventually the Meech Lake Accord died when two legislatures failed to ratify it within the two-year time limit. Quebec, its pride wounded, reacted as if betrayed. In a fury Mulroney's principal Quebec lieutenant, Lucien Bouchard, resigned from the government to form a group called the Bloc Québécois, dedicated to full independence for Quebec. Far from settling the constitutional impasse, the Conservatives had raised tensions to new levels and significantly increased the stakes.

Mulroney did not give up. His government continued to explore ways of recognizing Quebec as a distinct society by broadening the package of constitutional reforms to achieve wider agreement. In subsequent negotiations First Nations self-government, the gradual elimination of trade barriers within the country, and measures to give provinces greater influence over federal institutions such as the Senate and the Supreme Court were added to the agenda. Once again, in August 1992 the federal government, the provinces, territories, and aboriginal leaders, meeting in Charlottetown, struck another agreement, one that required approval in a national referendum in October 1992 to take effect.

The more ambitious program of constitutional change embodied in the Charlottetown Accord certainly attracted a wider constituency of support, especially among First Nations people. But the broadening strategy also attracted a wider array of dissidents who might approve some parts of the package but disapprove others. The ambiguity surrounding Native self-government aroused concern, particularly in Quebec, where it was seen as a means of dividing the territory of a heretofore indivisible, sovereign Quebec. A national plebiscite on 26 October 1992 rejected the constitutional amendment by 54.2 per cent to 44.8 per cent. Support for the Accord was strongest in Newfoundland, PEI, New Brunswick, and the Northwest Territories. Opposition was strongest in the West, particularly in Manitoba, Alberta, and British Columbia, where over 60 per cent voted against the Accord. Quebec voters too rebuffed the proposal by a vote of 42 per cent in favour and 55 per cent against. The province of Ontario split evenly with 49 per cent voting yes and 49 per cent no, with a slight decimal-point advantage on the yes side. Constitutional reform by negotiation ended with the defeat of the Charlottetown Accord in the fall of 1992. The Trudeau legacy would stand, though it would face one more crucial test.

Throughout the 1980s the fundamental social and economic changes previously noted continued apace. About 70 per cent of the 2.5 million immigrants arriving during the decade originated in India, Hong Kong, Pakistan, China, the Philippines, the Caribbean, the Middle East, South America, and Africa. A Sikh turban had acquired official standing as regulation Royal Canadian Mounted Police headgear alongside the traditional Stetson. Immigration spurred economic growth and brought needed skills to the country, but it also imported troubles from previous homelands, as the 1986 bombing of an Air India flight demonstrated.

The female higher education and labour force participation rate rose to equal that of males. The First Nations population continued to grow on the strength of a higher-than-average birth rate. Moreover, it grew in self-confidence as well: indigenous peoples expressed new-found pride in claiming Native status. Immigrants, women and aboriginal peoples could now appeal to the new Charter in their struggles for social equality and in defence of land claims and treaty rights.

Economically, Canada continued its long decline. The dollar fell steadily against its US counterpart, reaching a then new low of 70 cents (US) in 1985. Interest rates moderated to around 10 per cent annually after peaking at an astonishing 21 per cent in 1981. Macroeconomic management brought the inflation rate down from double digits in the early 1980s to less than 5 per cent after 1984. Nevertheless, as government expenditures annually exceeded revenues, the total federal debt rose from under 20 per cent of GDP at the beginning of the 1980s to well over 50 per cent by the end. There was a crunch coming. The Mulroney Conservative government talked a good deal about fiscal responsibility. Though the record of the government in many respects belied that profession, in one important respect the Conservatives did make a heroic and ultimately fatal effort to put the government's fiscal house in order. Mulroney removed a host of hidden taxes at the manufacturing level and replaced them with a comprehensive Goods and Services Tax (GST) at the point of sale, modelled in part upon European-style Value Added Taxes. Henceforth, all Canadians when selling or billing for goods and services would have to collect federal GST of 7 per cent. Though initially introduced as a revenue-neutral tax, in the long run it was expected this federal sales tax would greatly assist in the balancing of the books. Consumers and taxpayers across the country, however, rose in revolt. The GST deeply offended much of the Conservative party's core support across the country.

With all the constitutional discord and the GST, Brian Mulroney passed something of a poisoned chalice on to his successor, Canada's first female prime minister, Kim Campbell. It was hoped that her fresh face, candour, and gender would help people put the divisive past and unpopular policies behind them. The voters, alas, remembered and punished the Conservatives unmercifully; in the 1993 general election they retained only two seats. Never in Canadian history had a major party, a governing party, been virtually destroyed overnight. The Liberals formed a government by taking almost all of the seats in Ontario, a scattering in the East and the West, and about one-third of the seats in Quebec. In what must surely rank as one of the most curious anomalies in constitutional history, the separatist Bloc Québécois, which returned the largest number of members from Quebec, technically became Her Majesty's Loyal Opposition. In the West a populist, conservative political organization, the Reform party, gained a large amount of support by channelling western frustration into a movement of political and constitutional reform. Its program called for the election of a reorganized Senate in order to give the regions, especially the West, a greater control over the federal government. It championed debt reduction, fiscal conservatism, and in particular the dismantling of many parts of the welfare state.

~

A country politician was once asked in front of an academic audience what he thought of Canadian foreign policy. After a pause for reflection he replied: 'I think there should be more of it.' After all of the sound and fury of the Mulroney era, Canadian voters appeared to take a similar quantitative view of public affairs. Of politics, they wanted less of it. The new Liberal prime minister, Jean Chrétien, promptly delivered less politics. He managed expectations downward and stayed off the front pages, while authorizing his minister of finance, Paul Martin, to do whatever might be necessary to get Canada's deficit under control. In the early 1990s the Canadian economy was widely regarded as an international basket case. Annual deficits regularly exceeded 6 per cent of GDP; the total accumulated deficit had risen to above 60 per cent of GDP. The public sector accounted for more than half of all economic activity. On the right the Reform party had begun to make electoral inroads with its campaign against big government and ballooning deficits. Martin designed a program of federal spending cuts, reduced transfers to the provinces, offloaded responsibilities to the provinces, and retained the hated GST. He boldly promised a five-year program of fiscal restraint, which, to almost everyone's surprise, the government stuck to. The provinces instituted their own draconian fiscal regimes to reduce their mounting debts, passing these cuts on to the municipalities; they in turn cut services. To cut costs governments at all levels devised schemes of charging users, contracting out services, and privatizing.

In the mid-1990s, after a generation of welfare state expansion, accompanied by consistent annual deficits and mounting accumulated debt, the Canadian state began to contract. Later in the decade Canada experienced the most rapid rate of economic expansion among G7 countries (second highest on a per capita basis), a level of economic buoyancy that did much to assist government in its deficit-cutting goals by raising revenues without necessarily increasing taxes. Immigrants from China, India, the Philippines, Hong Kong, Sri Lanka, Pakistan, Taiwan, Ethiopia, Somalia, and the West Indies continued to flood into the country at a rate of about 250,000 per year, attracted by the flourishing economy, already well-established communities, and a generous immigration, refugee, health, welfare, and social security system. By the end of the century almost 20 per cent of the population had been born outside the country, a legacy that created a built-in constituency favouring continued immigration. The face of Canada, particularly urban Canada, greatly changed. Visible minorities were the majority in some areas of Vancouver and Toronto. The astonishing cultural and racial diversity of Canada had become one of its most striking and distinctive characteristics.

In subsequent elections, Chrétien would recapture a majority of the Quebec popular vote for the Liberal party, but not a majority of the seats, though with each election the number would increase from about one-third to about one-half of the total. The Liberals could make a claim to being the only national party. The Reform party in the West split the Conservative vote; the Bloc Québécois in Quebec reduced both Liberal and Conservative popularity. The social democratic party of the left, the NDP, had shrunk along with its core constituencies, farmers and the working class, but it acquired support in the disadvantaged regions of Atlantic Canada. It posed no threat on the Liberals' left. Well positioned in the centre of the political spectrum, while pursuing a fiscally conservative economic agenda, the Liberals achieved majorities in large part because the opposition was divided and regionalized. Across a wide range of public policies, Chrétien managed to turn politics into administration in his disarmingly folksy, seemingly amateurish style. But one factor, which he had hoped to bury with neglect, lay beyond his control: Quebec.

In the late 1980s following the collapse of the Meech Lake Accord, a commission of the provincial Liberal government in

Quebec had recommended a referendum on sovereignty if a deal could be reached with Canada satisfying Quebec's conditions for constitutional reform. The subsequent defeat of the Charlottetown Accord heightened Quebec's sense of rejection by Canada—even though Quebec too voted against the measures. In 1994 the Parti Québécois took power once again in Quebec, promising to hold a referendum within its term of office to settle the question of sovereignty once and for all. The federal government, following its 'less politics' instincts, largely ignored the agitation in Quebec.

But in the early summer of 1995 the PQ government of Quebec announced a referendum for the fall. Though Prime Minister Chrétien hailed from Quebec, he did not command a majority in the province where he was widely disliked both for his style and his firm defence of a Trudeau vision of federalism. Chrétien had been a Trudeau protégé; he had brokered the backroom deal with the provinces in 1981 that made Trudeau's constitutional revolution possible. He had campaigned against the Meech Lake and Charlottetown accords. He was widely seen in Quebec as intransigent on fundamental revision of the Trudeau constitutional legacy. This referendum asked Quebecers 'Do you agree that Quebec should become sovereign, after having made a formal offer to Canada for a new Economic and Political Partnership?' as outlined in a bill passed by the National Assembly.

At first the pro-sovereignty campaign appeared to be going nowhere; then in mid-campaign Lucien Bouchard, the charismatic leader of the Bloc Québécois opposition in Ottawa seized command. Under his leadership the referendum took on the character of a religious revival. With his extraordinary oratorical skills, media charisma, and emotional appeals to Quebec's sense of wounded pride, Bouchard made Quebecers want to say yes. The No campaign lacked an effective leader; Jean Chrétien seemed awkward and diffident, though he was not one to shrink from combat. In the campaign something astonishing happened. Thousands of young Canadians converged on Montreal, in one of the most massive popular demonstrations in Canadian history, to affirm their desire that Quebec should remain in Canada. Democracy witnessed one of its finest moments in Quebec that autumn. The debate was focussed and lucid; voters were presented with a clear choice—or at least the stakes were well understood—and an astonishing 97 per cent of the eligible voters participated in the referendum. By a very narrow margin, 50.6 per cent of Quebecers voted no and 49.4 per cent voted yes in answer to the referendum question.

An act of Parliament declared Quebec a 'distinct society'.

In the traumatic aftermath of the referendum, the federal government launched a campaign of reassurance. By an act of Parliament it declared Quebec a 'distinct society', though that declaration did not put Quebec's status above the Constitution and the Charter. For its part Quebec was part of the Constitution whether it liked it or not. The Charter applied in Quebec, and Quebec had to use federal institutions and Charter language to defend its legislation against legal challenges. The Supreme Court, when asked to clarify the legal situation surrounding possible separation, declared firmly that Quebec lacked the powers to make a unilateral declaration of independence, but it also ruled that if Quebecers decided to separate in a democratic election by a meaningful majority in response to a clear and unambiguous question, the government of Canada would be obliged to negotiate. The federal government then passed legislation, the Clarity Act, requiring a forthright question on independence be posed in any subsequent Quebec referendum.

That is roughly the point of standoff at which we presently find ourselves. To a certain extent the matter has been suspended, as popular support for sovereignty has faded under the deficit-cutting of the PQ. More recently Quebecers have elected a federalist Liberal provincial government. For 30 years the question of Quebec has been the pole star around which Canadian politics has revolved, and the Trudeau Constitution and Charter, despite the hostility of sovereignists and unsuccessful attempts to undo it, remain the collective response to that question.

The funeral of Pierre Elliot Trudeau in September 2000 represented a key moment when the country recognized the extent to which it had been remade under his influence. As television cameras followed the train bearing his coffin from Ottawa to Montreal through the blazing autumn leaves and announcers intoned their tributes, Canadians openly expressed their admiration for his statesmanship, some for the first time. He had been for many, a figure more respected and admired than loved. The death of one of Trudeau's sons in a mountaineering accident the previous year had revealed another side of Trudeau—a vulnerable, wounded, more human figure. As Canadians first shared his tragedy and soon after mourned his death, they began to think more about the man and his ideals, and understand what they owed to his fierce intellect and indomitable political will. Quebec and Quebecers were still dynamic elements of Canada. French and English seemed now a traditional and expected aspect of public discourse. His 'Just Society' had in large measure come to pass and been elevated by public opinion to the level of the 'sacred trust' of social programs as defining characteristics of a distinct society. The law and the courts now led the cause of equality and social justice.

Parliaments, legislatures, and national assemblies were no longer above the law. As the presence of Fidel Castro on the one side of his casket and Jimmy Carter on the other attested, under Trudeau, Canada had asserted a distinctive voice in a polarized world.

another opening

Canada has been 'becoming' for a very long time. From the year 1000, the time of first European contact, until after 1500 when transatlantic contact became more or less continuous, Canada underwent its first slow but wrenching transformation. French and British colonization efforts, and especially the diseases associated with those undertakings, fundamentally altered indigenous societies one after another. With extraordinary élan the French stretched a thin veil of empire and commerce across much of the continental interior. In the 100 years after the 1740s, the British Empire replaced France, but had to come to terms with the persistence of a French people in Quebec. Through revolution, war, and rebellion, the British sustained their colonial enterprise on the northern borders of the United States. Economically, politically, and ideologically these peoples in Canada were British, but in other social, political, and cultural respects they were also resolutely American. Over the next 100 years aspirations of nationhood were to a large extent realized. After Confederation, the nation of Canada took its place in the northern half of North America and assumed a role in the world, initially within a quasi-dependent relationship to the British Empire, and then as a full member of the Commonwealth.

The federal union of widely dispersed British North American colonies succeeded territorially, but social and economic cohesion were strained by regional, cultural, and religious tensions. A further transformation during the second half of the twentieth century would see a distinct society—within an independent, economically prosperous, bilingual, multicultural welfare state—take shape. Nonetheless, the supremacy of the federal government would be constantly challenged by the provinces; from time to time the integrity of the federation itself would be placed in jeopardy by Quebec; and an economy fully integrated with those of the United States and Mexico struggled to sustain social expectations.

$\backsim$

The process of transformation continues. At the millennium it might be ventured that the epoch of statist Trudeau federalism had reached its apogee. It had made Canada a distinct society. But this was not the end of history. This Canada, too, was in the process of being transformed at its height. Business now aimed for global or at least continental reach, rather than national or provincial markets. Globalization replaced Americanization as the leading Canadian insecurity. Opposition parties had made popular issues of shrinking the state and reversing the trend to bigger government. Canada had become better known abroad for its human talent—novelists, singers, actors, filmmakers, artists, athletes, academics, engineers, and business leaders—than for its natural resources. Social and cultural change continued to shift the ground beneath established politics.

Young people and newcomers had concerns different from the traditional ones of twentieth-century Canada.

Young people and newcomers had concerns different from the traditional ones of twentieth-century Canada. For this new, urban, and heavily foreign-born population, the old political quarrels failed to resonate. This was especially true outside Quebec. But immigration too had complicated the social composition of

Quebec and its politics. The 'pure wool' of ethnic solidarity was no longer a legitimate basis upon which to build the Quebec nation. Canada was being split and reconfigured. Race and gender, more so than language, religion, and provincial rights, framed a new political agenda over which the Supreme Court—on which three women, including the Chief Justice, sat—now conducted an ongoing dialogue with Parliament. The dominant belief that First Nations peoples would eventually disappear or be assimilated, the operative assumption for public policy for much of Canada's history, had been overturned by Native resistance and insistence upon their rights. Justice for First Nations peoples, based upon land claims, human rights, and a broader interpretation of treaties, re-posed one of Canada's long-standing, unanswered questions in a new and compelling form: How could indigenous peoples fully share in Canadian prosperity and citizenship while maintaining a separate, self-determining identity?

Canada had unconsciously become a nation of cities, but provinces occupied the seats at the table where resources were allocated and jurisdictions carved up. Externally, the end of the Cold War and the alarming commencement of a direct political-religious war on the United States opened an entirely new phase in international relations. Canada now had to negotiate the perilous dilemma of either being with its neighbour the United States in its heightened security concerns, or against it.

～

Out of all these tensions, hopes, and opportunities, another Canada is forming, one whose ultimate character we cannot predict. But just as surely as in the past, history is tugging at the strings and the Transformation Mask is opening yet again.

index

Acadia, 36–7, 40, 58–61

agriculture, 94–6, 206, 207;
Native, 3, 6–7, 141; in New
France, 34, 39–40; Norse, 11,
14; *see also* farmers

Alberta, 153, 178, 206, 240

alienation, western, 147, 234,
240

American Revolution,74–82

Arctic, 8–9, 53, 135

army, 146, 164–8, 186; *see also*
militia

Asia: immigrants from 155, 156,
204, 229; passage to, 16, 21,
49

assimilation, 71–2, 108, 109,
141

Baldwin, Robert, 118

Balfour Declaration, 174

Bennett, R.B., 174, 177, 181

biculturalism, 160, 222, 227,
229–30

bilingualism, 183, 222, 227,
229–30

birth rates, 9, 37–8, 45, 122,
204–5

Black Americans, 80, 155, 156

Bleus, 128, 159

Bloc Québécois, 245, 248, 250

Boer War, 161–2

Borden, Robert, 163, 167–8, 181

Bouchard, Lucien, 245, 251

Brant, Joseph, 79–80

Britain: change of policy in,
115–17, 118–19; colonial
administration of, 68–74;
colonies of, 56–61; Dominion
Status and, 114; foreign affairs
and, 137, 173–4; French and
Indian War and, 61–8; independence and, 116–17, 125,
126, 133, 174; Second World
War and, 187–93; ties with,
121, 124, 152, 155, 160–4,
185–6, 210–11; US and,
126–8, 201; *see also* England

British Columbia, 112, 119, 135,
137

British Commonwealth of

Nations, 174, 202, 210

British Empire: Canada in, 68–74, 78, 111–12, 124, 160–4

British North America Act (BNA), 134, 210, 232, 237

Brock, Isaac, 89

Brown, George, 128, 129

buffalo, 5–6, 53, 136

Caboto, Giovanni (John Cabot), 16

Canada: naming of, 18–19; as term, ix–x

Canada First, 138

Canadas, East and West, x, 109; politics in, 119–20, 128–9; responsible government in, 117–18, 119–20

Canadian National Railway (CNR), 166

Canadian Pacific Railway (CPR), 144–5

Cartier, Georges, 128, 129

Cartier, Jacques, 17–20

Centennial of Confederation, 222–3, 224

Champlain, Samuel de, 23–5, 47

Charlottetown Accord, 245–6

Charter of Rights and Freedoms, 185, 238, 239, 252

Chrétien, Jean, 249, 250, 251, 252

Churchill, Winston, 191, 201

Clark, Joe, 235

class, social, 41–2, 157–8, 169

Clear Grits, 120

Cold War, 208–10

colonies: British, 51–61, 68–74; French, 17–20, 23–54; Norse, 9–14

Confederation, x, 114, 125, 130, 131–3, 135, 138

conscription, 166, 167, 170, 187–8, 194, 195–6

Conservative party, 128, 138, 149, 163, 167, 170, 172–3, 174, 177, 212–15, 243–4, 250

Constitution: Quebec and, 221, 226, 244–5, 252; reform, 185, 226, 233, 237–9

Constitution Act (1791), 81

Continental Congress, 75–6

Cook, James, 87

Co-operative Commonwealth Federation (CCF), 178, 200

coureurs de bois, 34, 46

courts, 185, 239; provincial rights and, 148; *see also* Supreme Court

Criminal Code, 218, 225

Cross, James, 227–8

debt: Confederation and, 131–2; provincial, 199; public, 176, 197, 247
defence: colonial, 126–7; imperial, 162–4; New France, 35; spending on, 187; US and, 186, 189, 190, 209, 214–15
deficits, government, 232, 249
De Gaulle, Charles, 224–5
deportation, Acadian, 59–61
diamonds, 17
Diefenbaker, John, 212–15, 216
diseases: European, 20, 52–3; immigration and, 98
distinct society, 186–7, 244, 252, 256
Dominion Lands Survey, 143
Dominion of Canada, 134, 167–8
Dominion Status, 113–14, 173–4
Douglas, Tommy, 218
Durham, Earl of, 108

economy: (1850s), 121–2; (1870s), 137 (1890s), 149; (1900–14), 150–4; (1920s), 172: (1930s), 175–6, 179; (1950–60s), 205–8; (1970s),

232–4; (1980s), 247; (1990s), 243, 249–50; growth of, 184; New France, 34; North American, 186, 217, 242–3, 256; wartime, 166, 196–7
elections, 129, 159, 163, 167, 170, 177, 213, 215, 235, 248, 250
energy policy, 234, 239–40
England: exploration and, 16–17; fishery and, 14; new territories of, 36–7; war with France, 35–6; see also Britain
environment, 2, 11, 13–14, 83, 94, 97–8
Evangeline, 61
exploration: European, 15–16, 21; fur trade, 85–6; interior, 24–5, 47–9; official, 87–8; Norse, 12
Expo '67, 223
exports, 110–11, 121–2, 206; from New France, 32, 40; wheat, 91, 95

Family Compact, 100, 108
farmers, 169–70, 175–6, 178; see also agriculture
Fathers of Confederation, 114
federalism, 130, 185, 226, 236, 251

federal-provincial relations, 199, 226, 237, 244

Fenians, 105, 134, 135

First Nations, 231, 246, 247, 257; see also Native peoples

First World War, 164–8, 187

fisheries, 14–17, 21–2, 57, 68, 83–4, 152

flag, national, 218

foreign affairs, 137, 160–4, 179–80, 185–6

foreign policy, 172–4, 202, 214, 233, 241

forest products industry, 91–4, 111, 121–2, 152

Fort Whoop-Up, 141–2

France: colonies of, 17–20, 23–54; exploration and, 16–20; in French and Indian War, 61–8; imperial, 55, 58; Quebec separatism and, 224; territorial claims of, 48–50

free trade, 115–16, 119, 121, 138–9, 163, 242–3

French Canada: British Empire and, 112; Confederation and, 133–4; Riel's execution and, 147

French and Indian War, 56, 58, 61–8

Front de libération du Québec (FLQ), 222, 227–9

fur trade, 22, 26–7, 34, 40, 51–2, 72, 99; competition in, 84–8; expansion of, 48–9; Iroquois and, 28–9; Métis and, 46–7; Pacific, 87–8

gold, 16, 17

Goods and Services Tax (GST), 247–8

Gourlay, Robert, 100

government: British colonial, 72–3, 74–5, 81–2, 107–10; Great Depression and, 176–9; growth of, 184; levels of, 130–1; railways and, 144–5; responsible, 109, 117–19, 123–4; wartime, 166–7, 196–7

governor general, 160, 162, 210

Great Britain, 55; see also Britain; England

Great Coalition, 129

Great Depression, 174–80

Great Peace of Montreal, 35

Great Plains, 53

Great War, 164–8

Guzenko, Igor, 208

habitants, 41–2

Halifax, 56, 167

health insurance, 200, 217–18
Hitler, Adolf, 180
Holland, 55, 194
homesteading, 143, 153
honours, 124, 181, 222–3
horses, 44–5, 53–4
Howe, Joseph, 102, 117, 133
Hudson's Bay Company, 57, 84–7, 99, 119, 129, 135
hunting: Arctic, 8–9; buffalo, 5–6, 53, 136; Native, 2, 4, 6–8
hydroelectricity, 151–2, 224

immigration, 149, 154–6, 183, 246, 229, 249–50; British, 96–9; to British North America, 58, 70–1; Irish, 83, 97, 122, 123; to New France, 33–4, 37
immigration policy, 138, 203–4, 217
imperialism: free trade and, 115–16; nationalism and, 161–4
independence: colonies', 116, 123–4; Dominion, 160–4, 173–4
Indian Act (1876), 140–1
Indian Territory, 69–70
industrialization, 122, 138–9, 151–2
intendant, 31–2
Inuit, 8, 22
investment: domestic, 152–3; foreign, 151, 152, 233–4; manufacturing, 207
iron and steel industry, 12, 40, 151
Iroquois: people, 6–7, 8, 20–1, 23, 24–5, 35–6, 79, 80; Confederacy, 25, 28–9

Jews, 149, 156; as refugees, 181
Johnson, Lyndon, 219
Johnston, Daniel, 221
Judicial Committee of the Privy Council, 148, 160, 210

King, William Lyon Mackenzie, 171, 174, 177, 179–80, 181–2, 187, 189–90, 194–6, 200–1, 211
Korean war, 208–9

Labrador, 14
La Fontaine, Louis-Hippolyte, 118, 124
LaMarsh, Judy, 218
land: Crown purchase of, 80; French claims to, 19–20; Native, 70, 139; Native claims

to, 231–2; policy, 143; tenure systems of, 81

languages: conflict over, 147–9; Native, 141; official, 109, 183, 227; trade, 22–3

L'Anse aux Meadows, 11, 12

Laporte, Pierre, 228

Laurier, Wilfrid, 159–60, 162, 167, 181, 211

law: British, 70–1, 74, 81; Charter and, 239; French civil, 74, 81; language, 235

League of Nations, 173, 179

Lesage, Jean, 220

Lévesque, René, 224, 235, 236, 239

Liberal party, 128, 159–60, 163, 167, 170–1, 173, 179, 211–12, 213, 215, 216, 225, 248, 249; Quebec provincial, 220, 221

liberalism: economic, 115; radical, 119–20

'limited identities', 114

liquor: prohibition of, 148, 166, 171–2; trade in, 141–2

Louisbourg, 37, 49–50, 56, 61

Lower Canada, 81, 101–3, 104

Loyalists, 78–82

Macdonald, John A., 128, 129, 134, 137, 138, 181

McGee, Thomas D'Arcy, 125, 135

Mackenzie, William Lyon, 100, 103, 105, 106, 107

Manitoba, 136, 148, 159–60

manufacturing, 122, 138, 188, 207, 217

Maritime Union, 126, 129–30

marriage, 45, 184, 204

Martin, Paul, 249

medicare, 218; see also health insurance

Meech Lake Accord, 244–5

mercantilism, 32, 110–11, 119, 138–9

Mercier, Honoré, 147

Métis, 46–7, 86–7, 136, 139, 145–7

migrations: fishing and, 14–15, 21–2; global, 9; Native, 7–9; to New France, 29–30, 32–3

militia: British command of, 160, 162; rebellion and, 105, 106, 107; role of, 43–4; War of 1812 and, 89, 90

monetary policy, 176, 214

Montcalm, Marquis de, 62, 64–6

Montreal, 50, 76, 84–8, 252

Mounties, 141–3

Mulroney, Brian, 241–3, 247

multiculturalism, 155–6, 183, 230

National Energy Program (NEP), 239–40

nationalism: economic, 138–9, 233–4, 243; imperialism and, 161–4; Irish, 134, 135; Quebec, 219–22, 224, 225

National Policy, 138–9

Native peoples, 2–9, 23, 140–1, 183, 208; American Revolution and, 79–80; British Empire and, 69–70, 112; European fishermen and, 14–15, 21–3; French alliance with, 24–5, 35–6, 57; French colony and, 17–21, 52–3; Norse and, 10–11, 12, 14; political revival of, 230–2; Rebellion of 1885 and, 145–6; treaties and, 139–41; War of 1812 and, 90; *see also* First Nations; Inuit; Métis

navy: British, 56, 57, 66–7; Canadian, 162–3, 192, 193

Nelson, Robert, 105

New Brunswick, x, 80, 91–2, 102, 118, 148; Acadian revival in, 61

New Caledonia, 85

New Deal, 177, 179

New Democratic Party (NDP), 215, 250

New England, 28, 30, 35–6, 55, 71

Newfoundland, 11, 16, 83–4, 103, 116, 118–19; bankruptcy of, 178; Confederation and, 133, 135, 210; fishery and, 14, 21–2, 36–7, 50, 56–7, 78, 83–4

New France: expansion of, 46–54; population of, 37–9; 'private' development of, 23–30; 'public' development of, 30–7; society in, 40–4

New Nationality, 125, 135

New World, 16, 19–20

Norse, 9–14

Northwest Company, 84–8, 99

Northwest Territories, 129, 139

'notwithstanding clause', 238

Nova Scotia, x, 102, 117, 135; Acadians in, 58–9, 60–1; American Revolution and, 77–8, 80

October Crisis, 227–9

Ohio country, 56, 58, 62, 74, 75, 78

oil and gas industry, 206, 234

Ottawa, Ont., 124

Papineau, Louis-Joseph, 101–2, 103, 105, 106, 107
Parliament: sovereignty of, 185; upper and lower houses of, 130–1, 132–3
Parti Canadien, 101
Parti Patriote, 102, 104, 106
Parti Québécois (PQ), 235, 251
'patriation', 237–8
peacekeeping, 211
Pearson, Lester, 211, 213, 215, 216
pemmican, 87
pensions, 200, 243
Plains of Abraham, Battle of, 64–6
plebiscites, 195, 246
police, 141–3
Pontiac, 69–70
population, 95, 98, 122, 123, 154–5, 204–5; British North American, 58; Native, 4, 6, 7, 86; New France, 30, 33, 37–8; representation and, 120, 130–1; rural, 170
Port-Royal, 23, 28
Portugal, 14, 16
Prince Edward Island, 80–1, 102–3, 118, 133, 135

Progressive Conservative party, 235; see also Conservative party
Progressives, 170, 171
Protestants: in British North America, 71; Catholics and, 123, 148, 149; establishment of, 82; in New France, 26, 30
provinces: Constitution and, 237–8; farmers' parties and, 170; Great Depression and, 177–8; new, 153; powers of, 185; rights of, 147–8

Quebec: American Revolution and, 77–8; Church in, 148; Confederation and, 132; Great Depression in, 178; Liberals and, 170–1, 211–12; migration from, 99; nationalism in, 147, 219–22, 224; separatism and, 224–5, 235, 236, 245; sovereignty of, 185, 250–3
Quebec Act (1774), 69, 74, 75
Quebec City, 24, 50, 62–6, 76–7, 130
Quiet Revolution, 219, 220

racism, 156, 178
railways, 122, 123, 126, 138, 144–5, 146, 153, 166;

Confederation and, 132, 134, 135; scandal and, 137
Reagan, Ronald, 241, 242
rebellions: (1837–8), 103–7, 118; (1885), 145–7
Reciprocity Agreement, 121, 128, 133, 137, 163
Red River colony, 136
referendum, Quebec, 236, 251
Reform party, 240, 248, 249, 250
religion: accommodation of, 72–3; conflict over, 123, 147–8, 149; European, 19, 20–1; exploration and, 49; monopoly and, 23, 26; state, 82; *see also* specific religions
representation, population and, 81–2, 120, 128–9, 130–1
Riel, Louis, 136, 145–7
rights: bill of, 238; discourse of, 239; Native, 70, 232; 'regime' of, 185
Roman Catholic Church: in British North America, 72–3, 74, 75; Quiet Revolution and, 220–1
Roosevelt, Franklin Delano, 189–90, 201
Rouges, 119
royal commissions, 199, 222, 224, 230
Royal North West Mounted Police, 141–3, 146
Royal Proclamation (1763), 69, 70–1, 139
royal tours, 182
Rupert's Land, 119, 134–7
Russell, Lord John, 103

St Albans, raid on, 127, 128
St Laurent, Louis, 211
St Lawrence river: exploration of, 17–18, 19; as 'main street', 50–1; settlement along, 23–4, 34, 38–40; timber trade and, 92; as transportation, 110
St-Pierre and Miquelon, 68
Salaberry, Michel de, 89
Saskatchewan, 153, 200, 218
schools, 141, 159–60, 147–8
Second World War, 187–97
seigneuries, 33, 41, 42–3, 73
self-government: colonial, 99–103, 117–19, 123–4; First Nations, 246
Selkirk Colony, 85
servants, indentured, 30, 33–4
Seven Years' War, 61; *see also* French and Indian War
shipbuilding, 91, 111, 121
Sitting Bull, 142

slaves, 42, 80, 122–3
Snorri, 12
Social Credit Party, 178, 215
Social Gospel, 156
socialism, 200
social mosaic, 159
sovereignty-association, 113,
   236–7
Spain, 16, 55, 56
Spanish Influenza, 168
Stadacona, 20–1, 24
state: and citizen, 184, 185;
   colonial control and, 23,
   31–7, 48–9; as sponsor of
   exploration, 15–16, see also
   government
subsidy, provincial, 131, 133
Suez Canal, 211
Supreme Court, 160, 210, 232,
   252
surveying, land, 143–4, 145

Tadoussac, 22
Talon, Jean, 32
tariffs, 137–8, 139, 151
taxation, 184, 247–8;
   Confederation and, 131; fed-
   eral, 199; wartime, 166, 197
Tecumseh, 88, 89
Thatcher, Margaret, 241
Tilley, Leonard, 134

Tories, 100, 117
trade: with Britain, 110–11;
   Caribbean, 84; early fishery
   and, 14–15, 21–2; liberalization of, 203; monopoly and,
   23, 26; pre-contact, 3; see also
   free trade; fur trade
Transformation Mask, vi, 54,
   150, 257
treaties, Native peoples and,
   139–41, 231–2
Trudeau, Pierre Elliott, 225–9,
   233–9, 241, 253–4
Tupper, Charles, 134
'two solitudes', 219

Underground Railroad, 122–3
unemployment insurance, 198
Union government, 167
unionism, 157–8, 168–9, 178
Union Nationale, 220, 221
United Nations, 202, 203, 211,
   230
United States: Auto Pact and,
   217; Civil War in, 124, 127;
   defence and, 186, 189, 190,
   209, 214–15; immigration
   and, 97, 122–3, 137, 155,
   156; rebellion and, 105–6,
   107; relations with, 112, 114,
   119, 186, 218–19, 242;

Second World War and,
189–90, 201; trade with, 121,
137–8; war with, 88–91,
126–9

Upper Canada, 81, 100–1, 105

Vancouver, 144
Vancouver Island, 87, 119
Vaudreuil, Marquis de, 67

warfare: European, 28, 35;
guerilla, 57, 79–80, 105–6;
Native-European, 28–9
War of 1812, 88–92
War Measures Act, 197, 228–9

weapons: European, 25, 28, 27,
29–1, 52; nuclear, 209, 214,
215, 219
welfare state, 198, 200–1,
217–18, 221, 243, 249
whaling, 14–16
wheat, 91, 94–5, 111, 153–4
Winnipeg General Strike, 169
Wolfe, James, 62–6
women: equality of, 183, 223–4,
230; Loyalist, 79; Native,
46–7, 86–7; in New France,
30, 33, 44–5; voting and, 166,
171; war and, 197–8; work
and, 157